PROFESSIONAL RESOURCES

Supports
The Four-Blocks™
Literacy Model

Modifying the Four-Blocks™ for Upper Grades

by Cheryl Mahaffey Sigmon

Editors
Joey Bland
Erin Proctor
Tracy Soles
Louise Vaughn

 ISBN 0-88724-659-1

Table of Contents

Table of Contents

Chapter I

Why Four-Blocks™?

At the heart of the primary Four-Blocks™ Model are two basic beliefs. **The first belief is that there is not one sole approach that can be used to teach all children to read or to be better readers.** Children have different personalities, different learning styles, and have had different experiences that prevent a one-size-fits-all approach from being successful.

The second belief is that, through a teacher's careful planning and instruction, students can learn and can be nurtured in a heterogeneous classroom—without labels. To achieve this, a teacher's instructional planning must always be multilevel. This multilevel approach allows all students to gather what is necessary to help them grow, even though what they gather differs from one child to another. Heterogeneous instruction helps to erase lines of distinction—social, emotional, and academic—while supporting students.

Upper-grades teachers interested in Four-Blocks must investigate whether these two beliefs are central to their own classroom teaching and learning.

There can be little doubt that there is greater and greater potential for diversity among students as the grade levels get higher and higher. Differences in personalities and learning styles are more pronounced and the experiences are widely varied. The extremes between the more and less able readers and writers widen year by year.

Addressing this diversity is a tremendous challenge for the upper-grades teacher who is attempting to meet individual needs. Multiple approaches and multilevel instruction can be an answer for this dilemma—not an easy answer, but an answer.

Just as in the lower grades, older students need time for independent reading to develop and practice fluency and to apply the skills and strategies they have learned in the context of "real" reading. At the ages where students appreciate choice and autonomy, the self-selection of materials is both important and appreciated.

Additionally, older students need explicit instruction in reading skills and strategies as well as guidance in applying these to text that they can manage, given appropriate support. They need to be taught how what they are learning works in relation to all printed materials that they may encounter.

Older students need to explore words and patterns in ways that will empower them. Rather than memorizing lists of words for spelling and vocabulary, older students need to learn the how-to's of words: how to use a certain pattern to help spell words and how to use structural knowledge about word parts to figure out what a polysyllabic word means.

Older students need lessons and practice in writing and composition to develop as better communicators in written language and as a context and purpose for learning the useful skills of written Standard American English—grammar, mechanics, and usage. Some students may still need writing as a way to figure out their own reading. They must encode—think about the relationship between letters and sounds, choose the right symbols to match the sounds, then write them down—before they can be better decoders by reading back the symbols using the appropriate sounds. This is how writing is reading from the inside out (Atwell, 1998), and why it is one of the approaches used to teach students how to read.

The multilevel instruction of the Four-Blocks™ Model gives teachers an opportunity to plan instruction and activities that can meet a range of needs. For example, in the Writing Block, the teacher provides a model of writing each day, most often her own writing, though sometimes the writing of a published author. Within the context of this writing, the teacher takes the opportunity to teach a mini-lesson on a skill that she feels will benefit most of the class. Although this is only a fraction of what occurs in the entire Writing Block, the multilevel component is already in place. For students who are less able writers, the constant modeling of basic writing elements will be beneficial. These elements might include how to choose a topic, when to indent, what purpose the margins serve, and how to decide whether a sentence is relevant to the particular topic or paragraph where it is included. The mini-lesson may include how to vary sentence structures to make writing more interesting and more powerful. Not all students will be ready to apply this lesson in their own writing, and in a Writer's Workshop, not everyone will be required to apply what the teacher has modeled in the mini-lesson that day. Some students, however, will be ready for that lesson and will be eager to apply what they have learned in their writing. The fact that everyone, at the very least, is exposed to the lesson is important. The teacher will hold students accountable for the instruction as she deems it appropriate for each individual student.

Multi-approach and multilevel are the ways that Four-Blocks teachers will accomplish their goals—helping all students to be better readers and better writers.

Chapter 2

Creating a Supportive Environment

One thing is for sure: the classroom environment is an opportunity to promote what teachers value for their students. Because literacy is considered by schools and teachers to be a top priority, the room should reflect that emphasis. As soon as students cross the threshold—if not before—they should be aware of what is important to that teacher and to that class. In fact, even the main lobby of the building is an opportunity to make an impact on students about the literacy focus.

How Does a Supportive Four-Blocks Classroom Look?

☑ Books beckon from every corner of the room!

Because few students ever choose a book because it has a beautiful spine, as many books as possible need to be displayed with their covers out. Books should be placed on the ledge of the chalkboard, in the windows, in baskets, on magazine racks—anywhere books can be! At the intermediate and middle grades, children's trade books make colorful and appealing displays placed upright on shelves.

Some teachers have found that rain gutters (purchased at the hardware store) bolted horizontally on the classroom wall create wonderful, inexpensive display shelves. Another inexpensive, makeshift shelf can be made with J-channels that hold aluminum siding strips together, also purchased at the hardware store.

☑ **Seating arrangements encourage collaboration and interaction at all grade levels.**

Learning is a social process and providing the opportunity for interaction actually contributes to the rate and depth of understanding (Tharp and Gillimore, 1989). Additionally, in Four-Blocks™ classrooms teachers realize that the "sage on the stage" role of traditional instruction is not conducive to the kind of climate that they need and want to create. Teachers can be effective facilitators as "guides on the side." In some intermediate grades (3-5), students may be seated at tables of four to five students or may be seated with partners. In most middle grades (6-8), the students are seated at desks that are pushed together to form a common surface, much like a table.

☑ **A comfortable reading area provides a soft, casual area to relax and read or study.**

Such an area might be located in a corner of the room with a couch, a lamp, and several baskets of reading materials, including magazines, comic books, children's trade books, novels, and newspapers. The materials represent a variety of genres—mysteries, informational books, fiction, biographies, folk tales, fairy tales, drama, poetry, etc.

☑ **Words that support students in their writing and reading are accessible in the room.**

A Word Wall stretches over two walls. The words are large enough, legible enough, and positioned to be seen by all students from their desks. Words are written on brightly colored paper spanning the walls like a rainbow.

In some classrooms where words must be covered for frequent standardized testing or where attaching the words directly to the wall is prohibited, a simple solution has been found. Teachers purchase a long, wide roll of felt material. The felt is cut and hung from the top edge along the upper border of one wall. Words for the Word Wall are made and backed with colors that will contrast with the color of the felt material. A tiny piece of hook-and-loop tape is glued to the back of each word. The words will adhere to the felt without the companion piece of hook-and-loop tape and can be rearranged as necessary. During testing times, the felt is merely rolled up and tied or pinned. After testing, it is easily reopened so that students can continue to get the full benefit of the wall.

A similar solution is the use of an inexpensive shower curtain liner hung or tacked to the wall, on which words are individually attached with hook-and-loop tape.

☑ **Other words, besides the Word Wall words, are available for the students.**

Some teachers like charts of science words, math words, social studies words, health words, history words—whatever is helpful to the students as an easy reference. A "Nifty Thrifty Fifty" chart may hang in the room, reminding students of useful morphemic units—prefixes, suffixes, and root words (Cunningham, Hall 1999).

☑ **Homelike touches help to create a desirable climate—one that is nurturing and cozy for students at all grades.**

A lamp in the reading center emits cozy light, creating interesting shadows in that section of the room. Plants thrive and twine in different directions, running across the file cabinets and shelves. Curtains in some rooms frame the windows and diffuse the incoming light, casting a glow across the walls. Some teachers like to display some family photos, sharing some of their personal lives with their students.

☑ Student ownership is quite apparent in the classroom.

At the intermediate grades, bulletin boards are trimmed with purchased border strips that echo the class theme. Within the borders, however, there are canvases for students' creations. One board might say, "Writing from across the Oceans," where postcards from pen pals in foreign countries are posted—the results of a class project. At the middle grades, another board might say, "Our Thoughts on the Subject...," and represent a permanent display of current work published by each student. In some rooms, graffiti boards invite students to share their opinions about books they are reading or about topics in which they are interested. In some middle school classrooms, each student takes responsibility for keeping a current published composition in a two-gallon plastic storage bag labeled with his name and stapled on a bulletin board.

☑ Management systems are obvious at a glance.

Colored folders of students' compositions are neatly organized in one area. Boxes of different types of graphic organizers line a counter near the Writing Center. One organizational chart reminds students in what order and on what day they will come to the teacher for a conference, while another organizational chart tells with whom each student will be reading that day during the Guided Reading Block. In the middle grades, the folders require some additional organization since several classes are taught in the same classroom. The boxes that house the reading and writing folders are labeled "1st Period," "3rd Period," etc.

☑ **The Writing Center encourages students to polish their writing into a publishable format.**

In a corner of a middle grades room, there are several chairs around a table, which is against a wall. Two computers and a printer are on the table. Students enjoy using the software provided on these computers to add graphics to their compositions or to format their pieces into multimedia productions. Reference books, such as dictionaries, a thesaurus, a set of encyclopedias, and several composition handbooks, are stored in a cabinet on the other side of the table.

In an intermediate-grade Writing Center, there are numerous writing materials—pens, pencils, colored pencils, markers, scissors, construction paper, staplers, and paper of various sizes and colors—to stimulate students' creativity. A book binding machine is available for students who wish to publish in that format.

Teachers in classrooms such as the ones described above create a physical environment that loudly, clearly, and unmistakably says many things to their students. First and foremost, they say, "I value books, and we will be reading a lot this year!" With the warm touches around the room, they say, "This classroom is a nurturing one, created to make you feel comfortable during the time you're here to learn." Further, with several student displays they say, "This classroom belongs to you." The use of organizational charts says to students, "You will know what is expected of you every day, and you will have responsibility for your learning." The fact that the charts and decorations relate to learning, that they are not just pretty or cute, says, "We have a lot of work to accomplish this year!" So much is communicated in classrooms like these without a word from the teachers.

How Does a Supportive Four-Blocks School Look?

Schools, not just classrooms, can send clear messages, too. A school can communicate to students, parents, community members, and other visitors exactly what is central to its purpose. When a whole school adopts the philosophy of the Four-Blocks™ Model, the faculty often finds that they are more cohesive when driven by the same goals, when talking the same lingo, and when articulating the same type of curriculum. The physical environment, again, can send that message—loud and clear—to all who enter the building.

☑ **The entrance way is the first impression a school makes and should reflect an emphasis on literacy.**

In some middle schools where all teachers are focusing on Four-Blocks™ implementation, visitors and parents are welcomed by numerous displays related to writing and reading. A unique aspect of the displays is how they encourage collaboration among teachers, students, and parents. One display is entitled, "Viewpoints," and is divided into three sections by strips of colored tape. Headings for the three sections are, "Parents," "Teachers," and "Students." A topic or question is offered monthly, and responses are encouraged in classrooms and in newsletters. Sometimes the topics are serious and thought-provoking: "Does the government use our tax dollars wisely?" "Does education need to be fixed?" "Does media have a negative effect on society?" Sometimes the topics are lighthearted or of human interest: "What's your earliest memory?" "Who has influenced your life?" "What was your most embarrassing moment?" Responses relating to these topics are posted on the display for all to read and enjoy.

In intermediate schools, the entranceway might include benches with baskets of books and magazines, and racks or small tables displaying student publications for parents and visitors to peruse.

Creating a Supportive Environment

☑ The emphasis on literacy continues down the hallways.

Intermediate grade teachers use their doors to advertise popular books. Each classroom has decided upon a book that they want to share with everyone. One teacher's door has a huge eye looking out of the glass pane into the hallway. A dialogue bubble says, "I'm the BFG and I'm watching you!" On the bottom section of the door are the name of the book and the author, *The BFG* by Roald Dahl (Farrar, Straus & Giroux, 1982).

Another door is covered by green paper. Cards with plastic spiders attached to them are arranged on the door. On the outside of the cards are questions about spiders such as, "What is the life span of most spiders?" The answer can be found inside the card by lifting up the spider. In the middle of the door in large print is the book title, *Spiders*, and the author, Gail Gibbons (Holiday House, 1993).

For all grade levels, the hallways display different types of writing: compositions, pen pal letters, maps with reports about regions, news articles about a recent storm, and three-dimensional flowers with research about different varieties of flowers. In one hallway, a bulletin board contains work published by teachers, who are all strongly encouraged to write throughout the year.

☑ Even in the cafeteria, literacy is in the forefront.

There is a graffiti wall where the students stand in line each day. On the graffiti wall is the question, "Read Any Good Books Lately?" Students and teachers are asked to write the titles of books they've read along with a short synopsis and a recommendation. This wall is quite popular. Also alongside the lunch line is a vocabulary bulletin board with "Words of the Week." Classrooms take turns being in charge of this display which is usually filled with interesting word etymologies, the relationships among words that have the same Latin or Greek roots, catchy phrases or sentences with an interesting word or two, or riddles about words. In the middle grades cafeteria, SAT vocabulary might be displayed along the wall where students wait their turns in line, taking advantage of this opportunity to share words.

☑ School publications of different sorts also underscore literacy.

An annual literary magazine published by students with representation from all grade levels is appreciated by students and parents alike. There may also be a monthly newsletter that contains news from every grade level, book reviews for everyone to enjoy, and solicitations for writing submissions from parents.

☑ **The administration takes part in keeping everyone focused on literacy.**

The principal may keep a storage bin of books that she has gotten from vendors as samples. She often gives these to deserving students whom she has observed doing some good deed or who have achieved some academic feat. In one middle school, the principal has a book club that meets twice a month to discuss books. Occasionally he meets over lunch for book chats.

☑ **The parent-teacher organizations in these schools actively encourage reading and writing.**

These groups may supply money to supplement classroom libraries throughout the school, in addition to doing such things as awarding magazine subscriptions to classrooms in honor of teachers' and students' achievements.

Risk-Taking and Choice Are Hallmarks of the Four-Blocks Classroom Climate

The Four-Blocks™ classroom environment is not only created by its physical attributes but also by its affective attributes. Students are given much responsibility for their learning, and are expected to make many of their own choices and decisions:

> "I want to read about race cars today. Where's a good book on race cars?"
>
> "I love fiction best of all, but I think today I'll try to read something that's nonfiction during Self-Selected Reading."
>
> "I really want to write about what I learned about a car engine from my dad yesterday!"
>
> "This adventure story I'm writing about is really getting interesting. I can't wait to get back to it today!"
>
> "I love Cynthia Rylant's descriptions of the people of the Appalachian Mountains. I'm going to try her technique in my writing today."
>
> "What do I know about patterns that will help me spell this word that I need in my writing?"
>
> "Hey, that graphic organizer is quite a trick! I'm going to try that with my science book tonight and see if I understand it better."
>
> "What a great word! I'm going to put this in my writing notebook and remember to use it."

These are the sounds of students in the upper grades making choices about their learning. These are students who are drawing connections between what they're being taught and how they might apply it in their "real" reading and writing. These are kids who are beginning to take responsibility for their learning in a Four-Blocks classroom.

Must a school or a classroom do all of these things in order to have an effective program? No! Administrators and teachers, however, will surely want to take full advantage of the opportunity to use the environment to promote and support literacy. In some schools, a climate committee takes charge of what is done in the hallways and lobbies. In other schools, teachers and their students take the responsibility on a rotating basis. Clubs focusing on literacy are the advocates in other schools. It does not matter who does the work or who coordinates the efforts. The schools that use their environments wisely, however, are often the most successful schools as far as literacy development and appreciation. They learn that the environment should be stimulating for both the children and the adults who spend most of their waking hours in the school building.

Chapter 3

Self-Selected Reading Block

In the primary Four-Blocks™ Model, there are three basic components of the Self-Selected Reading Block (SSR):

1. A teacher **read-aloud** at the beginning of the block.

2. **A time for students to self-select books and, concurrently, a time for teachers to have book chats** with students, which include evaluating the students' reading performance and comprehension.

3. **An opportunity for students to share with each other, in various formats, what they have been reading.** These components are based on research findings and experiences of effective practices that contribute to reading success at all grade levels, not just at the primary grades (Anderson, et al, 1985).

Teachers at all grade levels who have utilized these components have discovered a number of benefits, some of which are far beyond what was originally expected. Teachers report these as some of the benefits:

- Students really appreciate the opportunity to choose their own reading materials.

- Students have a chance to read at their own reading level every day.

- The block provides a forum for sharing and responding to reading and books.

- The read-aloud exposes students to a range of genres that they otherwise may not have explored.

- Students have an opportunity to talk with their teacher about books.

- Both the read-aloud and the self-selected reading help build background knowledge that is necessary for success in reading.

- Students easily develop a sense of story.

- Students' own writing improves as they are exposed to more and more writing.

- The block facilitates the development of speaking and listening skills.

Certainly a long—but not inclusive—list of benefits!

Not everyone has embraced the practice of allowing students the time to read and the freedom to choose and read books that they want to read. In the upper grades—grades four and above—the read-aloud time has often suffered. Understandably, in the upper grades the curriculum is often more complex and demanding, and time is precious. Often, time allowed for actual reading is restricted to text selected by the teacher in an effort to cover core materials, thus eliminating any self-selected opportunities. **Sadly, creating a desire for reading often does not take precedence over**

coverage of content as schools prioritize goals for teaching and learning. Returning to the words from the report, *Becoming a Nation of Readers*, **"Children who read most, read best"** (Anderson, et al, 1985). How simple! There is no definition of which students or at what grade levels that truism might apply. It is just as likely to be relevant at grade one as at grade twelve.

A student's freedom to choose reading materials and the time to read these self-selected items are not the only elements missing from many upper-grades classrooms. Primary teachers have long recognized the benefits of daily read-alouds, and administrators at the primary grades have encouraged this practice. Although some sources have reported that the single greatest predictor of reading achievement is whether and how much a child has been read to prior to coming to school (Well, 1986), many teachers, through delivering daily read-alouds to their students, have attempted to compensate for this opportunity which may have been missed by a number of struggling students. **Good teachers see the read-aloud as a chance to create or recreate for children a literate homelike environment** (Allington, Cunningham, 1998). Students at the upper grades are no exception to the rule when it comes to reaping the benefits of being read aloud to. They just have longer arms and legs!

Let's explore the Self-Selected Reading Block as it may look in intermediate (4-5) and middle grades (6-8) classrooms.

Read-Alouds in the Upper Grades

A high school teacher shared the following:

> "When I first decided to start my English class every day by reading aloud, my students remarked that I'd 'lost it'—referring, I'm quite sure, to my mind! I read to them for about 10 minutes, sometimes a chapter of a novel, sometimes something from *Reader's Digest*, or even a clipping from the newspaper that I thought they'd find interesting. All I required was that they sit quietly. I told them I wouldn't be testing them on what I read—that it was just for their enjoyment. Well, the biggest, burliest guys put their heads on their desks, tuning me out totally, and I'll admit that was a little intimidating to me, but I went right on reading every day."
>
> "There were a few days when some students mumbled under their breath comments like, 'I can't believe you're wasting time reading to us,' or 'You must think we're babies,' but again I just kept reading."
>
> "Well, one day I was beginning to feel the pressure of the upcoming state testing, and I thought maybe we'd better start using every minute to review. So, I made a decision to suspend the read-aloud for a week. Well, I'll tell you, the first complaints came from those big, burly guys who had put their

heads on their desks. We had been in the process of reading a novel, and they exclaimed, 'How are we going to know how that ended?' 'We were just getting to the good part!' 'This isn't fair!' That's when I knew that the read-alouds were making an impression—not just providing a nap time for my students."

"That was twelve years ago, and I've been reading every day since I made that pledge to myself that read-aloud time should be a priority in my instructional day."

Where To Read

Bringing the class together in an area of the room where they can relax and listen quietly and comfortably still helps to create that literate, nurturing environment that some children have not experienced in their own homes. **There will come a day when students will no longer allow the reading in such close proximity.** Sometimes that is dictated by a teacher's personal style and comfort level, and sometimes it is dictated solely by the students and their perceptions of what is considered acceptable—or cool, as they might term it.

Some teachers like to sit in a rocking chair or on the floor with their students, again, as long as the students accept that format as not too babyish. **Creating or recreating the lap experience, even at the upper grades, can be rewarding for teachers and students alike.**

In some spacious classrooms at the intermediate grades, students sit around on a carpeted area near the teacher. In other rooms, the Reading Center, where beanbag chairs and carpeting provide comfortable surroundings, is the read-aloud center, too.

In other classes and more frequently at the upper grades, the read-aloud takes place with the teacher sitting on a stool or in a chair at the front of the class or reading as she strolls around the room. The students listen from their desks, which remain in cooperative groups throughout the day.

Some teachers dim the lights or switch on a soft lamp when they feel the lighting might add some ambiance to the reading time, depending upon the selection.

What Is Read During Read-Aloud Time?

What is to be read might be determined for a number of reasons. The reasons for choosing selections become the following planning goals or objectives for classroom teachers:

1. Expose students to a wide variety of genres this year.

2. Expose students to a wide range of written formats.

3. Introduce students to popular authors whose books they might want to read.

4. Introduce students to illustrators who use varied art to convey meaning.

5. Expose students to a wide variety of styles and techniques of writing within a genre that students might choose to emulate.

6. Read stories that inform students about issues they are interested in and even about things in their world they might not have noticed.

Additionally, one criterion for selection should be stories that have entertainment value—those that warm the heart (where tissues must be on hand); stories, articles, or riddles that make students laugh; and, certainly, some pieces that "gross them out"! Those are always favorites—within certain parameters, of course!

Genres that Teachers Will Want to Include in Read-Alouds

Fiction: Books with stories that are not true, though they may be based on situations, characters, and places that are believable.

Nonfiction: Books with true stories or information.

Informational Nonfiction: Books with facts and information that are true.

Science Fiction: Books with stories that are not true and which are based on situations not presently in existence.

Fantasy: A type of fiction that is not true and which cannot happen based on scientific knowledge and logic.

Biographies: Books that tell about someone's life, usually including a chronological account.

Poetry: Selections that focus on a topic using concise words, imagery, sometimes using rhyme and pattern and offer acceptable departures from the standard rules of grammar.

Autobiography: Selections that were written by the person whose life events are told.

Folk Tales/Fairy Tales/Fables: Stories that usually have a moral or lesson to be learned, featuring characters that are either good or bad, have elements of fantasy, and usually do not have an identifiable original author.

Mysteries: Stories with realistic settings in which the characters are involved in the search for a solution to a puzzle or problem.

Teachers will also want to include different formats in their reading, such as letters, newspaper articles, Internet selections, magazine articles, and, of course, books.

There are some good anthologies that include a number of the same genres or a mixture of genres. Jim Trelease's *Read All about It! Great Read-Aloud Stories, Poems and Newspaper Pieces for Preteens and Teens* (Penguin, 1993) is one that teachers of older students will want to add to their collections. Many of the selections are excerpts from larger works that will surely motivate students to want to read more!

Favorite Books Recommended by Teachers as Read-Alouds

Grade 4

Alexander and the Terrible, Horrible, No Good, Very Bad Day by Judith
    Viorst (Atheneum, 1972)
Babe–the Gallant Pig by Dick King-Smith (Econo-Clad Books, 1999)
The Best Christmas Pageant Ever by Barbara Robinson
    (HarperCollins, 1982)
Bridge to Terabithia by Katherine Patterson (HarperCollins, 1987)
By the Great Horn Spoon by Sid Fleishman (Little, Brown & Co., 1963)
The Chocolate Touch by Patrick Skene Catling
    (William Morrow & Co., 1979)
The Cricket in Times Square by George Selden
    (Farrar, Straus & Giroux, 1983)
Dog Breath!: The Horrible Terrible Trouble with Hally Tosis by Dav Pilkey
    (Scholastic Trade, 1999)
Duke Ellington: The Piano Prince and His Orchestra by Andrea Davis
    Pinkney (Disney Press, 1998)
The Giving Tree by Shel Silverstein (HarperCollins, 1986)
The Great Gilly Hopkins by Katherine Paterson (HarperCollins, 1987)
James and the Giant Peach: A Children's Story by Roald Dahl
    (Econo-Clad Books, 1999)
Jeremy Thatcher, Dragon Hatcher by Bruce Coville (Minstrel Books, 1992)
The Not-Just-Anybody-Family by Betsy Cromer Byars
    (Econo-Clad Books, 1999)
Patty Reed's Doll: The Story of the Donner Party by Rachel K. Laurgaad
    (Tomato Enterprises, 1989)
Ramona's World by Beverly Cleary (Aladdin Paperback, 2000)
Save Queen of Sheba by Louis Moeri (Puffin, 1994)
Sideways Stories from Wayside School by Louis Sachar
    (William Morrow & Co., 1998)

Snowflake Bentley by Jacqueline Briggs Martin (Houghton Mifflin, 1998)
Still More Two-Minute Mysteries by Donald J. Sobol (Apple, 1995)
A Taste of Blackberries by Doris Buchanan Smith (HarperCollins, 1987)
Tuck Everlasting by Natalie Babbitt (Farrar, Straus & Giroux, 1986)
War with Grandpa by Robert Kimmel Smith (Yearling, 1984)
Zia by Scott O'Dell (Yearling, 1995)

Grade 5

Alice in Wonderland and Alice through the Looking Glass by Lewis
    Carroll (Candlwick Press, 1999)
Animorphs Series by Katherine A. Applegate (Scholastic)
The Boys Against the Girls by Phyllis Reynolds Naylor (Yearling, 1995)
Castle in the Attic by Elizabeth Winthrop (Holiday House, 1985)
The Cay by Theodore Taylor (Random House, 1987)
Children of the Longhouse by Joseph Bruchac (Puffin, 1991)
Dog Breath by Dav Pilkey (Scholastic Trade, 1999)
Double Trouble in Walla Walla by Andrew Clements
    (Millbrook Press Trade, 1997)
Encyclopedia Brown: Boy Detective by Donald J. Sobol
    (Bantam Skylark, 1985)
Encyclopedia Brown and the Case of the Disgusting Sneakers by Donald J.
    Sobol (Bantam Skylark, 1991)
Five-Minute Mysteries by Kenneth Weber (Running Press, 1989)
The Great Brain by John D. Fitzgerald (Yearling, 1972)
Harry Potter Series by J. K. Rowling (Arthur Levine)
Henry Huggins Series by Beverly Cleary (Avon Books)
Island of the Blue Dolphins by Scott O'Dell (Houghton Mifflin, 1990)
J. T. by Jane Wagner (Yearling, 1972)
James and the Giant Peach: A Children's Story by Roald Dahl
    (Econo-Clad Books, 1999)
Johnny Tremain by Esther Forbes (Houghton Mifflin, 1943)
*Keepers of Life: Discovering Plants through Native American Stories and
    Earth Activities for Children* by Michael J. Caduto (Fulcrum, 1997)
*Keepers of the Animals: Native American Stories and Wildlife Activities
    for Children* by Michael J. Caduto (Fulcrum, 1997)
Keepers of the Night: Native American Stories and Nocturnal Activities by
    Michael J. Caduto, et al (Fulcrum, 1994)
Little House Series by Laura Ingalls Wilder (HarperCollins)
Mrs. Frisby and Rats of NIMH by Robert C. O'Brien (Atheneum, 1974)
Night of the Twisters by Ivy Ruckman (HarperCollins, 1987)
*No More Homework! No More Tests!: Kids' Favorite Funny School
    Poems* by Bruce Lensky (Econo-Clad Books, 1999)
The Noonday Friends by Mary Stolz (Econo-Clad Books, 1999)
Number the Stars by Lois Lowry (Yearling, 1990)
Randall's Wall by Carol Fenner (Aladdin Paperbacks, 2000)
Redwall by Brian Jacques (Ace Books, 1998)
Sarah, Plain and Tall by Patricia MacLachlan (Harper Trophy, 1987)
Sign of the Beaver by Elizabeth George Speare (Houghton Mifflin, 1983)

Sing Down the Moon by Scott O'Dell (Houghton Mifflin, 1970)
Skinnybones by Barbara Park (Econo-Clad Books, 1999)
Stuart Little by E. B. White (Harper Trophy, 1999)
Summer of the Swans by Betsy Cromer Byars (Viking, 1996)
The Tales of Uncle Remus: The Adventures of Brer Rabbit by Julius Lester
        (Puffin, 1999)
Tears of a Tiger by Sharon Mills Draper (Atheneum, 1994)
Where the Red Fern Grows by Wilson Rawls (Bantam Starfire, 1984)
A Wrinkle in Time by Madeleine L'Engle (Farrar, Straus & Giroux, 1990)
Books by These Authors:
    Avi
    Jan Brett
    Betsy Cromer Byars
    Beverly Cleary
    Paula Danziger
    Madeleine L'Engle
    Phyllis Reynolds Naylor
    Gary Paulsen
    Louis Sachar
    Shel Silverstein
    Donald Sobol
    R. L. Stine
    Laura Ingalls Wilder

Grade 6

Aldo Peanut Butter by Johanna Hurwitz (Econo-Clad Books, 1999)
Attaboy Sam by Lois Lowry (Econo-Clad, 1999)
The Best School Year Ever by Barbara Robinson (HarperCollins, 1994)
The Boys Against the Girls by Phyllis Reynolds Naylor (Yearling, 1995)
The Boys' War: Confederate and Union Soldiers Talk about the Civil War
        by Jim Murphy (Econo-Clad Books, 1999)
Brian's Return by Gary Paulsen (Delacorte Press, 1999)
Brian's Winter by Gary Paulsen (Econo-Clad Books, 1999)
Bunnicula: A Rabbit Tale of Mystery by Deborah and James Howe
        (Avon, 1979)
The Cay by Theodore Taylor (Random House, 1987)
Chicken Soup for the Soul Series by Jack Canfield and Mark Victor
        Hansen (Health Communications, Inc.)
Dog Breath: The Horrible Trouble with Hally Tosis by Dav Pilkey
        (Scholastic Trade, 1999)
Double Trouble in Walla Walla by Andrew Clements (Millbrook Press
        Trade, 1997)
The Egypt Game by Zilpha Keatley Snyder (Econo-Clad Books, 1999)
The Flunking of Joshua T. Bates by Susan Shreve (Econo-Clad Books,
        1999)
Frindle by Andrew Clements (Econo-Clad Books, 1999)
The Great Brain by John D. Fitzgerald (Yearling, 1972)
Harry Potter Series by J. K. Rowling (Arthur Levine)

Hatchet by Gary Paulsen (Aladdin Paperback, 1999)

The Indian in the Cupboard by Lynne Reid Banks (Doubleday, 1985)

J. T. by Jane Wagner (Yearling, 1972)

Joshua T. Bates Takes Charge by Susan Richards Shreve (Econo-Clad Books, 1999)

Journey to America by Sonia Levitin (Econo-Clad Books, 1999)

The Lion, the Witch, and the Wardrobe by C. S. Lewis (Econo-Clad Books, 1999)

Maniac Magee by Jerry Spinelli (Little, Brown & Co., 1990)

My Life in Dog Years by Gary Paulsen (Bantam, Doubleday, Dell, 1998)

My Name is Brain Brian by Jeanne Betancourt (Econo-Clad Books, 1999)

Nightmare Mountain by Peg Kehret (Leisure Books, 1999)

No More Homework! No More Tests! : Kids' Favorite Funny School Poems by Bruce Lensky (Econo-Clad Books, 1999)

Number the Stars by Lois Lowry (Houghton Mifflin, 1989)

Randall's Wall by Carol Fenner (Aladdin Paperbacks, 2000)

Read All About It! Great Read-Aloud Stories, Poems & Newspaper Pieces for Preteens and Teens by Jim Trelease (Penguin Books, 1993)

The River by Gary Paulsen (Delacorte Press, 1991)

Running Out of Time by Margaret Peterson Haddix (Aladdin Paperback, 1997)

Sarah, Plain and Tall by Patricia MacLachlan (Harper Trophy, 1987)

Saving Shiloh by Phyllis Reynolds Naylor (Aladdin, 1999)

Shiloh by Phyllis Reynolds Naylor (Yearling, 1992)

Shiloh Season by Phyllis Reynolds Naylor (Aladdin, 1999)

Stuart Little by E. B. White (Harper Trophy, 1999)

Tears of a Tiger by Sharon Mills Draper (Atheneum, 1994)

There's a Boy in the Girls' Bathroom by Louis Sachar (Random, 1994)

Where the Red Fern Grows: The Story of Two Dogs and a Boy by Wilson Rawls (Bantam Starfire, 1984)

Whipping Boy by Sid Fleishman (Troll, 1989)

Series:

   American Girl Series (Pleasant Company Publications)

   Anne of Green Gables Series by L. M. Montgomery (Bantam Skylark)

   Dear America Series (Scholastic)

   Help...I'm Trapped Series by Todd Strasser (Apple)

   Little House Series by Laura Ingalls Wilder (HarperCollins)

Grades 7 and 8

Basher Five-Two: The True Story of F-16 Fighter Pilot Captain Scott O'Grady by Scott O'Grady and Michael French (Yearling Books, 1998)

Behind the Attic Wall by Sylvia Cassedy (Avon, 1983)

The Bridge to Terabithia by Katherine Paterson (HarperCollins, 1977)

The Cay by Theodore Taylor (Random House, 1987)

Chasing Redbird by Sharon Creech (HarperCollins, 1997)

Chicken Soup for the Soul Series by Jack Canfield and Mark Victor Hansen (Health Communications, Inc.)

Dicey's Song by Cynthia Voigt (Atheneum, 1983)

Face on the Milk Carton by Caroline B. Cooney (Bantam, 1990)
Goodnight, Mr. Tom by Michelle Magorian (HarperCollins, 1996)
Goosebumps Series by R. L. Stine (Scholastic)
Hatchet by Gary Paulsen (Aladdin, 1999)
Holes by Louis Sachar (Farrar, Straus & Giroux, 1998)
Homecoming by Cynthia Voigt (Atheneum, 1981)
House of Dies Drear by Virginia Hamilton (Aladdin, 1984)
I Know Why the Caged Bird Sings by Maya Angelou (Bantam, 1970)
Imitate the Tiger by Jan Cheripko (Boyds Mills Press, 1998)
Killing Mr. Griffin by Lois Duncan (Econo-Clad Books, 1999)
A Long Way from Chicago: A Novel of Stories by Richard Peck (Dial, 1998)
Maniac Magee by Jerry Spinelli (Little, Brown & Co., 1990)
My Brother Sam Is Dead by James Lincoln Collier and Christopher Collier
    (Scholastic, 1989)
My Friend the Vampire by Angela Sommer-Bodenburg (Pocket Books, 1984)
Old Yeller by Fred Gipson (Harper Trophy, 1990)
*Read All About It! Great Read-Aloud Stories, Poems & Newspaper Pieces
    for Preteens and Teens* by Jim Trelease (Penguin, 1993)
Roll of Thunder, Hear My Cry by Mildred D. Taylor (Puffin, 1976)
Saving Shiloh by Phyllis Reynolds Naylor (Aladdin, 1999)
Scary Stories to Tell in the Dark by Alvin Schwartz (HarperCollins, 1981)
Shiloh by Phyllis Reynolds Naylor (Yearling, 1992)
Stone Fox by John Reynolds Gardiner (Ty Crowell Co., 1980)
Train to Somewhere by Eve Bunting (Clarion Books, 1996)
Visitors Series by Rodman Philbrick and Lynn Garnett (Apple)
Walk Two Moons by Sharon Creech (Harper Trophy, 1996)
Where Are the Children? by Mary Higgins Clark (Simon and Schuster, 1992)
Where the Water Lilies Grow by R. D. Lawrence (Natural Heritage, 1999)
Where the Red Fern Grows: The Story of Two Dogs and a Boy by Wilson
    Rawls (Bantam Starfire, 1984)
Wringer by Jerry Spinelli (Harper Trophy, 1998)

What Children's Tradebooks Have To Offer Older Children

Especially helpful in keeping with the pacing of the read-alouds included in the Self-Selected Reading Block is the use of children's tradebooks or picture books. **The publishing market is filled with delightful, intriguing, appealing books—not just for the younger audience, but books that appeal to all ages. Many of the writers of these books are masters of multilevel appeal.**

One example of the multilevel appeal might be the humorous book, *Dog Breath* by Dav Pilkey (Scholastic Trade, 1994). On one level, this is a simple story of a dog with bad breath and a family at wit's end with the odor so offensive that it wilts wallpaper right off the walls! The book is filled with pictures that evoke "laugh-out-loud" responses from children and adults. On another level, however, the book is also filled with delightful puns that will keep the attention of older children and adults, from the dog's name (Hally who lives with the Tosis family) to their solutions for his problem such as taking him to a scenic overlook (a "breathtaking" view!).

The entire genre of tradebooks is a most interesting study for older students. Upon analyzing the books, teachers will find that most picture book authors must deal with certain specifications for their writing. One of the most important of the specifications is the restriction of length, which is 32 pages for most books. Yet, within these few pages, good books can evoke a wide range of emotions. Readers and listeners laugh with Agatha as the geese flock to her bedroom to reclaim their feathers in Carmen Deedy's wonderful story, *Agatha's Featherbed* (Peachtree Pub., 1993), a story rich with figurative language. Likewise, kids and adults giggle through Jon Scieszka's *Math Curse* (Viking Children's Books, 1995). To the contrary, readers and listeners are brought to tears with stories such as Patricia Polacco's *Pink and Say* (Philomel Books, 1994) or *Thank You, Mr. Felker* (Philomel Books, 1998). Many teachers have admitted to not being able to read *Faithful Elephants* (by Yukio Tsuchiya, Houghton Mifflin Co., 1988) aloud to their classes because they cannot get through the book without sobbing. **How powerful a story must be to evoke these kinds of emotions within so few pages and with so few words!** This is a good lesson in itself for older students.

In addition to the power of the stories provided in the context of children's books, the display and range of illustrations included in the pages of the stories is often like taking a trip to an art museum. Diane Stanley displays period art in her biographies *Charles Dickens: The Man Who Had Great Expectations* (William Morrow & Co., 1993); *Bard of Avon: The Story of William Shakespeare* (William Morrow & Co., 1998); *Cleopatra* (William Morrow & Co., 1994); *Leonardo da Vinci* (William Morrow & Co., 2000); and *Shaka: King of the Zulus* (William Morrow & Co., 1994); among many others.

One reason for reading children's books to older students is the fact that these students are not far from the stage of their lives where they will be parents of children to whom they will need to read. **Acquainting students at this age with the types of books available and with what those books have to offer is important. This could help perpetuate the cycle of literacy that is created in a teacher's classroom.** What could be more valuable?

Short and to the point is what children's books are all about. They fit nicely within the time allowance of the read-aloud and meet all of the "3 E's" (described in the next section) as well!

Favorite Children's Tradebooks for Older Students' Read-Alouds

The Stranger by Chris Van Allsburg (Houghton Mifflin, 1986)

Oh, The Places You'll Go by Dr. Seuss (Random House, 1990)

The Bunyans by Audrey Wood (Scholastic Trade, 1996)

The Frog Prince Continued by Jon Scieszka (Puffin, 1994)

Water Dance by Thomas Locker (Harcourt Brace, 1997)

More than Anything Else by Marie Bradby (Orchard Books, 1995)

Schmoe White and the Seven Dorfs (Happily Ever Laughter) by Mike Thaler (Cartwheel Books, 1997)

The Teacher from the Black Lagoon by Mike Thaler (Scholastic, 1987)

The Music Teacher from the Black Lagoon by Mike Thaler (Scholastic, 2000)

Stephanie's Ponytail by Robert N. Munsch (Annick Press, 1996)

Dog Breath: The Horrible Trouble with Hally Tosis by Dav Pilkey (Scholastic Trade, 1994)

Agatha's Featherbed: Not Just Another Wild Goose Story by Carmen Deedy (Peachtree, 1993)

Pink and Say by Patricia Polacco (Philomel Books, 1994)

Thank You, Mr. Falker by Patricia Polacco (Philomel Books, 1998)

Faithful Elephants: A True Story of Animals, People, and War by Yukio Tsuchiya (Houghton Mifflin, 1998)

Animalia by Graeme Base (Harry N. Abrams, 1987)

The Eleventh Hour: A Curious Mystery by Graeme Base (Harry N. Abrams, 1993)

Rose Blanche by Roberto Innocenti (Creative Education, 1996)

The Lotus Seed by Sherry Garland (Harcourt Brace, 1993)

A Regular Flood of Mishap by Tom Birdseye (Holiday House, 1994)

Snowflake Bentley by Jacqueline Briggs Martin (Houghton Mifflin, 1998)

Hooray for Diffendoofer Day! by Dr. Seuss (Knopf, 1998)

Smoky Night by Eve Bunting (Harcourt Brace, 1994)

Fly Away Home by Eve Bunting (Clarion Books, 1993)

The Wall by Eve Bunting (Houghton Mifflin, 1992)

Delivering a Good Read-Aloud

The read-alouds for the upper grades need to be read within approximately 10 minutes. Why such a short amount of time spent on something obviously so important? **Teachers need to remember the "3 E's" as a rationale for the short duration of the read-aloud:**

Entertainment

The read-aloud is a time to hook students on reading. This is the time to let them know that there are books for everyone, for every interest, for every emotion, and for every place in time.

Exposure

Read-alouds allow students to know that reading and writing serve a variety of purposes through the appropriate use of a range of formats and genres—all at their disposal as readers and writers. All formats and genres will not appeal to every student. Teachers need to realize that and need to make students aware that they will develop favorites among the genres and formats. Nevertheless, everyone needs to know that a variety of printed materials exists and need to know how they are different.

Encouragement

Primarily, the read-aloud is a time for teachers to invite students to read and to motivate them. This is the time that teachers "bless books," a term coined by Dr. Linda Gambrell (2000). For as soon as a good book is read and placed in the classroom, most students seek that book. Teachers need to bless lots of books throughout the school year.

Teachers who focus on the "3 E's" will surely be successful in choosing their read-alouds! Also, in adhering to the pacing guideline for an effective read-aloud, teachers need to remember that "entirety" is not one of the E's. **It is not important to read all pieces in their entirety.** Teachers can still accomplish the "3 E's" without always reading the whole text. Here is an example of a teacher delivering her read-aloud from the book, *It's Disgusting And We Ate It* by James Solheim (Simon and Schuster, 1998):

> "Has anyone in our class ever eaten seaweed before?"
>
> A couple of hands go up, but many students wrinkle their noses in response to let the teacher know that they haven't done so and never hope to!
>
> "Well, I'm going to read a segment from this informational book that will let you know that maybe everyone here has eaten seaweed without even knowing it! Listen and find out!"
>
> She begins reading: "'Do you have ice cream in your freezer? If so, pull it out, brush off those ice crystals, and read the ingredients list on the container. You'll find carrageenan in the recipe for most ice cream sold in America...'"
>
> The teacher reads on for another paragraph, and then concludes with, "Now that's just a taste—no pun intended!— of what's included in this book. Can you imagine eating rattlesnake salad? Are you curious about what U.S. Air Force Captain Scott O'Grady ate to survive after his plane crashed during the war in Bosnia? Do you know who eats spiders, caterpillars, and insect larvae and what those critters taste like? All of that and more is in this interesting book that will be in our classroom! I hope you'll want to read it. Today I'm going to put it in the Book Basket on Table #1."

A complete read-aloud that took no more than five minutes! Did it accomplish the "3 E's"? Kids of all ages are **entertained** by it (especially because of the high "gross-out" factor!). The teacher has **exposed** the students to informational nonfiction to let them know that the genre can be fun and enjoyable. Also, the teacher has certainly "blessed" this book and has **encouraged** many students in the class to choose it during their Self-Selected Reading time.

Snippets of texts that are appropriate for read-alouds might include the following:

☑ the beginning of a novel that has a particularly strong lead

☑ a section of a novel that paints a vivid description of a character

☑ a section of a novel that paints an interesting and mysterious setting

☑ a funny anecdote from a story

☑ an interesting fact from an informational book

☑ a poem from a poetry anthology

☑ a short story from an anthology

☑ an article or portion of an article from a magazine

Teachers who keep the "3 E's" in mind as they make their selections can't go wrong!

The way in which a read-aloud is delivered can determine its success or failure. This is where planning and practice are critical, especially at the upper grades where material is written with greater sophistication. When material is not practiced prior to reading, the listener might feel that it really would not matter whether the text was being read backwards or forwards. Even when teachers read aloud, practice makes the difference between whether the text is delivered merely as words or whether it is delivered with feeling. Practicing the piece helps the reader adjust the voice intonation to match the meaning. That is when comprehension will be heightened. The extra time spent by the reader on the practice makes a dramatic difference to the listener.

What Is Not Done in a Read-Aloud

Sometimes it is difficult for teachers not to take every possible opportunity for direct instruction in skills and strategies. That is certainly understandable with the educational crisis and with accountability issues as they are. However, **the daily read-aloud is not the appropriate time to deliver mini-lessons.** If the temptation is too strong and the text too inviting, then **the teacher can easily use the material again later in another of the language arts blocks when that skill or strategy is more appropriate.**

For example, if a teacher is reading *The Cay* by Theodore Taylor (Flare, 1995) to his students and feels that the dialect is a literary device that needs more attention, the brief read-aloud time is not the time to stop reading and write sentences of dialect on the board to explore them. More effectively, the teacher might choose to copy onto a transparency a page or two of the dialogue that demonstrates the effective use of dialect. Then, during the Writing Block, the teacher might use the transparencies as part of his modeling and mini-lesson to discuss dialect and dialogue. He also might attempt a model writing lesson using dialect in his own story to simulate this author's technique.

Teachers must trust that lessons are inherent in the read-alouds each and every day, with each and every piece read to the students. The value is there and is well worth the time spent!

How Students Self-Select Materials

The middle segment of the Self-Selected Reading Block at the upper grades is spent, on most days, with students choosing books of personal interest and reading those books or printed materials. On those days when students are selecting and reading, the teacher is holding conferences with students, usually individually, though sometimes in small groups.

On some days there are literature circles or book club groups that meet to talk about the books they have been reading more in depth than the usual sharing time allows. On those days, the teacher is likely to be monitoring groups and sometimes stimulating the discussions. Let's look closer at how these different formats are organized and managed and also at the materials that students are choosing during this time.

Motivating Students To Read

Teachers must know their students—really know their students—to have a successful Self-Selected Reading Block. One of the greatest challenges for every teacher is to try to connect kids to the right books. Getting them hooked on something that interests them is critical!

In the very beginning of the school year, teachers should begin to gather as much information as possible about the likes, dislikes, school interests, sports interests, choices of television programs, favorite types of video games, hobbies, and everything else possible about each student. With students in the upper grades, an interest survey is easily administered, taking little time but gaining strategic information.

Besides interest surveys, every conversation a teacher has with a student can be an opportunity to gather information that is significant in making that necessary connection. Teachers may want to keep a corner of their anecdotal records about each student for making notes about something in their conversation that was a clue to what that student might enjoy reading.

A student's comment, "I've got baseball practice this afternoon," might lead a teacher to offer that student Lee Bennett Hopkins's book of baseball poetry, *Extra Innings: Baseball Poems* (Harcourt Brace, 1993).

A child whose social studies report was on Martin Luther King might be offered Ellen Levine's *If You Lived at the Time of Martin Luther King* (Econo-Clad Books, 1999), a book that allows the reader to visit an important time in history.

A girl who is new to the school and has moved from far away might be offered *The Broccoli Tapes* by Jan Slepian (Philomel Books, 1989), the story of a girl who moves with her family from Boston to Hawaii, finds comfort in sending tapes to her Bostonian friends, and finds new relationships in Hawaii.

For a student who enjoys television shows of fantasy—elves, trolls, gnomes, fairies—the teacher might suggest Janet Taylor Lisle's Newbery Honor Book, *Afternoon of the Elves* (Orchard Books, 1989), a story of mystery and friendships.

For a child who says, "I've always wanted a horse of my own," the perfect book, now considered a classic, might be *Misty of Chincoteague* by Marguerite Henry (Simon & Schuster, 1990).

An animal-loving student might be directed to Sterling North's tale of *Rascal* (Puffin, 1990), the heartwarming story of a raccoon befriended by an eleven-year-old boy.

An older student who enjoys camping and backpacking may enjoy Gary Paulsen's *Hatchet* (Simon & Schuster, 1987), which is a survival story.

The boy in class who asks a million and one questions might enjoy, *I Wonder Why Spiders Spin Webs and Other Questions About Creepy Crawlies*, by Amanda O'Neil (Kingfisher Books, 1995), with its comical illustrations and interesting answers to life's puzzling questions.

A girl who mentions wanting to pursue a medical career could be offered Rachel Baker's *The First Woman Doctor* (Scholastic, 1999), the story of Elizabeth Blackwell in the 1840s.

A boy who collects model planes may enjoy reading *1000 Facts About Space* by Pam Beasant (Kingfisher, 1992), a book filled with illustrations and interesting facts.

The matches between children and books they may enjoy is almost limitless. What is required for the match is that teachers know their students and know what books are available (or know how to find a source to make the match!). No student can resist a book placed in his hands with the teacher's words, "This book is just for you!"

Richard Allington once shared his failure-free secret for motivating the most reluctant reader in the class. He said for teachers to find some deep, dark, secretive-looking place in their desks or, better yet, a locked cabinet. At some private time with the reluctant student—during a conference or just after lunch as others are coming into the class—he encouraged the teacher to pull the student aside and share, "You know, I've got a book that no one else in the class has gotten to read. I haven't shared it with anyone. It's one I bought with my own money." Allington says that here the teacher should stall and deliberate! "Well, I know you're dependable. I would really like for you to read this and let me know if you think it's something we should share with others in the class. I know you'll bring it back to me."

That is the "forbidden fruit" method. No child can resist having his hands on a book that no one else has gotten to see! Teachers report that it works like a charm!

Some motivating of readers is done by the teacher during the reading time as the teacher monitors the room and during the individual conference time with students. Just a touch on the shoulder and a remark such as, "Oh, don't you love this book? It's one of my favorites," or, "I haven't read that book yet, but I'm planning to read it soon. Please let me know if you like it and if you think I would, too," will go a long way toward getting students focused and motivated during the Self-Selected Reading Block.

Teachers might keep in mind, too, that some students might be motivated to read books that have been made into popular movies. Hopefully they'll discover that the book is almost always better than the movie—if they'll just give it a try!

One great—and very inexpensive—way to survey students about their likes and dislikes is to copy several pages of a book order catalog. Use a catalog that has pictures and synopses of the books. Make a set of order blanks for each student. Give the students an amount that they could "spend" if they were helping you purchase books for the classroom. Students will check the books, of course, that they would like to read. Compile the lists and make anecdotal notes of each student's choices: genres, topics they pick often, lengths of books that are appealing, etc. Transfer their preferences to their reading profile sheets so that you can help connect them to books when they have difficulty. This makes a great math activity, too, if students figure the totals, shipping and handling, and taxes to be included in their orders!

What Students Read During This Time

What students read is, of course, what they choose to read—within certain parameters. If the teacher has chosen to present the books in book baskets, then she has orchestrated the choices to include the printed materials to which she wants to expose students and which she knows will interest them. If book baskets are not used, then the choices may be broader for students but, hopefully, the students will still be encouraged to explore the variety offered in the classroom.

Obviously, the most critical element for the Self-Selected Reading Block is a good classroom library of printed materials. Teachers should not despair if their collections are inadequate but should start to build their collections. Administrators' support is definitely needed! There is nothing sadder than looking into a classroom with only a few books, none of which are proudly displayed, and the covers of which are dog-eared or missing. Kids deserve lots of pretty, appealing books. Otherwise, they are much less likely to reach for them.

What types of materials should be included in the book baskets and elsewhere in the classroom? Books, books, and more books! Teachers must consider the widest range possible to meet the needs of all children in the classroom. The range must satisfy varied genres, readability levels, interests, formats, authors, illustrators, and themes. Also, the baskets should include magazines, comic books, and lots of "real-world" reading materials (see the following section for suggestions).

Using the Environment To Motivate Students

Some classrooms shout, "We love reading!" as you walk through the doors. Books displayed with their faces out; books on shelves; books in every nook and cranny; books catalogued by topics; books in the reading center; books in every available area. If the classroom is immersed in books, kids can't help but reach for them. The environment will speak volumes to the students.

Where Do Books Come From?

Almost as feared as the toddlers asking, "Where do babies come from?" is the question teachers often ask, "Where do the books come from?" If only test-tube books could be propagated! But, alas! They come from bookstores and are purchased with the green stuff that is sorely missing from many of our educational institutions!

There are some immediate solutions that might get a class started with the Self-Selected Reading Block but that are not permanent solutions. Permanent solutions need to be sought from school budgets, business partnerships, parent-teacher organizations (PTO's), and parents. Everyone needs to work together on this!

Here are some solutions for obtaining adequate materials to get started:

☑ Laminate comic strips from Sunday's paper. Cut out the cartoons, hole punch the upper left corners of each strip, and put on a loose leaf ring to create a "flip book."

☑ Get free materials from pet stores. Usually manuals on pet care are written with kids as the targeted audience. The manuals might be on caring for dogs, cats, parrots, tarantulas, iguanas, and hamsters.

☑ Take pamphlets from your next visit to the doctor or dentist. Kids will love reading about gory subjects like tooth decay, root canals, and various diseases—the gorier, the better! Hope for pictures, too!

☑ The local veterinarian will have booklets on pet care and on pet diseases.

☑ Visit the local chamber of commerce or some local hotels where brochures abound. Students will enjoy reading about attractions of their own area through the eyes of a visitor. Maps might also interest them. Try packing several of these types of materials into a large resealable plastic bag.

☑ Take apart old basal readers or literature books, saving favorite stories that can be bound with laminated construction paper to make individual books.

☑ Find out when local drug stores and book stores dispose of books. Sometimes whole class sets can be found! (Maybe the store will agree to give them to you, rather than make you climb into the trash bin!)

☑ Use students' published work as part of the class collection. These will be some of their favorites!

☑ Get takeout menus from a variety of local restaurants. Students love reading them!

☑ Go to car dealerships and get brochures on trucks and cars.

☑ Even grocery stores often have pamphlets on nutrition, food care, and interesting food facts.

☑ Hunt at garage sales, flea markets, or used book stores for books of interest to your students. Remember that they deserve pretty books and might not pick up books with missing covers.

☑ At grade levels where birthdays are still class celebrations, ask parents to donate a book in the child's honor rather than sending the traditional cupcakes. Encourage them to inscribe their child's name inside the book. (Lasting memories of literacy are far better than the lasting memories on our hips!)

☑ Present the PTO or the school's business partner with a wish list of certain book titles you want to add to your class. Many partners say they don't know quite what to do for schools. Help them!

☑ Call or write your local extension service to request brochures on numerous topics of interest.

☑ Owner's manuals for appliances are welcomed by mechanically-inclined students.

☑ Recipe books might be appreciated by some students.

☑ Drivers' manuals are hits with the older students and are usually furnished at no charge by the Highway Department.

☑ College catalogs might catch the interest of some students.

☑ Clothes catalogs that fill mailboxes at home and usually end up in the trash are welcomed additions to the book baskets.

Many of the materials listed represent "real world" kinds of reading materials that will remind students that reading does serve a practical purpose in their lives. Surprisingly, many students, even those at the upper grades, have not really made this connection. They think that reading is what you do in school—read stories in the literature book and discuss them, or read the science or social studies book and answer questions at the end of the chapter. They have not processed that teachers are equipping them with lifelong skills that will help them not only to cope and survive in the world, but also to thrive in the world. **So, even when books are abundant, real-world reading materials should always be available with that constant reminder.**

The list of free and inexpensive materials is endless, but good books in plentiful supply are necessary for every classroom. Every child—at every age—deserves to hold these good books. **Schools must look for permanent solutions!**

Books Students Recommend

In a poll taken of several hundred students, these were their book recommendations:

Grades 4 to 6

Animorphs Series by Katherine A. Applegate (Scholastic)
Anne of Green Gables by Lucy Maud Montgomery (Bantam, 1909)
Babysitters' Club Series by Ann M. Martin (Scholastic)
Boxcar Children Series by Gertrude Chandler Warner (Albert Whitman & Co., 1990)
Bridge to Terabithia by Katherine Paterson (HarperCollins, 1977)
The Borrowers by Mary Norton (Harcourt Brace, 1989)
Calvin and Hobbes Cartoon Books by Bill Watterson (Andrews McMeel Publ.)
The Cat Ate My Gymsuit by Paula Danziger (Dell, 1974)
The Cay by Theodore Taylor (Random House, 1987)
Charlie and the Chocolate Factory by Roald Dahl (Penguin, 1964)
Charlotte's Web by E. B. White (HarperCollins, 1952)
Chasing Redbird by Sharon Creech (HarperCollins, 1997)
Dear Mr. Henshaw by Beverly Cleary (Dell Yearling, 1983)
Don't Make Me Smile by Barbara Park (Knopf, 1981)
Encyclopedia Brown by Donald J. Sobol (Bantam, 1963)

Eyes of the Amaryllis by Natalie Babbitt (Sunburst, 1977)
Face on the Milk Carton by Caroline B. Cooney (Bantam, 1990)
Freaky Friday by Mary Rodgers (HarperCollins, 1972)
Go Eat Worms by R L. Stine (Apple, 1995)
Goosebumps Series by R. L. Stine (Apple)
Harry Potter Series by J.K. Rowling (Arthur Levine)
Hatchet by Gary Paulsen (Aladdin, 1999)
Harriet the Spy by Louise Fitzhugh (HarperCollins, 1964)
Heart of a Champion by Carl Deuker (Flare, 1994)
Heartbeat by Norma F. Mazer and Harry Mazer (Bantam, 1988)
Henry Huggins by Beverly Cleary (Avon, 1950)
Homecoming by Cynthia Voigt (Atheneum, 1981)
The House with a Clock in Its Walls by John Bellairs (Dell, 1973)
The Indian in the Cupboard by Lynn Reid Banks (Camelot, 1999)
I Want to Go Home by Gordon Korman (Scholastic, 1981)
A Job for Jenny Archer by Ellen Conford (Little, Brown, 1988)
The Leaves in October by Karen Ackerman (Atheneum, 1991)
A Light in the Attic by Shel Silverstein (HarperCollins, 1981)
My Teacher is an Alien by Bruce Coville (Minstrel, 1989)
Nightmare by Willo Davis Roberts (Atheneum, 1988)
Nothing's Fair in Fifth Grade by Barthe DeClements (Penguin, 1981)
Ramona Series by Beverly Cleary (Camelot)
Roll of Thunder, Hear My Cry by Mildred D. Taylor (Puffin, 1976)
The Secret Garden by Frances Hodgson Burnett (Harper, 1912)
Shel Silverstein poetry books
Summer of the Swans by Betsy Cromer Byars (Puffin, 1970)
The Snarkout Boys and the Avocado of Death by Daniel Manus Pinkwater
     (NAL, 1982)
Stuart Little by E. B. White (Harper Trophy, 1999)
Tales of a Fourth Grade Nothing by Judy Blume (Dell, 1972)
Tiger Eyes by Judy Blume (Simon & Schuster, 1983)
Trumpet of the Swan by E. B. White (HarperCollins, 2000)
Sarah, Plain and Tall by Patricia MacLachlan (Harper, 1985)
Slumber Party by Christopher Pike (Scholastic, 1985)
Wayside School Series by Louis Sachar
The Wind in the Willows by Kenneth Grahame (Bantam, 1983)

Grades 6 to 8

Another Fine Myth by Robert Asprin (Berkeley, 1978)
Are You There, God? It's Me, Margaret by Judy Blume (Dell, 1970)
Babysitters Club Series by Ann M. Martin (Scholastic)
Chronicles of Narnia by C. S. Lewis (Harper Collins, 1950)
The Chrysalids by John Wyndham (Penguin, 1955)
The Contender by Robert Lipsyte (Harper Collins, 1967)
The Counterfeit Tackle by Matt Christopher (Little, Brown, 1990)
A Day No Pigs Would Die by Robert Newton Peck (Random, 1973)
The Day of the Triffids by John Wyndham (Penguin, 1951)
The Diary of Anne Frank by Anne Frank (Pocket, 1947)

Dicey's Song by Cynthia Voigt (Atheneum, 1983)

The Dragon Reborn by Robert Jordan (Tor, 1991)

Dragonsong by Ann McCaffrey (Bantam, 1976)

Fahrenheit 451 by Ray Bradbury (Pocket, 1967)

The Fox Steals Home by Matt Christopher (Little, Brown, 1985)

Foundation by Isaac Asimov (Ballantine, 1951)

From the Mixed-Up Files of Mrs. Basil E. Frankweiler by E L. Konigsburg (Aladdin, 1967)

The Giver by Lois Lowry (Houghton Mifflin, 1993)

The Great Gilly Hopkins by Katherine Paterson (Harper, 1978)

Guinness Book of World Records Series (Bantam Books)

Hitchhiker's Guide to the Galaxy by Douglas Adams (Pan, 1979)

The Hobbit by J. R. R. Tolkien (Ballantine, 1937)

The Hockey Machine by Matt Christopher (Little, Brown, 1992)

I Know What You Did Last Summer by Lois Duncan (Pocket, 1973)

I Know Why the Caged Bird Sings by Maya Angelou (Bantam, 1970)

Island of the Blue Dolphins by Scott O'Dell (Dell, 1960)

Little Women by Louisa May Alcott (Price Stern, 1983)

A Long Way from Chicago: A Novel of Stories by Richard Peck (Dial, 1998)

Lord of the Flies by William Golding (Faber, 1954)

The Lord of the Rings by J. R. R. Tolkien (Unwin, 1954)

M. C. Higgins, The Great by Virginia Hamilton (Aladdin, 1974)

Maniac Magee by Jerry Spinelli (Little, Brown, 1990)

Number the Stars by Lois Lowry (Yearling, 1990)

On a Pale Horse by Piers Anthony (Ballantine, 1983)

The Outsiders by S. E. Hinton (Dell, 1967)

The Pigman by Paul Zindel (Dell, 1968)

Rumble Fish by S. E. Hinton (Dell, 1975)

Seventh Son by Orson Scott Card (Tor, 1987)

Shiloh by Phyllis Reynolds Naylor (Yearling, 1992)

Snow Bound by Harry Mazer (Dell, 1973)

A Solitary Blue by Cynthia Voigt (Atheneum, 1983)

Startide Rising by David Brin (Bantam, 1983)

Stranger in a Strange Land by Robert A. Heinlein (Ace 1961)

The Summer of My German Soldier by Bette Greene (Puffin, 1999)

The Sword in the Stone by T. H. White (Harper Collins, 1975)

The Way Things Work by David Macaulay (Houghton Mifflin, 1988)

Tiger Eyes by Judy Blume (Simon & Schuster, 1983)

True Colors of Caitlynne Jackson by Carol Lynn Williams

Turtle on the Fence Post by June Rae Wood (Philomel, 1997)

Voice on the Radio by Caroline B. Cooney (Econo-Clad, 1999)

War of the Worlds by H. G. Wells (Econo-Clad, 1999)

Weird on the Outside by Shelley Stoehr (Laurel Leaf, 1996)

A Wrinkle in Time by Madeleine L'Engle (Dell, 1962)

Organizing for the Reading Time

Students' easy access to books during the Self-Selected Reading Block can be accomplished in a number of ways at the upper grades.

The Book Basket Method

In some classes, teachers provide book baskets that are delivered to the cooperative groups' tables. In these baskets are a wide range of materials, based on the interests and reading levels of the students at each table. Approximately 25 selections are included in each basket, and each basket has a different mixture. The same basket will come to the same group of students for one to two weeks, depending upon how many students are reading longer books. Once most students are reading novels, one week is not adequate. For the students who may not choose novels or lengthy books, however, there must be a plentiful supply of other materials in the basket if it remains with them for two weeks.

Advantages: A distinct advantage of this system of bringing books to the tables is that it limits movement and distractions in the classroom, so that the time spent reading is maximized. Often, the student who most needs to be engaged in a book spends the entire reading time roaming the room in search of a book, which he often does not find! Also, this method of bringing the books to the students further encourages students to be exposed to materials they might not otherwise choose if they were given freedom to select anything in the classroom to read. Many students tend to get "stuck" on a particular genre and will read it exclusively, never discovering other types in which they might cultivate interest.

Disadvantages: Some teachers find at the upper grades that their students' interests cannot be met with such a limited range of materials as the 20 to 30 books, magazines, and other printed literature that are included in a book basket. Also, in classrooms where most students have moved into reading chapter books and novels, some teachers find it difficult to manage replacing chapter books in baskets when a student holds back a book to complete it after the basket has rotated to another table. This method can be used by self-contained classrooms as well as upper grades classes that are departmentalized, though it may be difficult for students to place bookmarks to continue reading a selection.

Organizational Tips:

1. If cooperative groups can be organized with no more than five students to a group, **each student can have a day of the week on which she is responsible for getting the basket and delivering it to the table for the other group members.** Because there are many tasks that can be accomplished by students throughout the day, appointing Monday, Tuesday, Wednesday, Thursday and Friday students can be most helpful to the teacher.

2. **The book baskets will stay with each group of students for approximately one to two weeks**, depending upon the depth to which the kids at the upper grades are engaged in the materials. When baskets are filled with novels, magazines, and books that require longer reading time, one week may not be sufficient for students to explore all that is offered. The chapter books, too, will often take longer than a week of 20-minute segments to read.

3. **After the baskets have remained at the tables the prescribed amount of time, the baskets must be rotated to the next table.** This will continue until all tables have had an opportunity to read from each basket's selections.

4. **Then, the teacher will need to reorganize the book baskets with new selections.** While many kids in the lower grades are quite content to see the same selections return time and time again, students in the upper grades are not usually satisfied to reread the printed materials. So, restocking the baskets to keep the supply fresh and appealing is necessary.

5. **Students will likely appreciate having their own personal bookmarks with this system.** Once they have begun reading a selection without the opportunity to complete it, they will mark their place with a bookmark. The rule for the class is, "Once a bookmark is placed in a selection, it's hands-off for everyone else until the bookmark is removed!" (Reproducible Bookmarks are provided on page 217 of the Appendix.)

6. While some teachers may choose to allow each student to personalize a bookmark for her own use, **having color-coded bookmarks might also serve a good purpose.** For this organizational method, teachers should purchase baskets in a variety of colors, with a different color for each cooperative group of students. Then, bookmarks are made, enough for the largest group of students in the classroom. The bookmarks are made in a color that corresponds with the basket (e.g., five blue bookmarks, five green, five yellow, five purple, and five red). The bookmarks are kept in the baskets that are the same color. When a student is unable to complete a selection within the time allowed for Self-Selected Reading, he places that bookmark in the stopping place and then can easily return to that book and that page on the following day. If a child has not finished reading a book when on the last day that book will be available to her group, she may still place the bookmark in that book. Books that still contain bookmarks on the last day may be kept in one of several places: a) a reserved bookshelf in the room; b) in the students' desks (unless more than one group of students shares the classroom daily); or c) in the basket that will be coming to their group the following week. When the book is finally completed, the color of the bookmark will allow them to replace the book in the basket of the same color, no matter how long the reading takes, so that the range of materials remains intact.

7. **In schools where books are not plentiful, teachers may want to share their baskets**, staggering their Self-Selected Reading Block time so that the books can move from one class to another between two, three, or even four classes. This is not ideal but can help a school get the model started.

The Book Basket Plus Method

In classrooms where book baskets are used to deliver a carefully arranged assortment of books to the groups but where many students are reading novels, some flexibility may be built into the system. Here each student is given a pocket file folder. On one side of the folder is a reading log for recording the titles of books read, the dates, and the numbers of pages read daily. (See the reproducible Book Log on page 218 of the Appendix.) This is especially important in keeping students focused as they move into longer books. Most books will fit into the right-hand pocket. The student can place the book in the pocket and then either store the folder in the basket, in his desk, or on a reserved bookshelf in the classroom. For classes that change rooms, the reserved bookshelf may be the only solution.

An alternative to the folder could be the use of a large resealable plastic bag for each student. In the sealed bag, a student's reading log, bookmark, and book can be kept together in the book basket.

Advantage: Books are still easily accessible and time spent on the task of reading is maximized. Students are encouraged by this method to read books for longer periods of time.

Disadvantage: Some students who need to be reading easier materials (pre-chapter books) may feel intimidated by not having books in folders that are read over long periods of time. This can be solved merely by giving every student a folder and having them keep the folders in the baskets daily. It is much less noticeable that some students are reading chapter books and some are not. If a teacher has more than one class sharing the same baskets, a box will need to contain each class's folders.

Management Tips:

1. If **each student within a cooperative group has a different colored folder** in the basket, all students can quickly identify and pick their own folders.

2. If **the baskets are large enough to accommodate the book collection and the folders for each of the four or five students in that cooperative group**, no time is spent out of the desk. This maximizes the time spent on task.

Shopping for Books

In classrooms with generous supplies of reading materials, teachers might allow some shopping time for students daily or weekly. In self-contained intermediate grade classes, this time might be when students are coming into class in the mornings. In schools where time is more limited and instruction is departmentalized, students might have five minutes to shop as they first enter the classroom. Students are told to choose at least three to five selections for reading. Usually the rule is that once the materials are chosen, those materials should satisfy the student for that day. No students are allowed to be up during the reading time.

Advantages: Students have the widest range of materials possible from which to choose, with greater assurance that they will find something to please them. Also, if students are not allowed to wander during Self-Selected Reading time, there are still few distractions for other students, and everyone has the opportunity to be on task.

Disadvantages: Students often will gravitate towards their favorite genre, failing to explore the other genres. Also, sometimes there is such a wide choice that it might actually overwhelm many students, making them less able to choose an appropriate book.

Management Tips:

1. **Teachers should teach students how to find appropriate books that they will enjoy.** This will require modeling many times the process of thinking about the types of materials available, reading over the book jackets, reading the lead of the book or a paragraph to get a feel for the text, and making predictions about the text.

2. Teachers will want to **limit the time students have to make book choices** so that most of the time provided for reading is actually spent doing just that!

3. **Folders will need to be provided** so that students will have some way of holding on to books in which they are engaged.

SSR Bingo

Another organizational method for teachers who have a generous classroom library and who feel that their students may need more freedom in their reading choices is SSR Bingo. Each student is given a sheet that looks much like a bingo playing card. (See the reproducible SSR Bingo Card on page 219 of the Appendix.) Different genres are written in the grids on the card, such as fictional novel, historical fiction, magazine article, science fiction, biography, etc.

Students are free to make choices from materials in the classroom and from their frequent visits to the media center. However, they must also document on the bingo sheets that they are reading from a wide range of genres by writing bibliographical information in the space alongside the genre as they complete the reading of that piece. Teachers may want to require that students read at least one complete straight line of selections each marking period. For reading beyond what is required, the teacher might offer some small incentives, such as additional points on grade averages for additional lines of reading completed, free homework passes for additional lines completed, or whatever small treat might be the right incentive. The rewards should not be so attractive, however, that the reading becomes more a "means to an end."

Advantages: Students have greater choice in their selections of printed materials. Also, students pay close attention to the various genres available and readily begin to identify the characteristics of the genres.

Disadvantage: For students to make choices from all materials available in the room, they will be moving about the room, some settling quicker than others. Teachers will need to notice whether some students spend their entire time roaming, rather than reading. This can be distracting to the teacher during conference time and for students who need the room quiet to attend to their own reading.

Management Tips:

1. **The SSR Bingo cards can be duplicated for class use.** Students may want to keep the cards in reading folders for easy access during the SSR Block.

2. **Teachers may want to have a stamp or may initial a completed line as "validation" that the student has received credit for that line.** Then, the student can continue with the same sheet to fill up more lines or to earn additional points by making scattered selections from the card.

3. **This card might also be used as an ongoing homework assignment to encourage outside reading.** Again, students enjoy earning grade points for their efforts when possible.

Establishing Rules for the Classroom To Observe During Self-Selected Reading

Many teachers who have had great success with Self-Selected Reading time report that **allowing students some input into the rules to be observed during Self-Selected Reading greatly contributed to their success.** It is amazing how cooperative students can be when establishing rules in the context provided when a teacher says, "Let's talk about the conditions in the room that would help YOU to be able to concentrate on your reading and to enjoy this time. Let's make up some rules that we all feel we can abide by to help each other." This sounds much less punitive than other warnings and edicts that could be issued! Students should appreciate ownership in establishing their own rules of conduct.

Some classes decide that students should be allowed to sit comfortably on the floor or in the Reading Center during this time. If the movement in the classroom becomes disruptive, then the rules may need to be reviewed and revised.

Teachers will need to walk through the entire procedure and all expectations for this time period—how to make a book selection, how to reserve a book, how books are to get to tables, how and when to record the book and pages read in the book log, the noise level expected, what interactions are allowed at tables, where folders and bookmarks will be kept, and what to do with books at the conclusion of the reading time. **Modeling this and discussing it prior to implementing this block will make the entire process go much more smoothly!**

The Teacher's Role During Self-Selected Reading

Beginning of the Year

In the beginning of the school year, spending time modeling and encouraging are all that can be expected of a teacher. This is time well spent in setting expectations and getting students focused. For some students, this may be the first time they have ever experienced such freedom in their reading.

Prior to this year, reading, perhaps, always involved an assignment book and was always for a purpose that was far different from mere enjoyment. Now, suddenly, a teacher tells them to choose a book—any book—settle back in their desks (or on the floor, or in a bean bag chair), and read—just read! No pencil and paper test will be required! No essay questions will follow! Kids are thinking, "Could this be real? There must be a catch!" Some students, naturally, will be tempted to test the system—"If there's nothing required of me, then why must I do anything? I can just take advantage of this time to goof off!"

This is where Role #1 of the teacher comes into play! **Role #1 is that of encourager.** As students choose their selections and settle into reading, the teacher monitors the classroom, stopping occasionally to ask questions like, "Why did you select that book?" or "Have you read other mysteries?" The encourager tries to keep students engaged in books by thinking about their choices and their patterns of reading. This sets the tone for the formal conferences that will soon occur in the classroom. Students will soon realize that they need to be ready with some "defense" of why and how they make certain choices as readers.

The encourager also begins to delve a bit deeper into students' reading while making the rounds in the classroom. With comments such as, "When I read that, I didn't understand why the character reacted the way he did when his boss fired him. What did you think?" students will know that you expect them to be able to talk about the books with a certain level of understanding.

The encourager is also at hand when reluctant readers have difficulty with book choices. That's where teachers' knowledge of students and of books is critical! "I know you love the outdoors since you talk about going camping with your family so often. You really might enjoy Gary Paulsen's book, *Hatchet* (Simon & Schuster, 1987), about a boy who survived a plane crash and had to depend on what he knew about the out of doors to survive." Putting the right book in their hands is what it's all about!

Role #2 of the teacher is that of a good role model. In the beginning of the year, the teacher will want to offer an example of the expected behaviors of students during the Self-Selected Reading time. She will pull up a chair to a group, announcing that she would like to read today, too. She will peruse the books in the basket until finding something of interest. She will model, without calling attention in any way other than through her actions, how to stay engaged in a magazine article or other material during the 15 to 20 minutes of reading time. This also allows the teacher to voice any opinions about classroom behavior from the perspective of a reader—not just from a teacher's point of view: "Today I had trouble concentrating on the article I was reading because of the noise level. Maybe we should look at our rules to see if we're following them or if some adjustment needs to be made."

Later in the Year: Conferences

The time at which classes will have settled down will, of course, vary from classroom to classroom. For some teachers, only a couple of weeks are necessary to get the students focused and on task. For other teachers, six weeks might be needed to settle into a routine. **When students understand what is expected and when they are able to engage in their materials for the 15 to 20 minutes allowed, then it is time for the teacher to add Role #3—that of conference leader.**

Many teachers report that their favorite part of Four-Blocks™ is having the opportunity to talk one-on-one with students, to see them individually in a casual setting that promotes a comfortable, nurturing tone. All students appreciate being seen as individuals rather than as a class, and this conference time allows that special, personal time. Every student deserves the undivided attention of the teacher on a regular basis, and setting this time aside ensures that will happen.

Length of Conference

There is flexibility for conference scheduling at the upper grades. In the lower grades, teachers see each student once a week. With between 20 and 25 students in a classroom, the calculations of children per day and minutes per child reveal about four to five minutes of conference time per child per week.

In the beginning of the school year in the upper grades, the fast-paced schedule used at the primary grades is advised to get students focused on their reading and to provide some level of comfort with the conference format, especially if the students have not experienced a one-on-one conference before. As the year progresses, teachers may find that four to five minutes does not allow for the depth of discussion that some students are willing to have and need to have with the teacher. An eighth grader's desire to delve into the character's motives behind a certain action cannot and should not be confined to four minutes.

To include every student on some rotational basis and to allow some depth to the discussion, the teacher may need to move to a two-week schedule, seeing every student once every two weeks. This should allow each conference to last for approximately 10 minutes.

Organizing for the Conference

Teachers must have some method for determining which students will have conferences on which days. Assigning students to certain days may not be an equitable system, since students assigned to Fridays and Mondays will surely be shortchanged due to holidays and assembly programs. Instead, **assigning students by group numbers that can easily be rotated may be a fairer system**. For example, a teacher may randomly assign students to Group 1, Group 2, Group 3, Group 4, and Group 5. The teacher will see each group consecutively and will then start over, regardless of the day's events. If one group has fewer students assigned, that might be the day the teacher can see students who were absent on their assigned day.

If a teacher chooses to assign students to a group, care should be taken not to assign by achievement levels. Also, if one child from each cooperative seating group can be assigned to each group, this will help with other classroom management. Group 1 students might be called to get materials for their group at some point during the day or to share what they have read that day.

SSR Conference Schedule				
Group 1	Group 2	Group 3	Group 4	Group 5
Tyra	Julie	Michael	Ty	Caroline
Eugene	Ashley	Josh	Michelle	Jerome
Thomas	Byron	Meg	David	Alice
Cindy	Shenika	Jason	Beth	George
	Raymond		Marian	

If a chart in the room lists the students' names under the heading of the group to which they are assigned, the students can take responsibility for knowing when they are to be prepared to come to the conference. There is no need for the teacher to disturb the class by calling for the students individually.

Getting Started with the Conference

Teachers will likely want to start their conferences with three to five minutes in the beginning of the year just as the lower grade teachers do. Students are to bring a book that they are currently reading to the conference. The primary goal of this conference is to motivate students to read. In order to achieve this goal, the teacher must encourage the students to make appropriate book selections that they can enjoy. A book chat for this purpose might proceed as follows:

Teacher: "Rob, what book have you chosen today?"

Student: "*Navajo LongWalk* by Nancy Armstrong (Roberts Rinehart, 1994)."

Teacher: "What kind of book is it?"

Student: "I guess it's historical fiction. Isn't that the kind of story that is based on historical facts, but the story didn't really happen?"

Teacher: "Yes! Good! You remembered our discussion about that genre. Did you choose the book because you like that genre or because of the subject of the story?"

Student: "Both, I guess. I like to read about real things, or at least stories that could possibly happen. I don't care for fantasy at all. I also like stories from this time period, stories about settling the American West especially. We talked about this time period in social studies, and I got interested in it."

Teacher: "Has the book gotten off to a good start? Has it kept your interest?"

Student: "The author started by letting you know what life was like for Navajos at the time the U.S. Cavalry was beginning to set up camps for Indian tribes. You can tell in the first chapter that something's going to happen to this Indian tribe. So, I guess you could say there's a lot of suspense."

Teacher: "I often find myself thinking about how I could use an author's style or technique in my own writing. Did this author begin her book in a way that you would like to start a piece of your writing?"

Student: "I think so. There's a little short introduction that has the historical background. I liked reading that briefly before starting to read the story. Also, I like the way she started with a peaceful beginning but let you know, too, that something was about to happen—the suspense."

Teacher: "How much of the book have you read?"

Student: "I'm on the fourth chapter. This isn't a long book, though, and the chapters are short. I'll probably finish it in a couple more days."

Teacher: "I like the way you're thinking about what you read. It lets me know you're growing as a reader and as a writer at the same time! Let me know if you like the way this story ends when you're through and whether you'll recommend it to your classmates."

Chatting about books is what this conference is all about. **The teacher's main goal is to motivate students to read and to guide them to be engaged in books.** For students who still may think that reading is only "calling words," being engaged in a book is something that must be learned. The skillful teacher teaches this through conversation.

Another goal of the book conference, secondary but nevertheless important, is that this is an ideal time to gather information about students. From this brief conversation, the teacher above has learned that this student:

☑ can identify historical fiction by its characteristics

☑ understands the term genre

☑ comprehends elements of suspense

☑ has identified two favorite subjects in which he is interested (settling the West and realistic fiction)

☑ has identified a genre that he does not enjoy (fantasy)

☑ makes connections from what he has read to his prior knowledge (the previous social studies unit)

☑ knows how to talk about books with little prompting

☑ can gauge his own reading rate

☑ expresses that he enjoys reading something

So much is learned from so few minutes spent with the student! All of the information this teacher gathers is valuable in planning mini-lessons for her class, and in planning for the individual growth of this child. For this student reading *Navajo Long Walk*, she has intentionally planted a seed to help this student grow as she said, "I often find myself thinking about how I could use an author's style or technique in my own writing. Did this author begin her book in a way that you would like to use in your writing?" She feels that this student would benefit from making a stronger connection from his reading to his writing, to experiment with techniques and styles. The notes she makes on her conference form will remind her of this when she has writing conferences with this student.

Admittedly, not all students will talk about books with ease. This reluctance may have grown for a number of reasons. First, not all students have had an opportunity to talk with an adult about a book. Not surprisingly, there are not a lot of students who sit and chat with their parents in the evenings about books! If they did, teachers' jobs would be much easier. Some children come to us, too, not having been conditioned to this opportunity by the previous year's teacher, so this may be a brand new experience for them. Their first feelings about the book chat may not be that it is a grand opportunity, but that it is an awkward time. They would, in fact, rather be handed a ten-item test instead of sitting down one-on-one and chatting. For the reluctant student, a conference may progress like this:

Teacher: "What are you reading today?"

Student: "This." (Shows the book rather than telling the title.)

Teacher: "Oh, that's *Little House in the Big Woods* by Laura Ingalls Wilder (HarperCollins Juvenile Books, 1953)! I love that whole series of Laura Ingalls Wilder's books. Do you like them, too?"

Student: "I guess."

Teacher: "These are stories about families who lived long ago. Do you like those stories that took place before cars and televisions, when people lived in log houses on the prairie and weren't dependent on modern conveniences?"

Student: "Not really. I like stories that happen today."

Teacher: "When you looked at the cover on this story you probably noticed a family that doesn't look like ours today. Did you have a reason for picking this one even though you like another kind of story?"

Student: "It was the only chapter book left in our book basket."

Teacher: "Do you think you'd like to try to read it or change books? I have a collection of Betsy Byars books on a shelf over here that you could choose from. Her stories are about modern-day boys and girls your age with the problems many of you experience. There's usually lots of humor in her books, too. *The Cybil War* (Econo-Clad Books, 1999) might be one that you would enjoy. Let's read the back jacket of the book and see if it's one you think you'd find fun to read."

So, in the real world, teachers will find some kids very reluctant to share, some who choose books because that is all that is left in the basket, some who choose books because they are the skinniest books in the basket, and some that don't have a clue how or why they've chosen a book. Teachers, like Boy Scouts, must always be prepared—with the right book or a suggestion of one. That link is critical. Maybe there will not be time left for talking about the book or reading anything other than the cover but, hopefully, the match between reader and the perfect book has been made. If not, there's always the next conference!

The best advice to be offered to teachers for whom the conference time is difficult is to hang in there! Teachers must continue to greet children during the conferences with a smile, with enthusiasm for books and reading, and with encouragement. They must be ready with a recommendation of a book that should interest that child if the child is having difficulty making a selection. They must use their greatest level of expertise in closely observing the habits and strategies employed by the child throughout the conversation, and the teacher must do this without intimidation as she inconspicuously jots some notes on a record keeping system of her own design. Not at all an easy task!

Conference Information

Much of the information to be gathered during the Self-Selected Reading Block conference is affective, not objectively measurable nor skills-based. **This is the time for teachers to detect whether reading is a positive experience for children and whether reading has yet become a habit in the life of each student.** Some of this information can be gathered through observation. A student who is well on his way to a lifelong habit of reading often exhibits all or some of these characteristics:

☑ eager to talk about books

☑ speaks confidently about what has been read

☑ expresses why he has made a book selection

☑ makes book selections with relative ease

☑ expresses likes and dislikes about reading

☑ relates books or portions of books to other texts he has read

These are subjective measures of how far along the continuum of developing a habit of reading a student might be. They are, nevertheless, important factors to watch for in the conference since **encouraging the lifelong habit of reading is the primary purpose of the Self-Selected Reading Block.**

Other information that is useful to collect during the conference is more concrete and measurable, and questions usually can be asked to elicit responses. Teachers may choose to focus on one particular aspect of a student's engagement with the text or may choose a broader focus for the information gathering.

For example, **when a teacher wants to know if a student is able to transfer knowledge about literary elements and text analysis that have been taught, he might ask questions to elicit focused responses.** Of the list of questions on the following pages, teachers would not need to ask all of the questions listed. Notice, however, that for the upper-grade students, these questions are not usually at the recall level. They encourage the student to read with depth and understanding and to look at reading from a writer's point of view, hoping to prompt transfer to the Writing Block as well.

Conference Questions

Setting
- ☑ What is the setting of your book?
- ☑ Can you find a passage that tells something about the setting? (You might have the student read this aloud.)
- ☑ Why do you think the author chose this setting?
- ☑ Do you think another setting would have been equally effective?
- ☑ Did the author do a good job in describing the setting so that you can clearly picture it?
- ☑ How important do you think the setting is to the story?
- ☑ If you were the author, would you have chosen this setting and described it just as this author did? If not, what would you have done differently?
- ☑ Did this setting remind you of any place you've ever been?
- ☑ Did this setting remind you of any other stories you've read?

Mood
- ☑ What is the mood that the author has created in this story?
- ☑ How did he/she achieve that mood—through narrative description, through dialogue, or in some other way?
- ☑ Have you written anything in our Writing Block where you've intentionally created a mood for the reader? Were you successful?
- ☑ Did the mood of this story remind you of any other story?

Character
- ☑ Who was the main character in your story?
- ☑ How did you learn the most about this character—through actions, through what others said, or through what the author directly told you?
- ☑ Can you find a passage that tells something about your character and read it aloud to me?
- ☑ Do you think the author did a good job of developing the character?
- ☑ Did the character change from the beginning of the story to the end? Can you tell me a little about how he/she changed?
- ☑ Was there another character in your story who created some conflict or tension with the main character?
- ☑ Did the author do a good job of creating and describing the secondary characters?
- ☑ Were the characters believable?
- ☑ Did the characters in this book remind you of characters in another book or of people in real life?

Genre
- ☑ What type of book are you reading?
- ☑ How did you determine that? What characteristics help you decide that it is _____?
- ☑ Is this a genre that you enjoy reading? Why or why not?
- ☑ Have you read similar books by this author?
- ☑ Have you read similar books by another author?
- ☑ How do those books compare to this one?
- ☑ Do you enjoy writing this genre?

Plot
- ☑ Can you summarize the main plot of this story?
- ☑ Are there subplots in the story, too?
- ☑ Are there any special techniques, such as flashbacks, that the author used in presenting the plot? If so, what were they?
- ☑ Was it easy to predict what was going to happen in the story? If not, did that make the book more or less interesting?
- ☑ Did this plot remind you of anything in real life that you've experienced or that you've heard about?
- ☑ Did this plot remind you of any other stories you've read?

Illustrations (where applicable)
- ☑ Do you feel that the illustrations add to the text? Why or why not?
- ☑ Do you usually choose books that are illustrated?
- ☑ Do you think that the style of art was appropriate to this text?
- ☑ Is this the kind of art you would have chosen for this text (photographs, watercolors, cartoons, charts, graphs, etc.)? Why or why not?
- ☑ Did you feel that the illustrations were as equally important as the text?

Point of View
- ☑ What was the point of view the author chose for this story?
- ☑ How could you tell the point of view?
- ☑ Did you feel that this was the best choice for this story?
- ☑ What are advantages of choosing this point of view?
- ☑ Do you think there are disadvantages in presenting the story from this point of view?
- ☑ Have you used this point of view in your own writing?

Theme

☑ Have you gotten far enough along in your reading to detect a message that the author might be conveying through his story?

☑ What message do you think the author is telling?

☑ Is this a theme that can be transferred into everyday life experiences?

☑ Do you think the author did a good job of conveying this message?

☑ Have you written anything using a similar theme?

Purpose

☑ What do you think was the author's purpose in writing this selection (to entertain, persuade, inform, etc.)?

☑ Was this the best genre to use in achieving that purpose?

☑ Do you think the author presented the purpose clearly?

Nonfiction

☑ What kind of nonfiction are you reading?

☑ How did you determine it was nonfiction?

☑ What kind of nonfiction is it (biography, informational book, etc.)?

☑ Is this a genre you enjoy? Why or why not?

☑ Have you written anything like this before?

☑ How does this author keep your attention?

☑ What is something new you've learned from this selection?

☑ How does this apply to your life?

Fiction

☑ What kind of fiction are you reading (historical, realistic, science fiction, fantasy, etc.)?

☑ How did you determine what kind of fiction it is?

☑ Is this a genre you like? Why or why not?

☑ Is this story like any other you've read?

☑ Have you written something like this before?

Conflict/Resolution

☑ What is the conflict in the story?

☑ What contributes to the conflict?

☑ How is the author building the tension throughout the story?

☑ How do you think the problem will be solved, or how was the problem solved?

☑ Was this a realistic solution?

☑ Is this the solution you would have chosen? Why or why not?

Opinions/Connections

☑ Are you enjoying the book? Why or why not?

☑ Why did you select this book?

☑ Are you enjoying it enough to read another similar one?

☑ Have you read any other books by this author? If so, were they similar? In what ways?

☑ Would you recommend this book to other classmates?

☑ Which readers would enjoy this?

Teachers may wish to copy the questions above and glue each section to a separate index card. Keeping the selected index card on hand during the conference may help the teacher stay focused. Teachers must consider each child individually in determining the difficulty level of the questions used to stimulate discussion. **Teachers must remember three things during the conference:**

1. Retain the comfort level of the book chat atmosphere.

2. Collect some information to help plan more effective whole group and individual lessons.

3. Use questions to stimulate and focus the discussion, taking care to gauge the appropriate depth of discussion without intimidating the student.

Conference Forms

With conference time at a premium, teachers may feel the need to have a conference form that will help them make the most of the time they have. **A conference form can help teachers to focus daily on important elements and to make decisions that will maximize their efforts in gathering good, useful information from the students.**

Although some forms are shared in this book (see Appendix), conference forms can be designed easily by the teacher who knows best what information will be helpful for planning instruction and for addressing the school's curriculum.

Some teachers may find that making anecdotal records about the conference is a sufficient way of gathering information. These notes might include documentation such as the following:

☑ Elaborated on her description of the character

☑ Showed notable progress in fluency development

☑ Applied knowledge of context clues during reading

☑ Linked this story to something previously read

☑ Needed the term "conflict" defined

Whether the teacher keeps anecdotal notes or has a conference form, **the record system is most effective if it allows the teacher to see whether patterns are developing over a period of time.** If notes are taken and filed without regard to these patterns, much valuable information is lost. Here are examples of these patterns:

☑ Is a student reading appropriate materials weekly? Too many easy books? Too many difficult books?

☑ Is the student varying genres, at least occasionally?

☑ Has the student's fluency changed according to the type of materials?

☑ Does the student continually need terms studied in Guided Reading defined?

☑ Does the student's comprehension change according to the type of genre he chooses?

Noticing the patterns over a number of weeks will help the teacher build a more complete profile of the student and plan more individualized instruction.

Sharing at the Upper Grades

Sharing books is something adults do in "real life." Oprah Winfrey has set a prime example of how enjoyable book discussions can be among adults. She models for many adults how to do this, knowing that some adults have never just talked about books with each other. Similarly, teachers must model this for students in many different formats until students feel comfortable with the book talks.

Formats

Book Chat Chair or Stool

Often the curriculum in the upper grades calls greater attention to speaking skills and oral presentations. Providing the comfortable book chat format paves the way for more formal presentations to come. With this format, students will come up before the class, sit on a stool or a chair, and "chat" about a book they've been reading during the SSR Block. Teachers may either take volunteers or may randomly draw names from a basket.

Group Chat (or Oprah Time!)

In this format, classmates participate as the "audience" while someone functions as the moderator—either the teacher or a student who feels comfortable being the center of attention. The lead questions or issues raised by the moderator (the "Oprah" figure) are generic enough to apply to many books which have been read or are being read by students during the SSR Block. The moderator poses the question/issue and then facilitates the sharing and discussion. Students are encouraged to use specific book titles and evidence in the discussions.

> Questions and issues are usually along the lines of the following: "Today we're discussing books that deal with problems and issues that students our age are facing. We want to explore these points: 1) what authors think our problems are; 2) whether the books we're reading are realistically portraying those problems; and 3) whether they are offering solutions that are practical."
>
> Another Group Chat might begin, "Today we're discussing how authors of fiction and nonfiction get us interested in their books. Because we write daily in this class, we want to look at reading from a writer's point of view to explore different styles and techniques we've noticed that get us interested in the text."

The moderator facilitates discussion, encouraging students to contribute. In some classrooms, the moderator passes a microphone to the person who has "permission" to speak to keep order in the classroom and to simulate the TV format.

Leader Chat

If students have been assigned to groups for their conference time, teachers might ask that each Group 3 student share that day at their table or cooperative group. For this to work, teachers must have formed groups from selecting one person from each cooperative setting to be a member of the group. With this format, one student in each of the cooperative settings would be sharing with the three or four students sitting with them. This allows a total of about four or five students to share.

Buddy Sharing

If each student has a cooperative group buddy or partner, then the teacher can easily say, "Today we have just five minutes of sharing time. Turn to your partner and share what you read today and whether or not you would recommend that he or she read it." This allows everyone a chance to share briefly.

Writing Response Sharing

The teacher gives out note cards (or has students use sheets of notebook paper) and directs students to write a brief reflection about the book they are currently reading. This can be a free response or one directed more specifically by the teacher. When students are finished reflecting for a couple of minutes, the note cards for each group are collected by that group's leader and are traded with another cooperative group. Everyone in the new group randomly selects a card and writes some response to whatever is written on the card. If this person has read the same book, comments can reflect that. Cards can be displayed on a bulletin board entitled "Critics' Corner," or "Book Talk Board." Once students know that comments are displayed, their reflections are usually a bit more serious.

The Good, the Bad, and the Ugly

On some days the teacher might like to have an open forum on book recommendations—the "good, the bad and the ugly." For the time allowed, any student may offer her opinion of a book she is currently reading, making recommendations as to whether most students would enjoy the book, whether only certain students would enjoy the book, or whether she really would not be able to recommend it to anyone!

Graffiti Time

For Graffiti Time, a teacher needs to have a bulletin board area covered with butcher paper. Time is allowed for some or all students, depending upon class size, to go to the graffiti board and write the titles of the books they are reading and comments about the books. They should also sign their names or at least initial their comments.

Graffiti Response Time

On a group rotating basis, usually over the course of a week, each student is asked to go to the graffiti wall and write a response to a comment about a book he has also read beside the original comment. This activity would have to be completed after books have been circulating in the room for some time.

Most of these sharing formats take only five to ten minutes to accomplish, keeping students motivated and thinking about what they are reading.

Helping Students Share

Many students will lack confidence as they begin to share books. This may be a new activity for them. No matter what the grade or how old the students are, teachers must continue to model for students what is expected in a book sharing and the different approaches that can be taken.

Teachers may find it helpful to have a poster of ideas that can offer students support. With just a glance at the poster, students may receive encouragement and direction. The poster could contain the following tips:

In a Book Talk, You Could Tell...

☑ the name and the author of your book.

☑ the type of book and how you decided that.

☑ a part of the book that interested you.

☑ about an interesting character.

☑ your recommendation to others about reading this book.

☑ about something you related to in this book.

☑ how this book is like another book you have read.

Occasionally, the teacher should give book talks about something she is reading, choosing some items from the chart or just modeling the traditional things people discuss when they share books. Staying casual and enthusiastic will make students feel more confident about their upcoming book talks.

How Often

One of the main purposes for the sharing time in the Self-Selected Reading Block is to keep students motivated to read a variety of materials. The frequency of sharing time may vary at the upper grades, depending upon the interest of students and the need for this extra effort at motivating them to read. Teachers may wish to start the year by sharing daily and then watching for signs, such as the following, that the sharing time may need to be reallocated:

☑ Students are easily and quickly self-selecting materials to read.

☑ Students are reading a wide variety of materials and genres.

☑ Students are focused on their reading during the allocated time.

☑ Students appear upset when the reading time ends.

As attention spans and interest in reading increase at the upper grades, students may find it quite difficult to discontinue reading after 20 minutes once they have "gotten into" their books. If this is the case and students seem annoyed with stopping to share daily, then cutting the sharing time to a day or two a week might be all that is necessary to keep students motivated. **Because students need to learn to talk about books and need to have practical purposes for refining their speaking skills, the book sharing should never be totally eliminated.**

Book Clubs as a Variation in Self-Selected Reading

Occasionally a completely different format for Self-Selected Reading rejuvenates the block. The Book Club, often used in the Guided Reading Block, is also a popular format for the Self-Selected Reading Block. This format gives students an opportunity to read and discuss the same books. How often do we all enjoy running into a friend who mentions having read a book we have just finished and getting to compare notes about it? What fun!

The Book Club during Self-Selected Reading is less structured than the Book Club during Guided Reading time. There is much less of an instructional role played by the teacher. The purpose of this Book Club is to have students enjoy their discussions about books and to explore the different points of view that they will bring.

How to plan for the Book Club days:

1. Select several titles (one title per group) of books of which there are several copies. (Remember to offer different genres.)

2. Give a quick book talk on each book or read the book jacket and the beginning paragraph so that students might anticipate what they will read in each book.

3. Give each student a note card and tell him to list the books in the order in which he would most like to read them.

4. Collect the note cards.

5. Assign each student to a book other than her last choice. Consider that the groups will need to be a manageable size for discussions.

6. Give the students a certain number of days to read as much of the books as possible during Self-Selected Reading Block time. They do not have to be seated together with students reading similar titles at this point. Books might also be taken home to finish before the Book Club days start.

7. After reading the book, or at designated intervals, students reading similar titles will be seated in a group together.

8. Each student will either be assigned a discussion topic to lead or will generate his own topic. (See Deal-a-Discussion Cards on pages 222-224 of the Appendix.)

9. After the daily teacher read-aloud, the students will go into their Book Club groups.

10. Students will take turns daily, stimulating discussion of their Book Club members with their questions, and will be responsible for eliciting responses from all group members.

On many days the teacher might bring closure to the block by asking members of a group or two to share something they enjoyed from their discussion that day. Students not only learn a great deal about books and book discussions during this format but they also learn lifelong skills of collaborative learning and group dynamics.

SSR time can be used infrequently to accommodate the spill-over from Book Club groups and Literature Circles that are operating in Guided Reading. This will expedite completion of the novel or text being read during Guided Reading and will allow for more in-depth discussion otherwise prevented by time constraints of the blocks.

Summary of the Self-Selected Reading Block

The purposes of this block:

☑ to build fluency

☑ to motivate students to read a wide variety of materials

☑ to allow students to read printed materials at their own independent reading levels

☑ to allow students to discuss books

☑ to build confidence in students as readers

Segment One: Teacher Read-Aloud   **(5-10 minutes)**

The teacher reads aloud to all students from a variety of genres, topics, and authors.

Segment Two: Independent Reading and Conferences   **(15-25 minutes)**

1. Students read books independently.

2. The teacher holds conferences with a designated number of students.

Alternate Segment Two: Book Club Reading   **(25 minutes)**

1. Students read or discuss assigned books.

2. Teacher monitors discussions.

Segment Three: Sharing (Optional Daily)   **(5-10 minutes)**

1. Students share what they have read with others, at least weekly.

2. When time allows, classmates can ask questions about the shared selection.

A Typical Week in an Upper Grades Self-Selected Reading Block

Monday

Read-Aloud Title: *Holes* by Louis Sachar (Farrar, Straus & Giroux, 1998)—fiction

Segment 1

The teacher sits on a stool in front of the class with the novel, *Holes*. The class has been listening to this Newbery Award winner for over a week. "This is one of the strangest stories I've ever heard," exclaims one student. "But it's one of my favorite novels ever!" The teacher reads chapters 42-45 to a class in which everyone's attention is riveted on the story as it unravels. When the teacher stops, she shares that they have only three more chapters and that they'll probably finish *Holes* tomorrow.

Segment 2

Leaders from each cooperative group of students deliver book baskets to their groups. In this seventh-grade class, four or five desks are grouped, forming a solid work surface that the students share. The book crates are filled with novels, newspapers, magazines, and pamphlets of various types. The same leaders who bring the crates to the tables also gather each group's folders that are stored alongside the crates. (Each group's folders are designated by a certain color.) There is one folder for each of the students in this class. They write in their reading choices and page numbers read during this segment. Some students have novels stored in their folders so that their selections are protected from other classes that share the crates. Some students are making new selections from the crates. The students all begin to read, and the classroom becomes quiet.

One student who has just gotten his folder removes his book from the folder and heads to the conference area to meet with the teacher. They meet for approximately 10 minutes today, enjoying their discussion of the characters in the novel that this student is reading. As soon as this student returns to his desk, the next student knows from the chart in the room that it is her time to meet with the teacher now. After 10 minutes with this student, the teacher still has time to monitor the classroom to see what other students have selected today. After a total of 25 minutes of reading, the teacher signals the class that their reading time has ended.

Segment 3 (Optional)

There is no sharing on this day.

Tuesday

Read-Aloud Title: *Holes* by Louis Sachar (Farrar, Straus & Giroux, 1998)—fiction

Segment 1

The teacher reads the last three chapters of this story to the students. "Oh, wow! I can't believe how that ended!" "What a great story!" "Talk about coincidence!" were the comments heard around the room as the story they had been reading for over a week ended. "This was certainly a different story by Sachar—not at all his usual story line," the teacher shares as she returns the book to the shelf. "You may want to read more books by Louis Sachar to see for yourselves his usual style of writing and story line. Now it's time for our Self-Selected Reading. If the table leaders will get the baskets and folders, please!"

Segment 2

Students continue with their reading as they did the day before, and the teacher has a conference with two more students for 10 minutes each.

Segment 3 (Optional)

Today, the teacher asks the Group 1 members to share at their tables for the last five minutes of this block what they have been reading and whether or not they would recommend their books to their classmates. The students enjoy listening to what their classmates have to share and learning about some new titles. Afterward, everyone returns their books and folders as class continues.

Wednesday

Read-Aloud Title: *Wilfrid Gordon McDonald Partridge* by Mem Fox (Kane/Miller Book Pub., 1985)—children's book, fiction

Segment 1

The teacher reminds the students that they have been reading some inter-generational stories in their Guided Reading Block and that a couple of children's books came to her mind to share with them. She wants to share one of her absolute favorite books today, *Wilfrid Gordon McDonald Partridge*, written by one of her favorite authors. "It's a beautiful story that has a message for all of us at every age. I'll share the illustrations as I read. Listen carefully," she says as she begins to read this tender story. The students seem to appreciate what Mem Fox has written.

Next the teacher asks, "Students, can you believe that this book was banned in Japan?" The students are eager to hear why as they exclaim, "But there are no bad words or X-rated pictures!" The teacher explains, "The people of Japan abhor the accepted American practice of putting elderly parents in nursing homes, and so they banned the book."

The teacher announces that it is now time for the table leaders to get the baskets.

Segment 2

Students read just as they have before, some choosing new materials from the crates and some returning to books they have been reading for days. The teacher holds her planned conference with two more students, chatting with them and then quickly recording some information from the conferences.

Segment 3 (Optional)

There is no sharing today.

Thursday

Read-Aloud Title: *Thirteen Moons on Turtle's Back: A Native American Year of Moons* by Joseph Bruchac and Jonathan London (Philomel Books, 1992)—narrative fiction and poetry

Segment 1

The teacher tells the students that she has one more book to share that she was reminded of during their readings of some inter-generational stories in Guided Reading. There is a poem for each of the 12 moons, which are the months of the year, in this book. She selects just half of those to share. When she finishes, she says, "We didn't have time for all of this beautiful poem, but if you'd like to read more, the book will be available in the room. Jessica, would you like to be the first to read it?" She hands the book to an eager student. Then, she announces that it is time for the leaders to get the books and the folders.

Segment 2

Students read just as they have before, some choosing new materials from the baskets and some returning to books they have been reading for days. The teacher holds her planned conferences with two more students, chatting with them and then quickly recording some information from the conferences.

Segment 3

The teacher announces that there is time for two students to share today. She calls for volunteers, and quickly two students' hands shoot up. They come when called, one by one, to share something about their books with the class. The other students enjoy hearing their recommendations. Afterwards, books are returned to folders and baskets.

Friday

Read-Aloud Title: Newspaper article entitled, "County's Oldest Citizen Recalls the Century"—news feature article

Segment 1

The teacher says that instead of the story she had planned for today she came across an article in the morning newspaper that ties in with the inter-generational stories they have been reading. She shares that she found the article fascinating—stories told by a man from their own county who is 112 years old! "Can you imagine what this man has seen over his lifetime? Let me share with you some of his memories of the 20th century."

She reads the article to them and hears remarks such as, "Wow! I never thought about all that has happened over the last 100 years." "I wonder what the next 100 years will bring?"

The teacher tacks the article to a section of the bulletin board which the class has reserved for news articles of interest.

It is time then for the group leaders to bring baskets and folders to the tables.

Segment 2

Students are in the routine of choosing their books or continuing with the ones they have previously selected. The room is quiet except for the background music of Mozart to which the teacher treats them on certain days. The teacher continues to confer with students who are on the schedule.

Segment 3

Today as the reading time ends, the teacher reminds the class that the baskets have been at their tables for two weeks and will move on Monday. If anyone is engrossed in a book and cannot part with it just yet, he can hold it back for a couple of days but must remember to which basket it belongs. Because the baskets are moving, she asks if anyone wants to promote any of the books that they enjoyed for the next group that will get those books. Three students give brief recommendations of "must read" books.

Chapter 4

Guided Reading Block

Are the students in the upper-grades classrooms still *learning to read* or are they as proficient in their reading as we can wish for them to become? Some educators have phrased this in another way, "Primary students *learn to read* and upper-grades students *read to learn.*" Many national achievement reports provide documentation contrary to this belief. Data reveal that students in grades four through eight have not achieved proficiency or mastery of reading skills and strategies. Therefore, **teaching only content rather than including instruction in skills and strategies may be a disservice to students.** As educators reflect on their daily observations of students at all ages and grade levels as they interact with text of various types, the complexities are clear. **Even though the skills and strategies may be the same at first grade and at twelfth, the complexity of the texts necessitates continuing to teach and apply these skills and strategies.**

Much of the direct, explicit instruction in the Four-Blocks™ Model occurs during the Guided Reading Block. Instead of the past approach taken, however, where teachers tried to "do it all" during guided reading, **the Four-Blocks Guided Reading Block is reserved for teaching students comprehension skills and strategies.** In the upper grades, students will be taught skills and strategies, given opportunities to apply them to various types of printed materials, and provided time to explore and enjoy reading to greater levels of depth.

What Is Read During Guided Reading?

The texts chosen for students to read during this block are printed materials that allow students to learn about and practice many different aspects of reading. **Teachers must select those materials that will help students achieve the block's goals:**

1. **to increase the comprehension level of students through their acquisition of comprehension skills and strategies**

2. **to allow ample opportunity for students to apply their knowledge of skills and strategies**

3. **to explore a great diversity of printed materials**

Because the Four-Blocks classroom is a heterogeneous one, some consideration must be given to the level of the materials used. Teachers must consider a range of materials that, given support, all students can read on days when all members of the class are using the same title. What teachers must remember is that the acquisition of the skills and strategies is what is critical—not so much the level of the text. The fact that some students may be reading material that is below their instructional levels is inconsequential during this time. This makes the Self-Selected Reading block even more crucial, however, so that students will all have time to read level-appropriate materials during the day.

In order to find material that can be read—with support—by all students, teachers in the upper grades should rotate between grade-level and easier materials, much as in the design for the lower grades. There is, however, a difference in how long students are exposed to each of these levels. In the lower grades, the guideline is three days at grade level followed by two days of easier reading. The lengths of the texts for the upper grades does not make that a practical plan for the upper grades.

Grade-level text is still important—perhaps even more significant—for upper-grade students. In these grades, many of the students are accountable to standardized, high-stakes tests, written mostly at grade-level. All students need exposure to and practice with this grade-level material, rather than encountering it for the first time in a testing situation. Given the right amount of support, most students can be successful with the text, even though it may be a great challenge for some.

Teachers in Four-Blocks classrooms must also provide a fair amount of easier text for students. Some students will need this easier text more than others for fluency development, and all students will benefit from the mini-lesson of skills and strategies and the opportunity to apply it to this text.

In the upper grades then, teachers will alternate between grade-level selections which may be lengthy and easier texts which will offer the necessary boost for some students. The grade-level text might require a week, or perhaps sometimes even longer; whereas the class may spend only a couple of days on the easier material.

What some schools use for grade-level material:

☑ Literature book or anthology selections
☑ Content area textbooks (science, social studies, health, and even math)
☑ Books of fiction, nonfiction, poetry, etc.
☑ Reference materials
☑ Sample test booklets
☑ Grade-level periodicals and newspapers (i.e., *Weekly Reader, Scholastic News,* etc.)

What some schools use for easier materials:

☑ Easier selections in literature anthologies
☑ Poetry
☑ Internet selections
☑ Below grade-level periodicals and newsletters
☑ Children's tradebooks

Sample Month of Reading Materials Used for Guided Reading

Sixth Grade Unit on Insights Through Folk Tales, Fairy Tales, Fables, and Tall Tales

Week One

Monday–Wednesday (grade level): Basal story: "Pecos Bill, King of Texas Cowboys" by Walter Blair (*Harcourt Treasury of Literature*, Harcourt Brace & Co., 1995)

Thursday (easier reading): Aesop's Fables

Friday (easier reading): Aesop's Fables

Week Two

Monday (grade level): introduction of books for Book Club, using variations of Cinderella books from different viewpoints and cultures:

- ☑ *The Rough-Face Girl* by Rafe Martin (Puffin Books, 1992)
- ☑ *Princess Furball* by Charlotte Huck (Mulberry Books, 1989)
- ☑ *Mufaro's Beautiful Daughters* by John Steptoe (Lothrop, Lee & Shepard Books, 1987)
- ☑ *Moss Gown* by William H. Hooks (Clarion Books, 1987)

Tuesday–Friday (range of grade levels): Book Clubs reading Cinderella stories

Week Three

Monday (easier): *Johnny Appleseed* by Steven Kellogg (Morrow, 1988)

Tuesday (easier): Poetry in *Johnny Appleseed* by Reeve Lindbergh (Joy Street/Little Brown, 1990). Compare and contrast two versions of the Johnny Appleseed story.

Wednesday–Friday (grade-level): "Three Strong Women" (Japanese folk tale) by Claus Stamm (*Harcourt Treasury of Literature*, Harcourt Brace & Co., 1995)

Week Four

Monday–Thursday (grade level): "Peki, the Musician" from *The Crest and the Hide and Other African Stories* by Harold Courlander (*Harcourt Treasury of Literature*, Harcourt Brace & Co., 1995)

Friday–Monday (easier): Selection of children's traditional folk tales and fairy tales

The selections are varied in scope and length and the materials alternate between grade level and easier throughout the month. The variety between those choices and the choices of groupings will help to keep students motivated in the classroom.

Formats for the Guided Reading Block

There are two major formats for this block: 1) one format with teacher-directed lessons; and 2) a student workshop, where more responsibility is placed on the students. Both formats provide the context for students to practice and apply what they have learned.

Teacher-directed reading is the format that is used almost exclusively in the lower grades. It is still used the majority of the time in the upper grades, though no longer without exception. The elements of these lessons are borrowed from research on best practice. Integrated into one lesson, these elements provide effective instructional delivery. The delivery is in three basic segments, easy to remember as 1) what must occur before reading to set the foundation (pre-reading); 2) how students will practice and apply the skills taught; and 3) how the lesson will come to conclusion to reinforce and review the application of the skill.

Segment One: Pre-Reading— Teaching and Learning about Comprehension

The pre-reading segment sets the foundation that will help students make better connections to the text they will encounter. The teacher works with the whole class during this time. There are many elements that contribute towards the success of students' reading during this pre-reading time. As many of the elements should be included daily as possible for maximum impact.

☑ Establishing Prior Knowledge

Children come to school having had different life experiences, and they bring something from those experiences to the printed page to help construct meaning. When those experiences are limited in the area covered by a given topic, understanding may be hindered by text that assumes that the reader is at least somewhat familiar with that topic. Even an adult who doesn't know a spark plug from a carburetor would derive little from a manual on advanced auto mechanics. Schema and background knowledge can play critical roles in comprehension.

When teachers address new topics, they realize that not all students have the background necessary to be successful with the text. To compensate for lack of awareness or experiences, the teacher must help to build the knowledge base. For example, if a class is reading a story based on Japanese culture, then awareness of where Japan is located, as well as something about its history and customs, may be quite helpful in understanding the story. The teacher may help students locate Japan on the map in the classroom, have students research its history and culture, or read *Grandfather's Journey*, a children's book by Allen Say (Houghton Mifflin, 1993), to the class.

> "Having knowledge of the world is essential for comprehension, but it is useless if it is not connected to the passage being read. Readers need to know something about what they are reading; they also need to realize when their knowledge fits the particular passage they are reading." (Cunningham, Moore, and Cunningham, 1999)

Sometimes students have already covered material that relates to what the class is preparing to read but the teacher wants to be sure that they activate their prior knowledge, or that they recall or retrieve it for their benefit. Some time is spent reconnecting students to what they already know so that they can relate it to new information.

Whether the knowledge exists from prior exposure and experiences or whether the teacher establishes the prior knowledge, the teacher can greatly heighten comprehension by taking a brief time to do this.

The inclusion of prior knowledge in the pre-reading lesson is much like the following equation:

Prior Knowledge + New Information = Comprehension

Ways to Establish Prior Knowledge

Use graphic organizers: For students who are visual, graphic organizers help them to visualize the structure of the text. Once students understand the concept of graphic organizers, they will enjoy creating their own.

Share your experience: Often, the teacher may need to share some personal knowledge of the topic through a story, an anecdote, or a description.

Show pictures: Because a picture often is really worth a thousand words, teachers might choose to show pictures supporting the topic. Pictures are easily accessible from the Internet on any imaginable subject. Most libraries also have artwork that can be borrowed. Works of art may make impressions on many artistic students. Sometimes photographs related to the subject, taken by students, help to establish prior knowledge.

Go to the Internet: Most students are quite adept at "surfing the Net" and may enjoy the challenge of an assignment prior to starting a new unit or topic. Internet information can also be accessed by teachers to help construct prior knowledge through short excerpts of explanation, pictures, film clips, and even the voices of writers and historical figures.

Brainstorm together: One of the easiest and most effective ways to lay the foundation for beginning a topic is to stimulate discussion, jotting down on a transparency or on the chalkboard ideas and impressions shared by different students prior to reading the text. This gives students more ownership in their reading.

Use children's books: These should present the concept in a short, simple, appealing format.

Bring in artifacts: Quite often, a concrete object may help students make closer connections to what will be read. Teachers may want to send home with students a list of some of the topics to be covered during the semester with a request that parents consider sharing items that may help students' understanding.

Ask several students to share their personal connections: An impromptu sharing by students who have some knowledge of the topic might help others make a closer connection.

Have guests share their expertise with the class: If parents or community members have expertise in the area being studied, teachers might consider allowing the guest to help with a firsthand account of the topic.

Use key vocabulary words to stimulate discussion: Sometimes vocabulary can be a great springboard for discussion. Simulating a game show, the teacher can share a list of vocabulary words, asking students to guess what the topic might be.

Here is an example of a graphic organizer related to the book *Croc and Gator Attacks* by Patrick Fitzgerald (Children's Press, 2000). Prior to reading this book, the teacher asks students to share what they know about alligators. After reading, the class will return to this web to add their new knowledge.

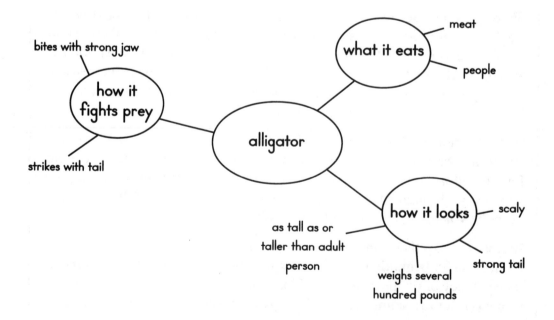

☑ Teaching Vocabulary

Vocabulary is included in the Guided Reading Block because it is a comprehension skill. It is the meanings of vocabulary words that are important, rather than the spellings. Vocabulary words are chosen for one of two reasons. First, they are chosen because they are critical to the meaning or concepts of the text. Second, they may be chosen because a teacher anticipates that the students will have difficulty decoding them and that the difficulty might hinder progress in reading.

Gone are the days of assigning 10-20 vocabulary words a week and then having students find them in the dictionary and write sentences with them. So often kids memorized these words for Friday's test, and then promptly forgot them. Why didn't the words "stick" with the students? Two ingredients were often missing from these vocabulary lessons: 1) applying knowledge of the word immediately in context, and 2) providing instruction that helped students store the words in the associative memory.

When addressing these two necessary ingredients, teachers in Four-Blocks classrooms must present the words to the students in some brief but powerful way. They must keep in mind that the more concrete the examples of the words can be and the closer and more personal the students' connection to the words, the more likely it is that the words will be retained by the students. Approximately four words are stressed daily, few enough for students to easily grasp and numerous enough to extend their knowledge base.

> "When students are given teacher-prepared vocabulary lists from which they much look up and memorize definitions, not only do they become turned off to reading, but they also do little meaning-making. Words in pre-selected vocabulary lists often lack connections to the real world or to the student's own reading." (Wilson, 1999)

Quick Ways To Introduce Vocabulary Words

RIVET

A game that is similar to the age-old game of Hangman, RIVET can be used to focus students' attention on several key vocabulary words for the text being read. (Cunningham, 1999)

The teacher begins by telling the students, "Today there are four words that are important to the text we're going to be reading. Let's see if any of you can guess these words." Then, on the board or on an overhead transparency, he numbers 1-4 and begins by supplying dashes rather than letters for the first word:

1. _ _ _ _ _ _ _ _ _ _

"Now, let me reveal the first letter to get us started with some guesses."

1. i _ _ _ _ _ _ _ _ _

"Any guesses for a word starting with 'i' that has ten letters?"

If the teacher has already helped students establish prior knowledge, their guesses are likely to be more reasonable than if they are making wild guesses. Also, teachers may want to prompt students by giving definitions as they go, such as "This word starts with an 'i' and relates to the people we are reading about today in the book, *If Your Name Was Changed at Ellis Island.*"

The teacher continues to reveal each letter in the order it occurs in the word, taking guesses each time. If a student makes a guess, the teacher has the student tell the next letter and then adds the correct letter to see if the spelling and the guess match.

The complete word (*immigrants*) is finally guessed or revealed. The teacher should take a brief opportunity to explain the definition of the word in the context of what they will read. The teacher may want to jot a simple definition beside the revealed word.

Picture RIVET

An additional step can be added to the game of RIVET to aid students in making more personal connections to the words being presented. This personal connection may be what helps students store these words in the associative memory, rather than in short term memory.

As the game of RIVET is played, each student will keep a sheet of paper on his desk. The paper will be folded into quarters or eighths, depending upon the total number of words to be presented over several days. Each time one of the words is revealed, the teacher asks the students to write the word in one of the cells of their folded paper and to draw a picture that will remind them of the meaning of the word. As the students read the text, they have a picture dictionary to use as a glossary of terms as they encounter difficult or keywords.

Vocabulary Clustering

With this activity, the teacher selects many words from the text, choosing only a few difficult words among many familiar words. The students work in their cooperative groups to find any relationships and categories for the words, using a graphic organizer to cluster the words.

This activity may look this way, using the text, *The Panama Canal* by Barbara Gaines Winkelman (Children's Press, 1999):

The teacher either writes on the board or overhead or gives the students a printed list of the words:

floods	merchants	crossing
United States	sea	Balboa
isthmus	buccaneers	build
Panama	dreamed	connected
canal	construction	interoceanic
passage	neutral	malaria
cholera	smallpox	transcontinental
Atlantic	Pacific	lock
landslides	humidity	Roosevelt
Carter	divided	treaty

Then students work together to group the words, inventing their own logical categories. One group's vocabulary clusters might look like this:

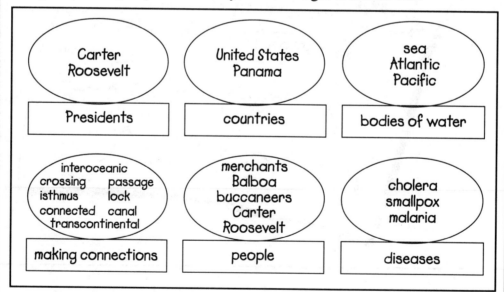

This activity requires higher-order thinking skills to think about words and their relationships and to verbalize those connections. Teachers are sure to find that students will be creative in coming up with categories, and that the categories are often springboards to further exploration and instruction.

Through this activity, students begin to see that the dictionary definition is not what teachers really want kids to know about words. The relationships among words and their connections to the meaning of the text are equally important, as well as far more interesting!

Also, because this activity can be time-consuming, teachers can assign the categorizing as homework to be done prior to the Guided Reading Block, or they can use some of the Working with Words Block time since this is a word exploration activity. (See page 225 of the Appendix for a reproducible Vocabulary Clustering Chart.)

Vocabulary Pop-Up

Another quick and easy way to present vocabulary is through the use of a device that actually lifts the vocabulary words from the text. Older kids (and teachers alike!) are amazed by this more three-dimensional display of the words. For this activity, the teachers will need to follow these steps:

1. Select key vocabulary words from the text to be read.

2. Make transparencies of the pages where the words are located in the text.

3. Construct a flag from poster board and a stick (tongue depressor, paint stick, etc.). The size of the poster board will depend upon the text to be used and the position of the screen to the projector, but will generally be about 3" x 10". The poster board should be stapled or glued to the stick so that the stick runs down the middle of the short side of the poster board as in the diagram.

4. As the teacher talks about certain words in the text, he scoops up the word with the flag by placing the poster board end flush with the projection screen so that the word appears on the flag. Then, the teacher gradually brings the flag forward so that the word stays on the flag. The added dimension of the word delights students and holds their attention as the teacher talks about the dictionary definition.

5. Then, the teacher slowly returns the word to the screen and adds, "Now, let's look at what the word means in this paragraph of our story."

Yes, it's a gimmick! But, it holds the attention of the students and that's what it's all about! (Routman, 1995)

Text Walk

Much like a picture walk that primary teachers routinely do, a text walk not only provides a preview and definition of words, but also lets students know where they will encounter the words in the text and how they fit into the context of what is to be read. In a Text Walk, all students will follow the lead of the teacher as they thumb through the book and pause on certain words. A Text Walk for the upper grades for the book, *If Your Name Was Changed at Ellis Island*, by Ellen Levine (Scholastic, 1993), might sound like this:

> Teacher: "Today we're going to be reading the section of our text entitled 'What Did Americans Think about the New Immigrants?' We want to look first at some of the important words. Let's all turn to page 68 of our book. On the first page, skim the first paragraph and find the word you think is 'descendant.' When you find it, put your finger on it." (Time is provided for students to locate the word.)

> Teacher: "Now, it looks like everyone has found the word. Let's read the sentence it's in and see if we understand the word. Would someone like to read it for us?"

After the sentence is read, students deduce the meaning of the word.

Here are some other good ideas that work well to engage students with this Text Walk:

☑ Have students use self-stick notes for this activity. Give each student one large self-stick note and have them cut or tear the note into strips so that each note has the sticky part on one end. As words are found, students can place the notes in the margins and can write definitions on the notes to aid them as they read.

☑ Use Wikki Stix™ for this activity. Give each student a single stick and have him press it into a circle. As a word is located, the student should place the circle around the word. This helps students stay focused on the activity, especially those who are more tactile learners.

☑ Use the removable book cover material that comes in bright, transparent colors to make strips. This inexpensive material usually comes in five-foot rolls with a peel-off backing. Strips can be cut in any shape or size for use with vocabulary highlighting or for marking text for other reasons (e.g., "As soon as you come to the first clue to help you solve the mystery, place your strip there." "When you find out the setting of the story...," "Place the strip wherever you find the answer to this question...").

☑ If consumable text is being used, students can use highlighters, pens, or pencils to mark vocabulary words and to write definitions in the margins.

☑ If nonconsumable text is used, students can use small strips of the bright colored static paper now available for book covers. The teacher cuts the strips (suggested size approximately ¹/₂" x 2") and places them on the students' desks. Students peel off the backing paper, and the strips can be used time and time again with students placing them on text and then peeling them up to move to another spot in the text.

Teaching a Mini-Lesson

Direct, explicit instruction occurs daily, concentrating on some comprehension skill or strategy. Instruction is brief and as concrete as possible.

There is a skill or strategy emphasized each day. The teacher continues with the same objective for as long as necessary, presenting it in new and different ways until the students demonstrate that they can apply their knowledge to the text. If students easily grasp concepts, the teachers may move to a new skill daily, or may choose to stay with one skill for a longer period of time if necessary.

Four-Blocks does not dictate curriculum for teachers, nor the scope and sequence of skills instruction. Four-Blocks is not *what* we teach; instead it is *how* we teach. Teachers may be guided in their preparation of mini-lessons by their school or district curricula, by their students' needs, and by guidance offered in resources such as literature series or teachers' guides.

Some Skills and Strategies To Be Included in Daily Mini-Lessons

Relationships	Antagonists/Protagonists	Setting	Point of View
Cause/Effect	Tone	Theme	Flashback
Drawing conclusions	Mood	Purpose	Main Idea
Making Inferences	Test-taking	Audience	Plot
Compare/Contrast	Foreshadowing	Diction	Subplots
Supporting details	Conflict/Resolution	Propaganda	Irony
Characteristics of genres	Character Development	Text structure	Dialogue

Application Strategies:

How to reconnect to text when comprehension is lost
Rereading to build fluency and understanding
How to determine the main idea
How to summarize important points from the text
How to identify a genre by its characteristics
Setting a purpose for reading
Drawing connections: prior knowledge, personal connections, other texts
Reading with expression/intonation
Determining a character's qualities
Comparing characteristics of different texts
Comparing styles of different authors
How to apply test skills in the context of an authentic test

What is a Strategy?

☑ "An operation that allows the learner to use, apply, transform, relate, interpret, reproduce, and re-form information for communication" (Clay, 1991)

☑ The elevation of a skill to the level of application in the context of real reading (Routman, 1991)

Many upper-grades teachers have found great value in using children's books to introduce sophisticated concepts in a nonthreatening and concise format. Here are a few favorite books that can be used as examples of what is taught in Guided Reading:

The Stranger by Chris Van Allsburg (Houghton Mifflin, 1986)—symbolism

Dog Breath: The Horrible Trouble with Hally Tosis by Dav Pilkey (Scholastic Trade, 1994)—puns, word play

Tough Boris by Mem Fox (Harcourt & Brace, 1994)—characterization

Because of Winn Dixie by Kate DiCamillo (Candlewick Press, 2000)—voice

More Than Anything Else by Marie Bradby (Orchard, 1995)—plot, sequence, theme

Town Mouse, Country Mouse by Jan Brett (Putnam, 1994)—foreshadowing

Black and White by David Macaulay (Houghton Mifflin, 1990)—plot, subplots

Rose Blanche by Roberto Innocenti (Creative Education, 1996)—point of view with an interesting shift

Regular Flood of Mishap by Tom Birdseye (Holiday House, 1994)—cause and effect

Ashley Bryan's ABC of African American Poetry by Ashley Bryan (Atheneum, 1997)—sampling of 25 poems and spirituals; poetry techniques

Animalia by Graeme Base (Harry N. Abrams, 1987)—onomatopoeia

Faithful Elephants: A True Story of Animals, People, and War by Yukio Tsuchiya (Houghton Mifflin, 1998)—plot, sequence, cause/effect

Shaka: King of the Zulus by Diane Stanley (William Morrow & Co., 1994)—characteristics of biography

Snowflake Bentley by Jacqueline Briggs Martin (Houghton Mifflin, 1998)—characteristics of biography

Wilma Unlimited: How Wilma Rudolph Became the World's Fastest Woman by Kathleen Krull (Harcourt Brace, 1996)—characteristics of biography

2095 (Time Warp Trio) by Jon Scieszka (Viking Children's Books, 1995)—characteristics of fantasy

Insectlopedia: Poems and Paintings by Douglas Florian (Harcourt & Brace, 1998)—characteristics of poetry

Beast Feast: Poems by Douglas Florian (Voyager Picture Book, 1998)—characteristics of poetry

Heckedy Peg by Audrey Wood (Harcourt Brace, 1987)—characteristics of folk tales and fables

Zomo the Rabbit: A Trickster Tale from Africa by Gerald McDermott (Voyager, 1996)—characteristics of folk (trickster) tales

Outside and Inside Alligators by Sandra Markle (Atheneum, 1998)—characteristics of informational nonfiction

Agatha's Feather Bed: Not Just Another Wild Goose Story by Carmenagra Deedy (Peachtree Publ., 1993)—figures of speech; cause and effect

Fire on the Mountain by Jane Kurtz (Aladdin, 1998)—characteristics of folk tales

Sweet Clara and the Freedom Quilt by Deborah Hopkinson (Alfred A. Knopf, 1993)—characteristics of historical fiction

The Keeping Quilt by Patricia Polacco (Simon and Schuster, 1998)—characteristics of historical nonfiction

Setting a Purpose for Students' Reading

In the lower grades, pages generally offered more pictures and borders to interrupt the print. **Now, students are encountering more sophisticated print without the support of illustrations—just word after word after word. This can be quite daunting for some students in the upper grades, especially the struggling ones. These students need assistance with navigating the text. Setting a daily purpose for reading provides this assistance.** Elizabeth Wilson studied the approaches to comprehension among secondary readers and concluded that the primary division between good readers and poor readers is the tendency of the better readers to think about a primary purpose for reading. Poor readers lack "a vision of the kind of knowledge they are after in the first place." (Wilson, 1999)

Often setting a purpose is accomplished by asking the students a question, such as, "Why do you think the author chose this unusual title? Let's read today to find out," or, "Read today to be able to give three reasons why the main character couldn't leave his brother behind." Sometimes setting the purpose might be more creative and engaging, such as the following:

Sticky Note Strips

Cut slits in larger-sized sticky notes (towards the sticky end); do not cut through completely. Give each student a "whole" sticky note that has the number of strips needed for the purpose that is set. Direct students to tear apart the strips to use for identifying very important points.

For example, if the lesson focuses on characterization, the teacher might cut four times through the sticky note, creating five strips. She might say, "As you read today, find five clues for what kind of character we're reading about. Each time you see a clue, tear off a strip and place it there in the text. When we finish reading, we'll talk about what you've found."

Graphic Organizers

All types of graphic organizers are used to help set purposes. Graphic organizers are especially helpful to show text organization and to aid students who are highly visual. A few easy graphics follow:

☑ **The Hand:** Students can easily trace their own hands to use in a variety of ways at the direction of the teacher.

"Read today to find out five things that this main character says or does, or that someone else says about him, that will let us know what kind of person he is. Write the character's name in the palm of the hand and put your evidence in the fingers as you find it in the story."

"Let's read to find out the supporting details in this article."

"Let's read to find out what we can about the setting of this story."

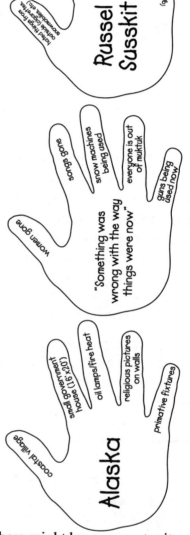

☑ **Someone Special Lends a Helping Hand:** There might be an opportunity to trace the hand of someone influential in the lives of your students. One teacher, who had the once-in-a-lifetime opportunity to travel on a plane with Shaquille O'Neal, asked to trace his gigantic hand that barely fit on a sheet of paper! The students loved using his hand as a graphic organizer.

☑ **Topic Maps/Webs:** The topic map is probably the most versatile graphic organizer of all. It merely has bubble or circles that show associations by connecting lines. A lesson might start by using a basic topic map outline in an attempt to search for details to complete it.

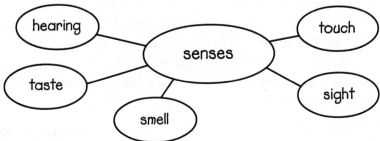

☑ **Invent an Organizer:** Once students understand the concept of a graphic organizer, they will become adept at creating their own, sometimes using shapes that relate to the topic, and certainly using graphics that help to capture the structure of the text or the relationships within the text being studied.

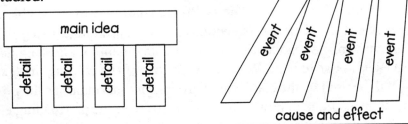

Making Predictions

Good readers make predictions before they read and constantly during their reading. Teaching students previewing and predicting as a strategy has been shown to be effective in helping students construct meaning (Cooper, 1997). Where younger students learn to predict from the title and the pictures that will support their texts, older readers, who sometimes will not have illustrations or graphics, will include reading the first few sentences or a paragraph. During the entire reading of the text, students should continue to make predictions and change them constantly as necessary. After proficient readers complete the task of reading, they confirm their original predictions. In order to have students internalize this concept, Four-Blocks teachers lead their students in making predictions daily about elements from the text. Sometimes students learn that the "unpredictability" of a story makes it even more interesting. They also realize, however, that without the reader making predictions first, the irony that makes the story enjoyable is lost.

> "Making predictions about what will happen in a story is a time-honored, student-centered knowledge activation strategy." Cunningham, Moore, and Cunningham, 1995)

Compacting and Integrating the Pre-Reading Elements

The more a teacher practices compacting the pre-reading portion of the Guided Reading Block, the easier it becomes to deliver within the time allotted. On days when some of the elements seem unnecessary, they may be omitted. For example, if the key vocabulary is presented on the first day of a week-long study of a topic with which many students are already familiar, then a quick review over a couple of days might be sufficient. After several days of prior knowledge building, the teacher may merely remind the students briefly of what they talked about the day before. **The bulk of the time for the Guided Reading Block still needs to be spent with actual reading and reading practice daily.**

A simple KWL chart is an excellent example of how some teachers integrate the pre-reading elements. In brainstorming about what students already know (the "K" of the chart), the prior knowledge is being shared. For students who do not have prior knowledge, they will hear knowledge shared that will help establish a foundation for them. As the students then decide what they want to know from reading the text (the "W" of the chart), they set their own purpose for reading and they make predictions about what might be included in the text. The skillful teacher may even be able to include vocabulary words in the K or the W sections of the chart, either using words some students share, rewording a student's question or statement, or allowing her own addition of a question or statement. What students learn from reading the text (the "L" of the chart) will be used by the class, small groups, or individuals as the post-reading activity. This is an example of how easy it can be to cover the pre-reading elements in a short amount of time, but to provide a great deal of support for reading the text.

KWL for: *An Author's Story*		
What I **Know**	What I **Want to Know**	What I **Learned**
• She wrote children's books. • TV show "Little House on the Prairie" based on her stories. • Lived in 1800's.	• Was her sister really blind? How did she become blind? • Did she read braille? • In what state did she live? • How did she start writing?	

Book: *Laura Ingalls Wilder: An Author's Story* by Sarah Glasscock (Steck-Vaughn Co., 1998)

The Time Factor

The approximate time of each of the segments is dependent upon several factors and must remain flexible in the upper grades. Some topics take longer than others to establish or create the prior knowledge. Some mini-lessons need more explanation than others. There are some general guidelines that can aid in planning.

Because the Guided Reading Block runs between 30 and 45 minutes in most classes, dividing the time into fifths might help with time allotments. The Pre-Reading Segment will take one- to two-fifths of the total time, depending upon how much foundation is needed and how much time is necessary for the mini-lesson. The During Reading Segment receives about two- to three-fifths of the total time, since practicing reading is what is most critical during this block. The Post-Reading Segment, then, receives another one- to two-fifths of the time. Teachers do not need to be guided by a stopwatch; they just need to be mindful that they allot the time as efficiently as possible to include all of the important elements of the lesson. By mixing and matching the topic and the total time according to the day, the schedule might look like this (all times are approximate, dividing the time into fifths):

45-minute block:		35-minute block:	
Pre-reading	9-18 minutes	Pre-reading	7-14 minutes
Reading	18-27 minutes	Reading	14-21 minutes
Post-reading	9-18 minutes	Post-reading	7-14 minutes

Segment Two: During Reading—Applying What Has Been Taught

The first segment of the Guided Reading Block allows the teacher to lay the groundwork for students to be successful at reading the text. Students now have a road map for where they are going—some familiarity with the topic, knowledge of key words, and a definite reason for reading the text.

Teachers must emphasize to students that this reading time is considered practice time so that they can improve their reading skills and fluency. Kids easily understand the concept of practice as it relates to sports. They will stand at the free-throw line and shoot baskets for hours, knowing that this will increase their chances of hitting the basket during that important game. They will dribble the ball endlessly up and down the court, practicing their ball-handling skills, realizing that this practice will improve their game performance. When it comes to reading, however, students have failed to understand that the same concept applies.

Guided Reading

The next step is to read the text. This is where the teacher must make a judgment about how much help students will need to be able to read with a certain level of understanding.

Teachers might think of levels of support much like a continuum from the highest level of support to the lowest level, considering the various formats used in the Four-Blocks™ framework. That support may look like the following chart:

Some Choices of Support for Reading

Highest Support

Teacher reads text aloud
Teacher directly supports individuals or small groups
Teacher directs whole group reading
    Shared reading (mostly at primary grades)
    Echo reading (mostly at primary grades)
    Choral reading (mostly at primary grades)
Students support each other
    Book Clubs and Student-Teacher Groups
    Readers' Theater
    Literature Circles
    Partner/Buddy reading
Students read independently

Lowest Support

Movement up and down the continuum does not necessarily occur according to the time of year. Daily, teachers must base their decisions upon the type and difficulty of the text as well as upon the needs and achievement levels of each child in the classroom. Formats might be mixed within one block and might also change each day of the week.

Teacher Read-Aloud

When material is particularly difficult or when the teacher needs to model the fluency or cadence of the material, the teacher may choose to read the text aloud to the students as the students follow along with their own copies of the text. The teacher may read the selection in its entirety or may get the students started on the piece using this method.

Whole-Group Reading

Used more often at the primary grades, whole-group reading of text allows the whole class to support each other in the reading. Struggling readers rely heavily upon others for help with decoding, expression, pacing, and fluency. Several whole-group methods can be practiced, with the teacher being as instrumental as is necessary.

☑ **Echo Reading:** A segment of text is first read aloud either by the teacher or a small, selected group of students (the girls, the boys, two cooperative groups, the Monday and Tuesday designated students, etc.) and then the remainder of the students "echo" or reread what the first group read. The segments of text can be any amount of text that the teacher feels is appropriate—a sentence, a paragraph, or a page.

☑ **Choral Reading:** All students read in unison, carefully monitoring the pacing as they read. The teacher can choose to be the most prominent voice to set the pace and to model the fluency and intonation or, once students have learned this method of reading (and realize that fast and loud are not the goal!), the students may read without the teacher's voice being heard.

These whole-group methods of reading are used less often in the upper grades and may be less beneficial in the upper grades, too. Many classes need to be less concerned about fluency and decoding at certain grade levels, especially with high-achieving classes. Socially, these methods may be less acceptable to the students, too.

Teacher-Led Small Groups

The teacher may want to work occasionally with an individual student, a couple of students, or a small group. The group should always be flexible—not always pulling the struggling readers or the advanced students. The group should work together because they have some common need—a skill or strategy that needs attention, some additional practice with reading, or perhaps more time on prior knowledge building.

Student-Teacher Groups

In the primary grades, this grouping is called "playschool group," but the name is changed to be more appropriate for upper-grades students. This format allows students to take more responsibility for their reading. The teacher usually conducts the pre-reading segment of the block as always and then charges cooperative groups with the reading practice and with completing the purpose that was set for reading that day. Occasionally, the teacher might allow the groups to cover the pre-reading activities, too, after giving the "student-teacher" some guidelines for brainstorming the prior knowledge, covering vocabulary, and setting the purpose that day. The teacher usually still covers the mini-lesson. The student-teacher can be appointed by the teacher or the group, or assigned on a rotating basis. Sometimes the cooperative seating groups work well since students are already seated this way and are heterogeneous. If each group has a "day of the week" student, the teacher merely elects the "Monday students" on Monday to be the student-teachers. The roles of the student-teachers are modeled and defined by the teacher. Students can read chorally with their whisper voices, silently, or they may occasionally choose to take turns reading. Sometimes this choice is made democratically by the group, and sometimes the choice is made by the teacher, especially when the teacher feels that there are students in the group who might not be able to read the text without support.

Book Club Groups

Occasionally, books are read during the Guided Reading Block rather than short basal or anthology pieces. Students in the upper grades need to learn to read longer pieces, to understand the intricacies of this extended text, and to apply skills and strategies to this text—not to mention to enjoy discussion and to appreciate books. The Book Club is a bit more difficult to coordinate, but is popular with students in the upper grades. This is how Book Clubs are organized for Guided Reading:

1. The teacher selects four to five book titles, usually finding books that are connected by some common theme. There must be multiple copies of each of the titles, usually four to six depending upon the number of students in the class.

2. The teacher previews each of the book titles for the class—reading a snippet of each, sharing the book jacket information, and telling a bit about the story or characters.

3. The books are placed on display in the room, and students are asked to preview the books during certain times to decide on the book they would most enjoy reading. The previewing can be done during spare time over the course of a few days or can take a day or two of the Guided Reading Block.

4. Students are all given a note card with the task of writing their top choices in order, starting with the one they would most like to read. There should be one less choice than the number of books (e.g., If there are five titles, each student would give her top four choices.). The teacher assures the students that they will be assigned to one of their choices—maybe not their top choice, but at least one of their choices.

5. The teacher collects the note cards and assigns students to books with which she feels they can be successful, attempting to build support in each of the groups.

6. The teacher reveals the Book Club assignments, arranges students in the groups, and gives them copies of the appropriate books.

7. The teacher conducts the pre-reading segment on most days, including all of the effective elements (prior knowledge, vocabulary, purpose setting, mini-lesson, and predicting). This is possible, especially when the books are tied together by a common theme.

8. Students read together in their groups—sometimes choosing to read chorally, sometimes independently, sometimes taking turns.

9. The teacher defines where each group will stop daily by placing a paper clip or sticky note on the appropriate page of each group's books. This helps to keep all of the groups together so that they will end on approximately the same day.

10. Most often, some type of whole group sharing is done daily or every other day. Students grow by learning what other groups have to offer about the same subject they are also reading.

Literature Circles

As students move into reading longer, more in-depth text, and as they grow in their understanding of and interest in books, they will likely appreciate quality time to discuss books with their peers. The Literature Circle time provides this interactive time to read and respond to literature. It operates in this manner:

1. The teacher usually selects the text to be read—often a novel, though sometimes other types of text lend themselves to this discussion format.

2. Then, the teacher puts the students in small groups, usually heterogeneous groups that provide structure and support for students.

3. Each student is assigned a daily task within the group. They perform the functions on the task cards they are given. (See the reproducible Roles Deck for Narrative and Expository Text on pages 226-228 of the Appendix to help with these assignments.)

If the text is narrative, the tasks are usually ones such as these:

☑ **Vocabulary:** This student records interesting vocabulary or key words in the text as the text is read. It is his duty to note the words or to elicit from group members the words that should be recorded. This person will facilitate discussion around the meanings of these words and their contribution to the comprehension of the text.

☑ **Characters:** This student records the main characters involved in the section being read that day and facilitates discussion about those characters (What kind of characters are they? How do we know that? How do they change?).

☑ **Setting:** This student makes note of the setting of the story and facilitates discussion about the impact of the setting upon the plot.

☑ **Problem/Solution:** This group member records the conflict of the plot and solutions developed within the story. She will promote discussion about the conflict, whether it is something to which the group can relate, and whether the solution is one that the group would have chosen or what alternatives might be offered.

☑ **Connections:** This group member looks for relationships both within the text and between the text and real life.

☑ **Summary:** This person is responsible for providing a summary of what is read that day. If this is done in a journal, the journal can be used to catch up students who have missed a session.

If the text is expository or informational, the tasks are ones such as these:

☑ **Main Idea:** This student makes note of main ideas delineated in the text that day.

☑ **Details:** This student records important details in the text as the text is read or upon conclusion of the reading. These should be details that support the main idea or major categories of text.

☑ **Text Structure:** This student makes note of the organization of the text that promotes comprehension (headings, subheadings, marginal notes, pictures, etc.) or any other parts of the book where additional information can aid the reader.

☑ **Key Words:** This group member records key words and vocabulary that are important to comprehending the text.

☑ **Illustrator:** This student sketches something important from the text that reveals major concept(s).

☑ **Usefulness/Connections:** This student makes note of the relevance of the information in the text to the real world and/or connections that exist within the text.

---

4. Some teachers provide journals that circulate for each of the tasks. Composition notebooks or spiral notebooks can be cut in half as economical journals. Each person in each group is given a journal with a label showing one of the tasks. The student may date and sign the page where he will record information for which he is responsible.

5. The roles and journals (if journals are used) rotate to a different person each day so that everyone will stay involved and will have different perspectives on the text. Some teachers like for the students to sign and date the backs of the task cards so that they are encouraged to keep up with the rotational plan.

The Literature Circles meet for as long as necessary to cover the material. The teacher may want to define the number of pages to be covered daily so that all groups conclude on the same day. Material can be read during the class and some can be assigned as homework to expedite completion of long texts.

Partner Reading

One of the most popular groupings for reading during the Guided Reading time is partner reading. The teacher usually assigns students to read with buddies to practice their reading. Sometimes teachers place a more able and less able reader together to provide the support necessary for all students to be successful. If that is done, teachers should narrow the gap as much as possible between the reading levels, providing enough to support, yet not making the differences too apparent. In the upper grades, teachers usually have a preference for the physical arrangement of students. This may depend upon the teachers' styles and the level of comfort students have working in close proximity. Some teachers let their students sit together on the carpet, on beanbag chairs, or on the sofa in the Reading Center. Some teachers prefer that their students remain in desks, positioning them either side-by-side or shoulder-to-shoulder in opposite directions. Teachers just need to experiment to find what works best for their students.

Independent Reading

Some text used in the Guided Reading Block can be read independently. Although they must also learn to work collaboratively, some students will prefer working alone and can concentrate better working independently. On days when some or all of the students read independently, all students will still be involved in whole-group activities in the pre-reading and post-reading segments of the lesson.

> As teachers make choices about the grouping of students for appropriate support, they must consider the support needed by every student to be successful at practicing the text. The formats will change depending upon the students, the time of year, the difficulty level of the text, and the variety needed to keep students motivated.

Making the Text Manageable

Upper-grades selections are often quite lengthy. This can make fluctuating between grade-level and easier text and still covering a certain amount of text difficult. Teachers must remember that they are not bound to the "three-day grade-level/two-day easier" guideline for the primary grades. Here are some hints to help make planning and delivery easier in the upper grades:

☑ **Decide that depth and understanding are more important than coverage.** Select fewer pieces from basals or literature books and anthologies. Perhaps only three-fourths of the basal can be covered, especially since some content area chapters may be used in Guided Reading.

☑ **Consider using some of the selections from the literature book for the read-aloud during the Self-Selected Reading Block.** This will give the students the opportunity to be exposed to some of the quality selections without having to use those selections during the Guided Reading Block.

☑ **Some of the selections from the literature book might also be used in the Writing Block as examples of style, technique, and good, standard English usage.**

☑ **Some of the selections from the literature book might be used in the Working with Words Block to explore diction, word patterns, or rhyme.**

☑ **Give students an opportunity to help organize what will be read during the year.** If a basal or anthology is used, let the students spend several days previewing the selections and ranking what interests them most. The buy-in from students having had some input into the planning has a big payoff! Students are far more motivated to read. It is rewarding to hear students remark, "Oh, this is the story I listed first on my sheet. It looks really neat! I can't wait to read it!"

☑ **Do not feel that everything must be read in its entirety.** Some sections of text can be used in class to apply the skills and strategies taught through mini-lessons. The remainder of the text can be assigned as homework, or sometimes it may not be necessary to complete it. Sometimes teachers hope that the text is interesting enough that students will want to finish it even though it has not been assigned.

☑ **When a piece is selected, the teacher should read it thoroughly, looking for "stopping points" or natural breaks in the selection.** Those will be the segments from which daily lessons are drawn—vocabulary words chosen, mini-lesson applied, purpose set, and reading practiced.

Example of Planning the Stopping Points in Text

Selection: "Pecos Bill, King of Texas Cowboys" (*Harcourt Treasury of Literature*, Harcourt Brace & Co., 1995)

Day One:
Mini-Lesson: Characteristics of a tall tale
pages: 185-187

Day Two:
Mini-Lesson: Foreshadowing
pages: 188-190 (second paragraph)

Day Three:
Mini-Lesson: Figurative language
pages: 190-194 (fourth paragraph)

Day Four:
Mini-Lesson: Continue with characteristics of a tall tale
pages: 194-197

So, in a Four-Blocks classroom, a teacher might cover only half to three-quarters of the selections in the literature book, include difficult chapters from science and social studies throughout the year, use some of the literature book selections as good read-alouds during the Self-Selected Reading Block, or might use some selections during the Working with Words Block or the Writing Block. There are many opportunities during all four blocks for students to be exposed to and engaged in a wide variety of printed materials. The Guided Reading Block is only one of those.

The Teacher's Roles During Reading

The teacher has many decisions to make in preparation for a successful Guided Reading lesson. He must decide what text lends itself best to the skills and strategies that need to be taught. He must decide how long the text will take to read and how it can be sectioned to make it manageable for the class. He must plan how to connect the students to the text, what vocabulary words are critical to their understanding, and what purpose will help to guide kids through the text. He must also decide how much support each class member needs to be successful with the text. Many, many decisions!

With all of this pre-planning, it would be nice for the "during reading time" to be free-time for the tired teacher! No such luck! There are several roles teachers should play during the middle segment of time.

The first role is that of monitoring the students as they read in their assigned groups or pairs. The teacher circulates, encouraging students who seem less involved than others, helping some groups to stay focused on the reading and completing the purpose set, and generally maintaining an acceptable noise level in the class ("healthy noise" should be expected).

The second role is that of evaluator, roaming the room to observe and listen as students read and discuss. Usually during this time, teachers make anecdotal notes that might help to gather a profile of the students and their progress. Teachers use these notes to plan more effective lessons for individual students when the teacher works with those students during conference and small group time. Teachers also use these anecdotal notes of what they have observed to plan mini-lessons that address the needs of the majority of the class.

The third role is an opportunity for more direct instruction, working either with an individual child, a couple of children, or a small group of students. Small groups are chosen because they have some common need that can be addressed in this group setting. Perhaps a group of students has had no obvious prior experience with the topic, and they could be more closely connected to the text through some further discussion, or the teacher may have observed that several students never apply a certain strategy when they are reading. The small groups remain flexible, not always the low or the high achievers. Likewise, when the teacher pulls aside individual students, she is careful not to always pull the struggling readers. All students need some special, individual attention from the teacher.

Fluency in the Upper Grades

Sometimes in the upper grades, teachers ignore fluency as a part of their lesson planning. It is true that many (and in some schools most) of the students in the upper grades are considered to be fluent readers with much of the text that they read. Fluency, however, is not judged solely by the fact that the words flow without hesitation. Teachers want to hear appropriate intonation that reflects understanding of the text. Reading is, of course, all about comprehension and understanding.

There will be a level at which all students in the upper grades can be considered fluent, even though that level might be below grade level. With the Four-Blocks planning providing regular below-grade-level experiences, the struggling readers should be able to read some materials fluently, although practice may have to occur to achieve that fluency.

Teachers should include in their plans ample opportunities for students to reread material in order to practice or build fluency. Students will understand the analogy of practicing to be better readers just as they must practice to get better at sports. After practicing reading printed material, students might have the chance to read aloud to the class to demonstrate their fluency.

Segment Three: Post-Reading—Evaluating the Application of Skills and Strategies

The conclusion of the teacher-directed format of Guided Reading provides an opportunity for the teacher to bring the lesson full-circle. In the pre-reading segment a skill is explicitly taught; in the during-reading segment, students have a chance to apply the newly taught skill. Finally, in the post-reading segment, students have the opportunity to see whether they were successful in their application of the skill and to get clarification and validation from the teacher about their attempt to apply what was learned.

Alignment is what should be achieved in the planning and delivery of an effective Guided Reading lesson. A clear thread should run throughout the lesson, especially evident in certain elements of the lesson. Emphasizing one particular aspect of reading will help students to focus more clearly.

In simple terms, alignment looks like the following:

Pre-Reading (whole group)

Mini-lesson: Teacher will share new skill or strategy.

Purpose: Teacher will set a purpose that will actively engage students in applying the new skill or strategy.

During Reading (chosen format)

Students will practice reading and will complete whatever purpose has been set that will allow them to apply the skill or strategy in the context of real reading.

Post-Reading (whole group)

Students and teacher will interact in some way that will allow teacher to clarify or validate students' attempts to apply the new skill or strategy.

With a mini-lesson involving characterization, the conclusion might involve each cooperative group of students sharing with the whole group something they learned about the character and how it was presented in the story. With a lesson on cause and effect, the class might complete a fill-in-the-blank chart on different causes and effects that they determined in the story. With foreshadowing, partners might offer to the whole group evidence for what they believe will happen in the next section of the story. Occasionally, some students might dramatize various parts of the story—beginning, middle, and end—according to their interpretation of the plot. **Here are some other creative ways to bring closure to a lesson:**

Beach Ball

In the primary grades, Four-Blocks teachers have been using the Beach Ball activity to stimulate discussion and summary text. Now teachers in the upper grades have found that this method is a favorite of their students. It's hands-on and engaging for tactile and kinesthetic learners and just plain fun for the others!

Expository/Informational Beach Ball: Take a beach ball and, using permanent ink, write on the segments such questions as the following:

- ☑ What was something new you learned?
- ☑ What was the main idea or theme?
- ☑ What was one supporting detail about the main idea?
- ☑ Where could you find more about this topic?
- ☑ How could this information be useful to you?
- ☑ How could you use this to write fiction?
- ☑ What does this relate to that you've read?

Narrative Beach Ball: Questions can include recall and higher level questions, too, such as the following:

☑ What was the problem and how was it solved?
☑ What was the theme of the story?
☑ What was the setting and was it important?
☑ What were the main events of the story?
☑ What would you like to ask this author?
☑ How was this story realistic?
☑ What other stories does this remind you of?
☑ What personal connection do you have to this story?

Once the beach ball has been covered in questions, the ball is ready to toss around the classroom to review what has been read.

Deal-a-Discussion

There are a couple of different decks of cards that can be used for stimulating students' discussions. Both are shared here:

Question Deck

Teachers prepare a deck of cards with common questions to help students explore and analyze text. (See pages 222-224 of the Appendix for reproducible Deal-a-Discussion Cards.) The cards can be used in a number of ways:

☑ **Each cooperative group of students in the class is given a deck of cards.** Each member in turn draws a card and gives a response. One team member is the judge and decides whether the member gets a point for his response to the question. All groups work independently.

☑ **Students are in cooperative groups.** There is one deck of cards for the whole class. The teacher draws a card consecutively for each group. The captain/leader of each group is responsible for leading a brief group discussion about the question they have been given. The teacher or the class decides whether the response is adequate for a point.

Roles Deck

These cards are simply basic elements of either narrative or expository text. The cards provide roles for students during discussion of text. (See pages 226-228 of the Appendix for reproducible Roles Cards.) The cards are given to each student in a small group. At the end of the reading that day, each student shares something about that element that was included in the text. The cards can rotate over a multiple-day reading of the same text so that each student gets to focus on a different element each day. For narrative text, the cards contain the words *interesting vocabulary, characters, setting, problem, solution, connections,* and *summary.* For expository text, the cards are *main idea, details, text structure, key words, relationships, connections,* and *usefulness.* If teachers want students to be accountable for what they have contributed and when they participated, the students can sign and date the backs of their cards.

Puzzles

Students work together after reading the assigned text to put together a puzzle. On the backs of the puzzle pieces are questions relating to the text. The students take turns answering the questions as they place the puzzle pieces together correctly.

Generic Puzzles

These puzzles can be constructed on material that will last throughout the year and beyond. Some teachers use brightly colored place mats in various shapes or laminated paper prints that are appealing to students (stars, musical instruments, etc.). Questions are written on the backs. Each mat is then cut into pieces, keeping each question intact as one puzzle piece.

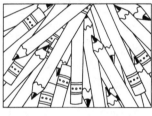

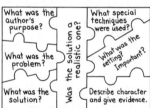

Specific Puzzles

The same idea as above is copied using a duplicated picture from the text, if one is available, or using any pictures that would appeal to the students' ages and interests. The front of the sheet would be the picture, and the back would be the questions.

Graphic Organizers

Quite often the conclusion of a daily lesson or unit is the completion of a graphic organizer. Sometimes the teacher uses the graphic organizer as the focus of the purpose setting for that day: "Now you've listed five different things you want to know about life on a submarine. Let's read to find the answers to these questions today." Quite often, students will work in their groups or with partners to complete the portion of the organizer as their purpose and will then share back with the whole group what they have included.

KWL

The teacher will use the "K" (know) and the "W" (want to know) portion of this organizer prior to daily reading or prior to starting a multiple-day lesson. The "K" provides an opportunity for the teacher to brainstorm with students what they already know about the selection (What do I already know?). The "W" allows the students to set their own purposes for reading the selection (What do I want to know?). After reading, the students would show what new knowledge they have gained (What have I learned?).

This organizer illustrates the thought process involved in reading—drawing on prior knowledge before reading, making predictions and setting a purpose for reading, and validating those predictions.

KWL for: *Freedom Rides*		
What I **Know**	What I **Want to Know**	What I **Learned**
• Deals with civil rights struggles. • This was a time desegregation legislation was tested. • Took place in the 1960's.	• What happened to the pioneers of this movement? • How did it feel to test the legislation? • Were most protests nonviolent?	

Book: *Freedom Rides: Journey for Justice* by James Haskins (Hyperion, 1995.)

Chapter Summaries

A simple chart is one that encourages students to recall and summarize what was read that day. This is also a great way for students who have been absent to catch up on what they have missed from the prior day's reading.

Chapter Summary Chart		
Chapter	Date	Summary

Hands

If the "hands" organizer (see page 78) has been used as a quick purpose setting for the students, the teacher might gather different ideas from each group onto a master organizer for the class as a concluding activity.

The Student Workshop Format

Whereas the teacher-directed format is used to teach the skills and strategies of reading—truly guided reading, the student workshop format is the time for applied reading. The student workshop format is used much like a culminating activity might be for a unit of lessons. This format provides students with an opportunity to demonstrate the many skills and strategies they have acquired in reading. The teacher becomes the facilitator during this format, with the main responsibility for reading, discussing, and applying knowledge placed upon the students—a shift that is necessary for preparing students for secondary education and beyond.

After a number of mini-lessons have been taught and learned, the teacher provides workshop time for students to read some text that the teacher feels will allow the students to apply their accumulated knowledge more comprehensively. Prior to this, mini-lessons focusing on one particular skill at a time have been presented to students. Now, students are expected to think about these skills more collectively and to apply them to text in a more aggregated fashion.

For example, in one classroom a teacher has spent seven weeks emphasizing the following:

Characterization	Analogy	Fiction/Science fiction
Plot	Figures of speech	Dialogue
Mood	Theme	Setting

After the teacher feels that the students have a certain level of understanding about all of these elements that contribute to reading, she may plan for a student workshop that will allow students the experience of applying what they know in a larger work. She expects them to use the terms they know. Also, she expects them to delve deeper into the meaning of this story, to analyze its plot and theme, and to make connections to other texts and experiences that they have had. She expects them to know enough to talk about books and other printed materials in an intelligent way.

The teacher may make the selection or may give the students some choice in the materials that they will all read. **Sometimes the teacher chooses a book (varying the genres, of course), sometimes a short story, sometimes a lengthy poem, or perhaps even a good magazine article or a chapter of a social studies or science textbook.**

In this class, the teacher previewed four books for the class, reading snippets of each and the book jacket summaries. Then, in this democratic classroom, students voted overwhelmingly to read Lois Lowry's Newbery Medal winner, *The Giver* (Houghton Mifflin, 1993). The teacher agreed that this was the perfect book for this seventh-grade class to read during their student workshop. She knows it will provide students with the opportunity to apply all of the skills they have learned to a riveting, provocative, futuristic story.

The planning begins! First, the teacher will need copies of the novel for each of the students to use during the workshop. She then begins to plan carefully how she will facilitate the learning, how she will give students the responsibility for their application of knowledge, and how she can make the text manageable for the students.

For *The Giver*, this teacher decides on the length of time that she feels they can devote to this activity. Given the curricular demands of the year, this teacher decides that two weeks is all that is available in her schedule. Now she must decide how to chunk the material so that she can keep the class together in their reading and in their discussions. Reading three to four chapters per day seems reasonable; however, she knows that the stopping points need to be strategically appointed so that students have information they need for discussing and predicting and so that suspense is created to motivate their continued reading. The teacher reads back through the book and decides on these stopping points. The book, she determines, will take around six class periods to read, allowing for some brief discussion daily. She also feels that the book and the discussions will provide wonderful springboards into other blocks, certainly the Writing Block and, most likely, the Working with Words Block, too. If the discussions are particularly lively, she may borrow some time from the Self-Selected Reading Block, though she will still try to allow some daily reading time in that block. When novels are completed, there is often the need to integrate more closely, both to maximize the benefits for the readers and to economize on the time spent.

The teacher can easily control the amount of reading by giving each student or each group a sticky note or paper clip to place on the page where they are expected to stop that day. No fair reading beyond!

This teacher decides that she will have the students read for approximately two days and will have them discussing briefly at the end of the second day. On the third day, the students will have time to discuss in depth what they have read, sometimes stimulated by a lead question provided by the teacher and sometimes totally guided by students' interests and curiosity. The third day can also serve as a catch-up day if the reading is lagging behind or can be a day that each group is asked to share something with the whole class—reactions, questions, or opinions.

After the teacher has determined the logical stop-points in the reading of this novel, she has many options on how she will proceed. **She will balance two main objectives during the days of this student workshop format:**

1. Students need to apply what they have learned with as little fragmentation as possible.

2. Students need to take responsibility for their learning.

The teacher knows that to ensure that students actually remember to apply what they have learned, she will need to facilitate that application. Remembering, however, that she wants them to take responsibility for their learning, she gives them the major role in the reading and discussing. She may start each day by giving each cooperative group a question to use to set the purpose for their reading that day. On some days, she might give each group a graphic organizer that will help them organize their thoughts as they read.

One favorite activity of the students is when they keep double-entry journals. Sometimes the teacher has jotted down critical quotes or thoughts on one side of the paper, and the students write down their reactions to the quote or thought as they reach that point in the story. They can do this individually or as a group. Sometimes the journal is kept by having students write down quotes or accounts from the story in one column as they read, and then respond in the other column. Sometimes the teacher invites students to jot down things that they want to bring up for group discussion in the left-hand column, and add the responses in the right-hand column as the group discusses the items.

This simple activity helps students to process information, to monitor their comprehension, and to reflect on the meaning and symbolism of the story.

In the story...	My thoughts...
pg. 20 Jonas' eyes are different from others	I think the author is telling us in discreet ways that Jonas is different from others in this society.
pg. 21 "Depth" in the baby's eyes	Might be a character trait. Is this foreshadowing?
pg. 22 Assignments in this community: Birthmother, Laborer, Speaker, Nurturer	All is not well in this society! They seem to have no choice in what they will become. Don't think I'd like that!
pg. 24 Jonas observes the apple changing.	I don't get this. Maybe later in the story I will. He seems to have special powers—maybe figures in with the different eyes again.

Just as for the teacher-directed reading days, the reading groups for the student workshop days are flexible. Although students usually start the block in their cooperative groups to set a purpose for their reading and for some brief discussion, the reading can occur in many different ways—partners reading together, independent reading, group members taking turns (all group members need to be fairly fluent readers for this—otherwise another format should be used!), or one member of the group reading to the others. Sometimes the way they read is determined by the group members, sometimes it is determined individually ("If you would prefer to read alone today, feel free to do that."), or sometimes it is orchestrated by the teacher who realizes the support that each class member needs to navigate the text and to understand it to the level required to contribute to the discussion.

The student workshop in this class begins with the teacher setting the foundation by stimulating discussion about the term "utopia." She asks students to share what they would consider to be the perfect society. After this brainstorming, the teacher distributes the books. She suggests that the way to achieve the perfect society might be found within this book. After choosing the way they want to read that day, the students read three chapters, and still a few minutes remain for the groups to reflect on what they have read.

The groups begin daily with some purpose setting. Sometimes the teacher directly gives a question or makes a statement to stimulate thought. Her questions will help to bring the elements studied into the students' discussions about the story. Sometimes a question is specific, "Why do you think the author uses this figure of speech in paragraph 4 of page 28? How do you think it is important to the plot?" Sometimes a question in writing is given to each group by the teacher for discussion.

On some occasions, each group is given a question or questions provided by another group from the day before—something that group was puzzled by or thought might be provocative for another group. With this method, the teacher gives each group a note card on which to write several questions or reactions to the story. The note cards are taken up and redistributed the following day. This way the students, again, are more in charge of their lesson.

In planning for each lesson, the teacher should be sure that the skills and strategies are applied and that students are enjoying the experience of interacting with text and with each other in a real-world context. Not often in the real world will they be asked to take a 10-item multiple choice test after reading a book, an article, or a manual. They will need to read, comprehend, and be able to react in a number of ways. That is the purpose of the student workshop, to give them this opportunity to put it all together!

Great resources for learning more about comprehension skills and strategies:

☑ *Guided Reading the Four-Blocks™ Way* by Patricia Cunningham, Dorothy Hall, and James Cunningham (Carson-Dellosa Publishing, 2000)

☑ *Improving Reading: A Handbook of Strategies, Second Edition* by Jerry Johns and Susan Davis Lenski (Kendall/Hunt, 1997)

☑ *Mosaic of Thought: Teaching Comprehension in a Reader's Workshop* by Ellin Oliver Keene and Susan Zimmermann (Heinemann, 1997)

☑ *Teaching Genre, Grades 4–8: Explore 9 Types of Literature To Develop Lifelong Readers and Writers* by Tara McCarthy (Scholastic, 1996)

Summary of the Guided Reading Block

> The purpose of this block is to teach students to apply comprehension skills and strategies to a wide range of texts.

Segment One: Pre-Reading   (10-15 minutes)

The teacher connects the students to text by the following methods:

- ☑ Establishing prior knowledge
- ☑ Introducing critical vocabulary
- ☑ Teaching a mini-lesson on comprehension
- ☑ Setting a purpose for students' reading
- ☑ Making predictions about text

Segment Two: During Reading   (15-25 minutes)

1. The teacher matches students to text with the correct amount of support through formats.
2. Students read and apply strategies, and sometimes discuss elements of text.

Segment Three: After Reading   (5-10 minutes)

The teacher brings the block to closure by returning to the comprehension mini-lesson in some way.

— or —

Student Workshop Format

Segment One: Pre-Reading/Discussing   (5-10 minutes)

The teacher sets a purpose for reading and/or discussing selected text.

Segment Two: During Reading/Discussing   (20-30 minutes)

1. Students read and/or discuss, usually in small groups, applying skills and strategies previously learned.
2. Teacher monitors groups.

Segment Three: Closure   (5-10 minutes)   **Optional Daily**

Closure can be brought in small groups or with whole group sharing.

A Typical Week in an Upper-Grades Guided Reading Block

Note: The text length and purposes below fit the "three-day grade level/two-day easier" format used in the primary grades. It is not necessary, however, to keep Guided Reading in the upper grades within this schedule.

Monday—Grade-Level Text

Segment 1 (Mini-Lesson: How Publishers Emphasize Text; Previewing Text)

The teacher begins by saying, "I hope that you all remembered to bring your social studies books with you today. I told you that we would be using them today even though these are the books you use in another teacher's class. We're going to take a close look at how publishers of informational text tell you when something is important."

Before they look at the books, the teacher asks the students to help her make a list of the ways that different publishers help readers know when something should be emphasized. "They don't have a stamp that says 'This is important,' but they definitely have ways to tell you what you should pay special attention to," the teacher adds. As students share items, she lists them: marginal notes, bold print, headings and subheadings, italics, underlining, colors, summaries, illustrations/graphs/pictures, etc.

She tells them that in most texts she feels that she could prioritize several of these as the most important: bold printed text, including headings and subheadings and graphics, including illustrations, photographs, and pictures, along with their captions. She says, "Today we're going to use these items to preview the text. I want you to see how helpful the publisher's signals can be."

"Now before we preview this chapter, let's see what you already know about this subject," the teacher says as she begins to sketch a topic map on an overhead transparency. She uses a green pen, writes the subject in the middle, and draws a circle around it. The subject is "Humid Subtropics." The teacher asks, "Does anyone know anything about this subject? What it might be or where it might be?"

A student starts with, "Well, it's a location, I think, maybe in South America." The teacher draws a line from the topic and writes "location" in a connecting, satellite circle. From "location" she draws another line and writes "S. America" with a circle around it. Another students says, "I think 'humid' is a clue about the kind of atmosphere or climate they might have in that region. The weather is humid here where we live." The teacher draws another line from "Humid Subtropics" and writes "climate" with a circle around it and another line and circle coming from that one with "humid" in it. Students who seem to be making some guesses about the topic offer a few other details.

Segment 2 (Abbreviated Time on This Day Due to the Purpose)

The teacher begins: "Okay. Now let's get ready to preview the chapter on humid subtropics. What I want you to do is to take two minutes and preview this chapter, concentrating on the items that the publisher has used to tell you that something is important. I would suggest that you look at the headings, subheadings, and illustrations. If you have any additional time, review any other items you feel the publisher might be emphasizing. I expect you to remember the major headings at the end of the two minutes."

Segment 3

After two minutes, the teacher asks the students to close their books and give her information to add to the topic map they started earlier. This time, instead of the green pen, she uses a red pen on her transparency to show the students how much information they have gained in this short amount of time by concentrating on the bold print, graphics, and other items. In addition to the headings they already had—"location" and "climate," they recall "urban centers," "manufacturing," "tourism," and "agriculture." From one of the pictures, students are able to help fill in many of the locations of the humid subtropics. From bold vocabulary words, they are able to add "revenue" under the section on tourism. Some students had read the definition offered in the text and shared that with the students. The words "urban," "agriculture," and "subtropics" are discussed and placed on the map appropriately.

The teacher finishes by saying, "Tomorrow we'll go back and begin to read the chapter. I think you may be surprised how much better your comprehension will be after spending the time we did today understanding how the chapter is organized."

Tuesday—Grade-Level Text

Segment 1
(Mini-Lesson: Using Previewing Strategies To Comprehend Text)

The teacher has the students review the topic map from the day before, paying close attention to the subheadings and the details that are included under each. They also review the vocabulary words on the map. "Now, what I want us to do is read the information in-depth today. Previewing the text the way we did yesterday won't tell us about the details that might be important to our understanding. So, today we'll be reading and seeing how much more we can learn about this topic. We're going to share our responsibility for the reading. Today, each group will read only one section of the text. I have prepared a chart for each of you to gather the new information you'll read about today. Each group will have a large sheet of chart paper with the information from yesterday about one of the subheadings. Some of you have a sub-heading written in green and some additional information written in red. You might remember that we used those colors yesterday—the green for our prior knowledge about the subject and the red for what we learned in our preview. Some of you have only the red because we didn't include this information in our prior knowledge."

"As you read today, I want each group to appoint a recorder who will add details from your reading to the chart you'll be given. I want you to use a third color (orange) to show you how we're growing in our knowledge from prior knowledge, to preview, to actually reading the text carefully. You may choose the way your group wants to read the text today—independently, chorally, or taking turns. I would like for each group to plan to share one fact that you think might be most interesting to the whole group when we get back together again."

Segment 2

Each group is given a large sheet of chart paper with one of the subheadings included. As they spend time reading, each group has a recorder. They occasionally stop in their reading to add to their chart. The orange words are concrete reminders of how much they have grown in their knowledge of the topic.

Segment 3

After each group has spent approximately 20 minutes reading their section of the text, the teacher has them tape their charts on the wall under a long strip of paper that says "Humid Subtropics." The colors stand out clearly—green for the portion that was offered on Monday as prior knowledge about the topic, red for the portion that was gleaned from the preview on Monday, and orange for the portion that was added from the thorough reading of the text. A spokesperson for each group shares with the class the facts that their group found interesting as they read today.

The teacher brings closure by remarking, "Do you think it was easier to read this text after previewing the chapter and making the topic map?" Students responded that they did find it helpful and that it was good to have the framework to guide their reading.

Wednesday—Grade-Level Text

Segment 1 (Mini-Lesson: Relationships in Text)

Today, the teacher tells the students that they are going to return to the text they have been working on for the past several days: "I want you to think about the relationships that exist in text. Sometimes we don't try to make text connections on our own. We should be thinking about these connections as we read."

She writes on the board, "Subheading + Subheading = Prediction about Connection," and says, "I would like for you to work for a few minutes in your groups to write down a combination of the subheadings from the "Humid Subtropics" chapter. For example, 'Tourism + Climate = ?' I would like for your groups to make guesses about the relationships between these subheadings. I'll give you about 10 minutes to do that." The students work quickly together on their worksheets.

Segment 2

The teacher says, "Now that you've made predictions about how one heading relates to another, I want you to pick two of the subheadings that you've listed and read them carefully today to see if you can find evidence that there is a relationship between these two topics. Jot down your evidence on the same sheet. We'll share some of these when everyone is finished."

Segment 3

Students come back together in a whole group. The teacher calls on groups to share the relationships between different subheadings and to tell whether they were able to validate their predictions in the text.

Thursday—Easier Text

Segment 1 (Mini-Lesson: Cause and Effect)

The teacher shares with the students that they are going to spend a couple of days reading another informational piece that she hopes they will find interesting. She has chosen a piece that she feels is high interest, although the readability level is slightly below the majority of the students.

"Before we get started," she says, "let's take a quick poll. Our story today is about cats. Let's see what kind of pets you have in your households." She creates an axis for a line graph on her overhead transparency. Across the bottom axis, she writes "dogs," "cats," "fish," "gerbils," and "other." Then, she proceeds with a show of hands of which students have which types of pets in their households. The count for cats and dogs is about equal for this class.

The teacher asks, "Have you ever wondered how long cats and dogs have been considered pets that live in homes? Today, our text is about the history of the domestication of cats. There is a very interesting history. I wonder if some of you would like to make a guess about how long you think we've had cats as pets?" Several of the students make guesses, anywhere from 100 years to 1,000 years, and the teacher jots the guesses on the same transparency as the graph. All of this introduction takes just a few minutes.

"Before we read today, I'd like for you to become familiar with some of the words that are important to our text today. If you would take your highlighter paper, I would like for you to hunt for the words and cover them quickly as we talk about them," the teacher says. The students keep small strips of brightly colored, transparent paper cut from book cover material on their desks for this purpose. The teacher guides them through locating and discussing four words by saying, "On the first page in the left hand column, you'll find the capitalized word *Egyptian*. If you'll cover that, we'll look at that sentence to see how the word is used in this piece." They cover and briefly talk about all four words that the teacher feels are important to the students' understanding of the portion of the text that they'll read today.

Next, the teacher takes the opportunity to teach a quick mini-lesson that will apply to the portion of the text that they'll read today. She has a sentence strip that she places in her pocket chart. On the left-hand side of the strip is the word CAUSE written in large, bold print with green marker. On the right-hand side of the strip is the word EFFECT written in red. Between the two words is a long arrow in green moving from CAUSE to EFFECT.

The teacher says, "Today we're going to talk about a relationship that we often see in text just as we see it in life. One thing happens and, as a result, something else occurs. Let's think about some common everyday occurrences that show this relationship." She takes the green marker and writes, "The alarm doesn't ring," on half a sentence strip. "Okay, now what might happen as a result of this?" One student replies, "I would be late to school." "Good," she says as she writes that response in red on half a sentence strip which she places beside the green strip. "Let's try another one," she says as she writes in green "It rains 10 inches in five hours." "Well, it would probably flood the town," replies one student. She writes this response in red and places it beside the green cause statement. "Yes, you all seem to understand this concept in our everyday lives. Today we're going to look for cause and effect statements in our text. I want you to read as partners today, and when you and your partner have read to page six, I want you to stop and raise your hands. I'll bring you a sentence strip that's going to be a statement from the story written in red or green. If it's in green, it's a cause in the story, and I want you and your partner to consider what happened as a result of this. If I give you a red statement, it's a result, and I want you and your partner to consider what made that happen."

Segment 2

Today, the students read as partners. They have six pages of text to cover before hands begin to go up signaling that they are ready for the teacher to give them the sentence strips they need to consider.

Segment 3

The teacher has all students come back together as a whole group. She calls on one pair at a time to stand and share their statement. The other pairs are asked to see if they think their sentence strip is the cause or the effect of what has been shared. The students enjoy matching the strips. The teacher reveals that there is a way to self-check for correctness once they have tried to make a match. They can simply turn their sentence strips over and put them side-by-side. A symbol is drawn on the back that matches if the answer is correct. The students enjoy this quick activity that checks their understanding of the relationships in the text.

Friday—Easier Text

Segment 1 (Mini-Lesson: Cause and Effect)

The teacher asks the students some general questions to review what they read the day before. Next, she has the students review their guesses for how many years cats have been household pets. They discovered the day before that the answer was not included in the text they read that day. The teacher tells them that they will find out the answer today. The teacher plays a quick round of RIVET (see page 70 for an explanation) to review five vocabulary words that are included again in today's text. The students do well in guessing the words for RIVET, and they enjoy this format to review words.

Today for her mini-lesson, the teacher returns to the pocket chart where the beginning of her lesson remains from yesterday: "Yesterday you did a great job of finding the cause and effect relationships in the story. Today, we've got something a little bit harder, although I think you'll do great with it. Sometimes we find that we have chains of events rather than just one cause and one effect. For example, we'll start with one of the sentence strips from yesterday—*The alarm doesn't ring.* Now, Marion offered the effect that we wrote down yesterday—*I'm late to school.* What if we take that effect and make it into a cause? If you're late to school what might happen as a result? Let's show this chain on the board."

She writes, "The alarm doesn't ring," and an arrow to "I'm late to school," and then draws another arrow. One student responds, "I have to go to the office for a tardy slip." The teacher writes that and draws another arrow. Another student says, "I'm late to my class." The teacher continues to write students' responses until the line of causes and effects stretches across the board. "Okay! I think you've caught on. Now, let's see if we can find this causal chain in the portion of text that we're reading today.

"As you and your partner read, I want you to try to find a string of these relationships. We'll come back to the board to see if these have been clear in the text." She directs them to read to the end of the text today.

Segment 2

The students read as partners today. They read to the end of the text and then most of the students have time for discussing the chain of events.

Segment 3

The teacher starts the causal chain by listing an event from the early part of the text on the far left side of the board: "Cats were thought to be evil." She calls on different partner groups to add to the causal chain they are creating on the board. The students do a great job of connecting these events.

Before the lesson ends, the students go back to their original guesses about how long cats have been pets. They've now discovered the answer! (What do you think?)

Chapter 5

Writing Block

In the Writing Block in the primary grades, teachers accomplish a number of goals, though two are most central: 1) development and application of phonetic principles, and 2) understanding the basics of written communication. First and foremost, in the primary grades, the Writing Block provides the greatest opportunity for students to apply their own phonetic understanding through creative spelling. Emergent writers and readers make a connection between the letters and sounds of words they wish to express and commit those to paper—a process called encoding. This encoding is the reason teachers don't spell for students during the Writing Block. If they did, it would be the teacher's own understanding of phonics that would be applied to the students' compositions—not at all our goal!

In the upper grades, most, if not all, of the students understand the basics of alphabetic principles and letter-sound relationships that will allow them to commit ideas to paper. **So, in most classrooms the primary grades' goal of providing students the opportunity to apply their phonetic understanding is no longer an emphasis, even though there are still misspellings that may commonly occur.** Teachers still won't find it necessary to spell for students during this block in the upper grades, however, since students still can use their creative spelling strategies and can use resources— dictionaries, thesauruses, rhyming dictionaries, etc.—to assist them. Writing will still provide practice for students to apply their understanding of patterns, rules, and guidelines that they have studied.

The second goal in the primary grades takes on greater importance in the upper grades and also becomes more sophisticated and complex. This goal moves beyond understanding basics to having students become effective communicators of written language and to empowering them with their use of the written word. Towards meeting this goal, students must learn and apply grammar, mechanics, usage, writing process, audience, purpose, etc., and the list goes on. Over the decades, high school teachers have complained that students entering the ninth grade insist that they have not been taught about prepositions, interjections, semi-colons, etc. Middle school teachers report the same strange phenomenon—students claiming to have no clue as to parts of speech, transitional words, active and passive voice, etc. What's going on here?

Well, what has actually happened is that we've all been teaching the parts of speech, the use of appropriate punctuation marks, active and passive voice, etc., but often we haven't had the students apply this knowledge in any practical way. Often, we taught the skills in isolation and had students apply their new knowledge to exercises in workbooks. So, students learned to underline subjects with one line and predicates with two lines and could do it beautifully in the workbook and on the test. However, transferring these skills into their own "real" writing rarely occurred. The reason was likely that students never related to these lessons—how knowing the appropriate verb to fit the case of the subject would clarify their writing; how wording their composition in the active voice would make their point more powerfully. It was the **context** of the instruction that was lacking—not the **content**.

Now, in the Four-Blocks™ approach, we match content and context for powerful instruction that transfers into students' real writing. Lucy Calkins and Shelley Harwayne remind us that, "Writing is lifework, not deskwork." (Calkins, 1990) In Four-Blocks, we explicitly instruct students using a context that demonstrates for them the practical reason for acquiring this skill—their lifework. We find then that they are more focused on the instruction, they absorb and apply the information with greater ease, and they file this away in their long-term memories.

Just because students are more fluid and fluent in their writing in the upper grades certainly does not mean that all students have the same instructional needs. For this reason, the writers' workshop approach works well to provide instructional time to meet the needs of the whole group, as well as time to address individual needs of students. **The challenge in the upper grades becomes elevating students' capacity to communicate to help them learn more about communicating effectively and powerfully to various audiences for varied purposes.**

The workshop time is divided into three segments, two of which are used daily and one of which is used at the teacher's discretion. Let's take a look at what occurs.

Segment One: Direct Instruction through Modeling

Just as with the primary Four-Blocks™ framework, students in the upper grades need models of good writing and good writing techniques. They need explicit, direct instruction, and they need it in the context of real writing.

Students are naturally immersed in models of spoken language in their environment. Written language models, however, are less frequent in the natural environment, especially the variety to which students should be exposed. Teachers must facilitate this exposure. In the primary grades, the teacher models daily a brief writing sample for students. In the upper grades, the teacher's own compositions and samples are still critical for the students. However, the variety of techniques, styles, and formats that students need to be exposed to will exceed what any one teacher is likely to feel confident in providing. As long as teachers can provide the models and encourage students to explore and experiment with those models, whether or not they are the teachers' own models, then growth in writing is likely to occur. So, besides the teacher's own writing, the models may often be the works of published authors or may come from other sources—even from students' own writing.

Getting Ready To Write for the Class

The best modeling a teacher can do will closely match the expectations the teacher has for her students. Sitting alongside an overhead projector, a teacher can simulate the posture of a writer, the way the writer holds the writing tool, and the way(s) he positions the paper. As the teacher faces the students, she can more easily maintain control of the classroom and can effectively keep students focused on the lesson.

Continuing to simulate what students will be doing as they write, the teacher's model is written on the same lined paper used by the students. This can be created easily by copying a sheet of notebook paper onto a transparency. Color transparencies can also be produced on the computer with blue lines and red margins. (For the modeling, teachers may need to slip these colored transparencies into clear protective sleeves so that they can be used many times since most colored transparencies will not erase.)

One teacher shares how effective using the lined transparencies has become in her model lessons:

> "Every year that I've taught middle school, I've had students who haven't understood the purpose of the margins on notebook paper and who've come to my class with no sense of spacing and order in their compositions. Over and over, I've struggled to make comments on their papers and tried to remind them individually about guidelines for organizing their work on the paper. Now, my job in the beginning of the year has been so much easier! In my model lessons, especially in the beginning of the year, I always include a 'think-aloud' about setting my left and right margins and about gauging how much text I can put on a line. Sometimes I intentionally put too much text on a line, running beyond the margins. When they can see the difference it makes in reading it back and in having the space to revise and edit, it makes sense to them. Miraculously, they begin to obey the parameters! Even for this seemingly small change in their habits, modeling has made an impact."

In the upper grades, teachers may want to write with fine-point transparency pens that, again, simulate more exactly the size of the line made by the students' pens and pencils.

Teachers will want to experiment with many different ways to organize their thoughts for prewriting. This is an attempt to give students a menu from which they can choose the most helpful method for them in their writing.

Mental Planning

Sometimes the prewriting activity is a mental exercise, rather than any written plan, especially for informal writing or journaling. The mental planning might sound like this as the teacher thinks aloud:

"This summer I had the opportunity to visit one of America's most beautiful natural land formations, the Grand Canyon in Arizona. So often we overuse the term 'awesome' to describe something that's special or good. The Grand Canyon, to me, was one of the few sights I think truly deserved using the word 'awesome' for its description. I want to write about what I saw even though it'll be hard to capture that incredible scene. I need to think about what part of the canyon and what time of day I want to tell about or whether I want to limit it to one part or one time of day. You know, I think my first glimpse of the canyon was so inspiring and breathtaking, that I should try to tell you about those few moments and what I saw. I think that just free-writing for a while and trying to recall exactly what I saw and how I felt might be the best approach today."

Jot Lists/Brainstorming

Often the planning consists of a free-flowing list of items for inclusion in the composition, often followed by prioritizing or narrowing the list to those things that might best be suited for the composition. The teacher might say:

"Today I want to write about my trip to Arizona to see the Grand Canyon. That trip was really a highlight of all my travels. There's so much that I could tell about that visit. Let me start by making a list of what some of the writing possibilities might be."

Then, she begins a list on her transparency:

Jot List on Trip to the Grand Canyon

Different ways to see the canyon:
- donkey ride
- helicopter ride
- hiking the canyon
- jeep rides through the canyon

Time of day to describe:
- early morning (hazy, shadows)
- midday (bright sunshine, vivid colors, position of clouds)
- evening (sunset, brilliant colors, shadows, darkness)

Plant life in the canyon:
- cacti
- flowers
- shrubs
- trees

Animal life in the canyon:
- jackrabbits
- bears

When I saw the canyon for the first time:
- mid-morning
- unexpected
- colors
- comments of family
- emotions: proud, excited, awestruck!

"Now, I don't think I can write about all of the things I've put on my list unless I want to write a book! So, I probably need to narrow down the topic to one or two categories that I've listed. As I glance down this list, I think I'm most inspired by my first glance of the canyon. That's the one that I'm most passionate about! I'll have a chance to include something about the time of day and how that affected the scene and about the plant life that was visible at that point. So, let me start writing, using those points."

Graphic Organizer for Pre-Writing

Quite often, people who are visual learners might choose to get organized for writing using some structural map for where they're going. Templates for organizing writing are limited only by the imagination of the writer. Many organizers graphically depict the purpose of the writing as well, such as a table construction with the main idea written on the table top and the supporting details written on the legs supporting the main idea.

Using one of the most common organizers, a web, a teacher might model as follows:

"Today I want to write about my summer trip to the Grand Canyon in Arizona. There are so many things I could write about, but I think I really want to try to describe what I saw and how I felt the very first time I saw the canyon. Let me use a topic map to organize my thoughts."

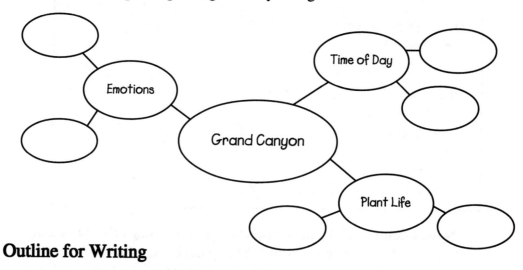

Outline for Writing

One of the trusty old methods used through the decades to organize for writing is the outline. If required by a standards or curriculum document to be a formal outline with Roman numerals, with ascending letters of the alphabet, and numbers, the formal outline can be modeled. Many teachers have moved towards using a more informal outline of showing students how to indent and organize. A teacher might model as follows:

"I want to share with you something about my vacation this summer, a trip I took to the most gorgeous natural land formation I've ever seen—the Grand Canyon of Arizona. I'm going to organize my thoughts in an outline so that I know where I'm going in my writing." She writes the following:

```
                    Trip to the Grand Canyon
My first glimpse
    • colors
    • time of day
    • emotions

Traveling through the canyon
    • hiking trail
    • route
```

Plant life in the canyon:
- cacti
- blooming flowers
- trees and shrubs

Animal life in the canyon
- observed
  jackrabbits
  prairie dogs
- unobserved
  bears
  cats

She may also use the formal outline required by some standards:

Trip to the Grand Canyon

I. My first glimpse
    A. Colors
       1. muted shades
       2. range of colors
    B. Time of day
       1. impact on colors
       2. shadows
    C. Emotions
       1. mine
       2. comments of others
    D. Traveling through the canyon
       1. hiking trails
       2. route we took
    E. Plant and Animal Life
       1. observed
          a. cacti and blooming flowers
          b. jackrabbits and prairie dogs
       2. unobserved
          a.
          b.

A teacher will offer various ways of organizing only to provide a menu from which students will choose the one that might be best for their style of writing. The recent trend in education has been for teachers to require that graphic organizers always be used prior to writing, or that a certain organizer always be used with certain modes of writing. Yet, many teachers admit that they personally don't use a graphic organizer in their own writing—even those teachers who consider that they are good writers.

So, we should admit that organizing writing is personal. Some writers need more help with structure than others. Occasionally, a teacher might require that students experiment with a format that the teacher has shared, but usually the decision is left up to the students. If, however, a student's writing lacks organization, the teacher can certainly take the liberty of insisting that a student use an organizer.

Writing the Model Composition

Once the prewriting is done using whatever method the teacher wishes to model, the teacher then begins to write. During the modeling, the teacher thinks aloud to model for students how a writer makes the necessary and constant decisions that must be made, such as choosing a topic or title, how far to indent and when to indent, when to start another paragraph, making the right word choice, when a sentence is irrelevant, what appropriate transitional word to use, what point of view would be most effective, whether the topic has been well-developed, what kind of internal punctuation would be most effective, etc.

The teacher writes and thinks aloud, but doesn't say every word as the word is written. Students should be anticipating the words, as well as reading the words, as they are committed to paper.

The teacher, just as the student, is free in the rough draft stage from the restriction of using her "best" handwriting, as long as the handwriting is legible. She makes decisions that cause her to strike words and substitute better word choices, to spell words phonetically or with her best guess and later check them in a dictionary if this piece is selected to refine, and sometimes to scratch out whole sections of text that just do not communicate the idea clearly.

Including the Editor's Checklist

Two tasks should be included in the daily model lesson. First, teachers should hold their own writing accountable to some criteria—a basic standard for rough draft writing that would make writing easier to read by the writer or by someone with whom the writer has shared the composition. The basics are those established for the class in the form of an Editor's Checklist. The checklist of items can be prominently displayed in the classroom and/or available in each student's writing notebook. Most teachers use the class checklist until the students all seem to have internalized the items and have moved beyond needing encouragement of the basics. This basic checklist is not comprehensive of all that students need to know about and include in their writing.

It likely includes items such as the following:

```
                        Editor's Checklist

☑ My name and date are on the paper.
☑ I've used appropriate punctuation marks at ends of sentences.
☑ I haven't overused certain words.
☑ All of my sentences relate to the topic.
☑ Words I'm unsure of are circled.
```

In the lower grades, this checklist is slowly evolving, often allowing months between the addition of items. In the upper grades, teachers may feel that students need less modeling on the basics, and that they can add the items more rapidly. **Although the basics of the Editor's Checklist are necessary to review, they are not the mainstay of instruction in the upper grades. Revision is the step of the writing process that becomes the emphasis, where there is so much room for students to expand their knowledge.**

Including a Daily Mini-Lesson

Along with the checklist, another element is included in the daily model writing: a mini-lesson. The mini-lesson is the opportunity the teacher takes to include direct, explicit instruction for the whole class. The skillful teacher matches the defined curriculum for the grade level with the needs of the students as reflected in their own writing samples. From the curriculum guide, the teacher is likely to draw the objectives or standards that best fit in the context of writing which would include grammar, mechanics, usage, process writing, genres and formats of writing, styles, and techniques, among other curricular items.

```
        Some Mini-Lessons That Might Be Included in the Modeling:

Class Procedures for Workshop
   ☑ Organizing folders
   ☑ Signing up for conferences
   ☑ Peer revising and editing

Grammar/Usage (Show how these make writing clearer, stronger, more effective)
   ☑ Pronoun agreement
   ☑ Correct antecedent
   ☑ Subject-Verb agreement
   ☑ Parts of speech
```

Punctuation/Mechanics
- ☑ Appropriate end punctuation
- ☑ Commas
- ☑ Semicolons
- ☑ Apostrophes
- ☑ Appositives
- ☑ Dashes
- ☑ Ellipses

Writing Process
- ☑ Pre-writing
  - Brainstorming/Jot lists
  - Graphic organizers
  - Narrowing a topic

- ☑ First Drafts
  - Dealing with spelling and correctness
  - Organizing for the draft
  - Paragraphing
  - Audience

- ☑ Revisions
  - Developing ideas
  - Relevance of topics
  - Sentence variety (including clauses, phrases)
  - Transitions from idea to idea
  - Voice
  - Diction
  - Multiple days of writing
  - Continuing drafts
  - Resources (thesaurus, encyclopedia, Internet, etc.)

- ☑ Editing
  - Conventions
  - Proofreading and proofreader's marks
  - Resources (dictionary, thesaurus, etc.)
  - Editing with peers (what to look for; being constructive)
  - Editing with the teacher
  - Final copies (setting standards, computer use, etc.)

When It's Time to Move from One Step of the Writing Process to the Next

How to Re-connect to Text When Writing Multiple-Day Pieces

Writing for Different Audiences

Writing for Different Purposes (to entertain, to inform, to persuade)

Responding to Literature

Creating Literary Elements (mood, tone, setting, character, plot)

Creating a Persona

Choosing an Appropriate Point of View

Genres of Writing (fiction, nonfiction, biographies, mysteries, poetry)

Characteristics of Various Genres

Modes of Writing (narrative, descriptive, expository, persuasive)

Forms of Writing (letters, research reports, scripts)

The mini-lesson is kept to a brief sound bite of instruction, which seems to suit the learning styles of so many students of the technological generation. Even though the direct instruction is kept to a bare minimum, the lesson is powerful because it is delivered in the context of what is meaningful to students—real writing. So, students get the *how* and also the *why* of the lesson.

A Model Lesson in Action

A teacher who is addressing his curriculum guide standard of teaching students to write book reports might plan a multiple-day lesson that looks like this:

Day 1 Mini-Lessons: Book Report Writing and Appositives

The seventh-grade teacher, Mr. Norton, sits alongside the overhead projector and addresses his class: "Students, I've just read a book that is one of the most thought-provoking adolescent novels that I've ever read. It's a Newbery Award book by Louis Sachar, the author of the *Wayside School* series. This book is a real departure for Sachar from the funny riddles of Wayside to a dark story of ironies. I thought I might use this book to write a report that would, hopefully, persuade others to read it. Let's see if I can accomplish that."

Then, Mr. Norton begins to write and think aloud: "First, of course, I need to put my name and the date on my draft in the upper right hand corner of my paper. Then, I'll just put the name of the book as my title, here in the center." Mr. Norton writes those basics on his transparency and then strikes his favorite pose as The Thinker, with his fist to his chin as he continues to think aloud, "Now, I probably need to include just the basics about the book before I talk about it. That would be stuff like the title, the fact that it's an award-winning book, and who wrote it. So, here goes. Of course, I need to indent to get started since this report will be several paragraphs long." And, at this point he slowly writes the first sentence. When he continues his sentence to the second line, he says, "I'll skip every other line when I write so that I'll have plenty of room to revise."

Mr. Norton
March 26, 2001

Holes

The recent Newbery Award book <u>Holes</u> was written by Louis Sachar the author of the <u>Wayside School</u> series.

Mr. Norton continues to think aloud: "Now, I've got to decide what I want to accomplish in this piece. Sometimes we write book reports to analyze something about the story—the characters, the plot, the symbolism, or maybe to compare it to another piece of literature or an event in history. Sometimes we write book reports to convince others to read the book we've read or, occasionally, we might write to discourage others from reading a book. There are many purposes for writing reports. For mine, I'm just going to write a report to encourage others to read this book, especially because I think it's so different and thought-provoking. I really want people to know about *Holes*."

He again puts his pen to the transparency and continues to write:

The recent Newbery Award book <u>Holes</u> was written by Louis Sachar the author of the <u>Wayside School</u> series. <u>Holes</u> is definitely a departure in storylines for Sachar. <u>Holes</u> is a story about a boy who was unjustly...

At the next word, he says, "So often, we get hung-up on words we can't spell. My next word is 'accused' and if I can't remember how to spell it correctly, I'll just put it down the way I think it may be spelled and circle it. Then, I'll keep on writing. When I edit this, I'll pay special attention to the words I've circled, and I'll look them up in the dictionary to check the spelling. Now, let me quickly sound out 'aaaccuuuuzzzzdd.' " He writes "acuzed" on the transparency, circles it, and continues to write:

The recent Newbery Award book <u>Holes</u> was written by Louis Sachar the author of the <u>Wayside School</u> series. <u>Holes</u> is definitely a departure in storylines for Sachar. <u>Holes</u> is a story is about a boy who was unjustly (acuzed) and convicted of a crime. The main character a young boy named Stanley Yelnats (Stanley spelled backward!) is given the choice of going to jail or of attending Camp Green Lake. His deprived childhood never allowed him to attend camp, and so his choice is made in hopes of capturing that experience. What a bad decision that soon proves to be! In this bizarre story of ironies, Sachar entertains readers and causes them to do a little soul searching as they follow Stanley on his journey to camp.

"Now," says Mr. Norton. "I need to read back over what I've written to see if what I've said so far makes sense. I'll use our Editor's Checklist to see if I've remembered my basics." The teacher reads through the checklist item by item and places a checkmark at the top of the transparency when an item has been completed.

"I see several places where commas would make my writing much clearer. This is an opportunity to teach you about something called an appositive. We use appositives to rename something that we've mentioned to give more information about it. Let me show you in my writing just what I'm talking about. In my first sentence, I've got two appositives. First, 'Newbery Award book' and *Holes* are the same. One renames the other and gives more information about it. What I'll need to do to clarify that for the reader is to set the title *Holes* apart with commas. Class, do you see another example in the first sentence?"

One student responds, "Yes, 'Louis Sachar' and 'the author of the *Wayside School* series' is the same person."

"Right! One just elaborates on the other. Where do you think we'll put commas?" Mr. Norton says picking up the pen to add the commas.

"With the first one, the commas went around the shortest of the pairs which was the word *Holes*. Would we put it around 'Louis Sachar'?" one student replies.

"Good observation, but there's another rule that guides placing commas for appositives. We always assume that the first mention announces and the second one elaborates. The commas always go around the elaboration as just giving a little more information about the topic. So, we'll put a comma after 'Sachar.' If this weren't the end of the sentence, we'd also put a comma after series, but instead there's a period there already," the teacher says as he places a comma after 'Sachar.'

"Do you see another example of an appositive?"

"How about 'A young boy named Stanley Yelnats' and 'the main character'? They're both talking about the same person. One is kinda renaming the other," one student offers.

"Right!" says Mr. Norton. "Where do you think we'll place the comma or commas?"

"Well, you said the second one is the one that just gives more explanation and that would mean that the commas would go around 'a young boy named Stanley Yelnats.' Is that right?"

"Exactly right! You're fast learners!" said Mr. Norton, placing the commas appropriately. "You all know most of the basics of writing, so I think that you're ready to learn about things like appositives to make your writing clearer to the reader. Those commas will help the reader because as you read back through now, you'll pause a little on the commas without reading right through them. Let's see if it helps a bit."

They read the piece again, agreeing that the commas do clarify the piece for them.

Day Two Mini-Lessons: Book Reports with Pizzazz and Review Appositives

Mr. Norton starts this block by saying, "Students, I read back over the book report that I started yesterday, and I decided that it wasn't very inspiring. Let's look at it again."

Sitting at the overhead projector, he reads his unfinished rough draft to the class and responds, "Now there must be a way that I can write a report that really grabs your attention quickly and makes you want to read more about this book. You know that I've read lots and lots of book reports over the years, and I'll have to say that this one I've started is pretty standard. I'm going to try giving it some pizzazz!"

He begins to think aloud, no longer directly addressing the class. "Okay. Now what about the novel *Holes* would really grab someone's attention? That should be easy since it's such a very different storyline. Let me jot down a few of the really bizarre things that first caught my attention while reading this story."

He begins to jot down a few of the outstanding elements of the story as he continues to think aloud:

Holes
• accused of crime he didn't commit
• choice of camp or prison
• Camp Green Lake
• no lake
• dig holes all day (5' x 5')
• looking for something?
• Camp Director paints fingernails with rattlesnake venom!

The students express interest in some of the items Mr. Norton has written: "That's some wicked director! Glad I never had one like that at camp!" "What were they digging for?" "Why was it called Green Lake if there was no lake?" "Those aren't things I think about when I think about going to camp!"

"I thought I needed to create more interest in this story. You didn't ask lots of questions yesterday while I was writing. Now, let me try to start again," Mr. Norton said as he gets a lined transparency for rewriting his report. "I don't think I'm going to try to just revise the piece I started yesterday, especially since I didn't write a great deal. I just don't think it got off to a good start. Sometimes a whole rewrite is necessary."

"I'm going to start by taking the most shocking, bizarre points of the story and hook the reader into reading my report and, hopefully, into wanting to read *Holes*. That's what a book report should accomplish, don't you think? It shouldn't just be fulfilling an assignment made by the teacher. There should be a 'real life' purpose in writing a book report."

"I think I'll use Joel's thought about the items on this list not being what he thinks about when he thinks of going to camp. That'll be my beginning." And, he begins his composition and takes items from the jot list and turns them into questions in his new report:

> Mr. Norton
> March 27, 2001
>
>
> <u>Holes</u>
>
> What do you think about when someone mentions summer camp? Do you think of a lake that's been dry for 100 years? Do you dream of spending your days digging 5' holes in the hard earth? How about spending time with an evil camp director who paints her nails with rattlesnake venom? Welcome to Camp Green Lake, created by Louis Sachar in <u>Holes</u> a recent Newbery Award winning book!

"Now which beginning do you like best? Be honest now!" Mr. Norton asks as he switches the two leads back and forth on the overhead projector. The class agrees that this report has opened with more pizzazz than the report from the day before.

"Good! I like this new one best, too. Now does anyone remember what we talked about yesterday related to commas?"

"Appositives," one of the students replies.

"Right! I see another example of one today where I didn't remember to put a comma. Can you help me?"

The students point out that the comma should be placed after *Holes* in the last sentence, and the teacher is delighted that they have recalled the mini-lesson from the day before!

Days 3, 4, and 5

Mr. Norton continues to work on his book report until he has a good draft. Each day he adds a mini-lesson—subject-verb agreement, word choice, the appropriate use of a dash in writing, etc. The students grow in many ways through his mini-lessons while receiving a great model of a book report format.

> Middle school teachers may find Don Killgallon's *Sentence Composing for Middle School* (Boynton/Cook, 1997) of special interest. Killgallon has sentences and passages from classic literature, as well as from contemporary novels and movies by Thornton Wilder, Ernest Hemingway, Stephen King, Michael Crichton, and Confucius! He uses their clever sentence constructions and punctuation to teach students to analyze and imitate more complex structures. This is a clever book of exercises!

Including Model Writing about Real-World Writing

Teachers should not forget that one of their goals should be to prepare students for the real-world tasks of writing. They should include as many of those tasks in their model lessons as possible throughout the school year. Such real-world writing tasks might include one like this:

> "Students, I ordered a product advertised in a magazine four months ago, and the product hasn't come yet even though the time they advertised as necessary to fill the order has come and gone. I want to write to the company to tell them that I'd like a refund after this length of time. Since I'm going to use the format of a business letter, I thought it would be a good time for me to share that format with you."

Some Real-World Writing Tasks		
Thank-you notes	Job inquires	Business letters
Friendly letters	Editorial letters	Job applications
College applications	Placing orders	Summary reports
Travel directions	Recipes	How-to directions
Taking messages	Taking notes	Writing memos

Students certainly need to understand that writing has real-world applications and life-long applications as well.

Going Beyond the Teacher's Own Model: Using Published Authors

As previously mentioned, there is an occasional need to move beyond the models that can be provided by only one writer. Producing "copycat" or "cookie cutter" writers is certainly not the goal of the teacher. Students will need exposure to many different examples, styles, and techniques. **Helping students develop their own unique styles is a goal in the upper grades.**

Towards this goal, teachers may find it helpful to use students' favorite authors as examples of styles and techniques, and even to teach grammar, usage, and mechanics. A transparency can be made of a particular page of that author's book. Sometimes the teacher may find it helpful to use the enlargement function on the copy machine before copying the page of text onto a transparency. The teacher, then, displays the text for the class and teaches the mini-lesson based on some pre-determined element of that selection.

A lesson using a published author's work might look and sound like this:

"Students, we've been talking for a couple of days about how sentence variety really has an impact on our writing. You'll recall that I felt my writing on Monday had sentences that were too short and choppy, too many sentences that were simple ones with subject-verb construction. I went back and combined some of my sentences by changing some of the independent clauses into subordinate clauses.

Today, I want to show you the work of one of my favorite children's book authors, Cynthia Rylant, who just happens to be one of the most skillful writers at sentence variety. Although some of her sentences are quite long and packed with details, they flow beautifully on the page. I want to show you a page from her book *Appalachia: The Voices of Sleeping Birds* (Harcourt Brace, 1991), where she's describing the people of the Appalachian mountains. She is portraying their unique personalities and qualities. Look at this paragraph with me," the teacher says as she displays a transparency of a page from the book.

"Let's take a close look at this one sentence that looks so interesting," she says as she touches each word with a pencil as she counts it. "Wow! Fifty words in this sentence! Listen, though, to how nicely the sentence flows." She reads the sentence. "Now let's make a list of all of the details Rylant has included in this sentence. We'll just write the details as simple sentences on the chalkboard as we find the details. Ron, would you step up to the board and list them as we call them out to you?" Ron agrees and steps up to the board to record.

"Okay, I'll get us started. First she says, 'The owners of the dogs grew up more used to trees than sky.' " Ron records this. "Okay, someone else find a simple detail."

A student offers, "What about 'The owners had inside a feeling of mystery about the rest of the world.'?"

"Good!" the teacher encourages. "Let's keep going!"

The class lists six separate ideas expressed in the one sentence that Rylant created.

"Students, please be sure that you understand that I'm not encouraging you to write long, unwieldy sentences that go on and on forever! I want you to think about making your writing more interesting by combining sentences that might be short and choppy. A composition of simple sentence construction is likely to be uninteresting. Think about compound sentences, compound/complex sentences—lots of variety—that will spice up your writing and will be more interesting to the reader."

Here are some examples of books that would appeal to students and would offer opportunities to teach mini-lessons:

Appalachia: The Voices of Sleeping Birds by Cynthia Rylant (Harcourt Brace, 1991)—character description, sentence combining and variety

Dogsong by Gary Paulsen (Bradbury Press, 1985)—effective use of fragments; style

Relatively Speaking: Poems About Family by Ralph J. Fletcher (Orchard Books, 1999)—poetry (rhymed, thematic connections between poems)

Because of Winn-Dixie by Kate DiCamillo (Candlewick Press, 2000)—voice, character development

The Cay by Theodore Taylor (Flare, 1995)—dialect, dialogue

The Mysteries of Harris Burdick by Chris Van Allsburg (Houghton Mifflin Co., 1984)—getting ideas for stories

Casey Over There by Staton Rabin (Harcourt Brace, 1994)—power of writing letters

Behind the Mask: A Book About Prepositions by Ruth Heller (Paper Star, 1998)—Parts of speech

Faithful Elephants: A True Story of Animals, People, and War by Yukio Tsuchiya (Houghton Mifflin, 1997)—concise plot that evokes emotions

Emma's Journal: The Story of a Colonial Girl by Marissa Moss (Silver Whistle, 1999)—journal techniques and features with a history connection

Brown Angels: An Album of Pictures and Verse by Walter Dean Myers (HarperCollins Juvenille Books, 1993)—poetry in response to photographs of family

Ashley Bryan's ABC of African-American Poetry by Ashley Bryan (Atheneum, 1997)—poetry techniques

The Butterfly Alphabet by Kjell B. Sandved (Scholastic Trade, 1999)—research combined with photographs and poetry

Going Beyond the Teacher's Own Model: Students' Samples

Another effective model for students can be the work of their peers. Teachers must be especially sensitive, though, in how and what they choose to share. Guidelines used by some teachers might be helpful to consider:

1. Ask permission of a student before sharing his work with the class. Never critique a student's work without permission and without being sure that this student will not be offended by the critique. Many students are sensitive about their writing. Writing is sometimes a very personal, private mode of communication.

2. Use student work as good examples whenever possible. They usually feel more confident that they can attain this standard, more so than the teacher's examples or that of published authors. (i.e., "I want to show you a good example of how Carrie effectively compared and contrasted characters in her report." "Look at the sentence variety in this paragraph of Mark's story." "Jerome really did a good job of using dialogue. Let's take a closer look.")

3. Transfer the student example onto a transparency. That will help the visual learners as you explore it together.

Students may find it interesting that many of the world's greatest writers were notable writers in their teens:

☑ Walt Whitman was editing a newspaper by the age of 19.

☑ Sylvia Plath had a short story published at age 17.

☑ Writer, abolitionist, and early feminist Louisa May Alcott wrote the play on which *Little Women* was based at the age of 16 and was published by the age of 18.

☑ Edgar Allan Poe published his first book of poetry at the age of 18.

☑ Ernest Hemingway wrote many poems and stories as a high school student and first published in his school's literary magazine at 16. By the age of 18, he was a reporter for the *Kansas City Star*.

☑ Langston Hughes's first poem was written for his eighth-grade graduation ceremony. He had two poems published at 18 and his first professional adult publication at the age of 19.

(*Merlyn's Pen Magazine*, Spring/Fall 2000)

The Time Element

The model lesson is a brief portion of the Writing Block. Usually it doesn't go beyond 15 minutes and many days is closer to 10 minutes—all depending upon the total amount of time available for this block. That's one reason why prior planning is necessary. Teachers have a short amount of time to make an impact on students' ability to communicate in writing. Teachers must review the curriculum and must study students' writing to see what would help most or all students grow during this lesson. The more technical aspects of writing, beyond the defined curriculum and beyond what most students are ready for, are the lessons taught individually to students during their conference times.

Storing the Lessons for Future Use

The teacher sets a clear expectation in connection with the daily mini-lesson: this is something that students should remember in their own writing to make it better, clearer, and more effective. Many teachers find it helpful to give students a few seconds to record what they've learned in a journal or a portion of their notebooks that can be used as a resource as they write. (See reproducible My Record of Writing Lessons on page 229 of the Appendix.) When a teacher conferences with a student, the teacher might ask the student to review his notes on a particular mini-lesson so that it can be employed in his writing. **Students need to see that paying attention to the mini-lesson and thinking of its application to their writing is their responsibility.**

Segment Two: The Student's Role

Especially if students in the upper grades have been in Four-Blocks classrooms before, they should understand that the middle portion of the Writing Block is a time that all students are busy writing. Just as in the primary grades, no one is ever "through," "finished," or "done." As soon as one piece is completed, the student's task is to begin another or to return to an earlier piece to refine it.

Organizing for Writing

Most teachers choose to help students organize their writing with certain tools—folders, binders, or notebooks. Some teachers require certain organizational methods and some allow the students to define their own, given certain parameters. Some suggestions follow:

Pocket Folders

Pocket folders give the opportunity to separate completed works from the ongoing work. Completed work goes in the left pocket along with a writing log where topics and dates are recorded. On-going work is placed in the right pocket.

Advantage: This method is simple, uncomplicated, and inexpensive.

Disadvantage: Some students tend to lose papers that fall from the pockets or that, once displaced, become difficult to reorganize. Pocket folders also have limited space.

Pocket Folders with Brads

This system gives an extra dimension to the plain-pocket-folder system. One pocket may be used for resources such as an Editor's Checklist, frequently misspelled words and/or Word Wall words, and a writing log. The back pocket might be used for completed works. The brads might store plenty of notebook paper, unfinished works, and works in progress.

Advantage: This system is simple, uncomplicated, and inexpensive.

Disadvantage: Disorganized students still tend to have trouble making papers fit neatly where they belong. Also, there is limited space in the folder.

Three-Ring Notebooks

This notebook system provides more options in organizing writing for the year. Within the 1½" notebook (or whatever size is appropriate for the class needs) inexpensive page dividers with tabs can help even the most disorganized of students to easily store their materials for quick reference and retrieval. Students can also personalize their notebooks, which is appealing to them.

> Here are some suggested divisions for sections:
>
> ☑ **Current Writing:** Used for storing the three to five pieces in the current writing cycle along with a log of all pieces written throughout the year with a date for start and completion. (See page 231 of the Appendix for a reproducible My Writing Log).
>
> ☑ **Achieves:** Used for storing all past compositions that were not published or polished.
>
> ☑ **Published Pieces:** Used to store the compositions that were selected to go through the writing process.
>
> ☑ **Hints:** A student's record of what has been learned from daily mini-lessons that should be remembered and applied—See "Storing the Lessons" in this chapter.
>
> ☑ **Words:** Portable Word Wall/commonly misspelled words, a personal collection of words with definitions that the student found appealing in reading or in vocabulary study that might be used in writing, small dictionary/thesaurus/synonym dictionary
>
> ☑ **Ideas:** Contains on-going lists of ideas for topics that can be used in writing. (Occasionally, the teacher might give students some time during the Writing Block to add to this list to keep it fresh.) Also used to store snippets copied from selections that the student has found interesting that might be adapted in his own writing. (The teacher might encourage students to collect such things as first lines, character descriptions, themes, story ideas from news clippings, neat names for characters, etc.).

☑ **Required Writing:** Used to store compositions that meet requirements stated by the teacher, such as a teacher's requirement that every student must write one each of these different types: one original poem, one poem that simulates the style of a published poet (include the published work, too), one persuasive piece of writing, one personal narrative, one informational piece, and one fictional piece.

☑ **Narrative/Expository/Persuasive/Descriptive:** Some teachers also have divisions for each type of writing they will teach that year. They have students keep notes and samples in that division.

☑ **Rubrics:** Contains rubrics that will guide students as they write or as they peer edit with classmates.

What Students Write: Self-Selected Topics

In a primary grade Four-Blocks classroom, students write, almost exclusively, on self-selected topics. They are busily learning a very basic concept: that writing is just communicating, or that anything that can be told or spoken can be written down. Students in the upper grades clearly understand that concept, although there are many students (and, admittedly, many teachers, too!) who remain a bit intimidated by this mode of communication. Given the opportunity to talk during class, students never show any hesitancy. However, if students are told, "Take this time to write whatever you want," many students are at a loss for words. Some of this hesitancy may be a conditioned response from having had teachers assign all of their writing topics over the years. The first generous offer from a teacher to, "write whatever you want to write about," may likely bring that startled "deer-in-the-headlights" look and a response of, "Well, what do I have to say?" followed by "How long does it have to be?" Teachers may have a lot of "unconditioning" to do with these students!

Consider the capabilities of students to write about what most interests them: By the time Charlotte Bronte was 14, she had compiled 22 volumes of text based on her creation of the imaginary Glass Town. (Krull, 1994)

Given frequent opportunities, students will grow to appreciate the freedom of writing about whatever they choose to write about, just as they have grown to appreciate the choices they are allowed to make in the Self-Selected Reading Block. Ralph Fletcher shared in his book *What A Writer Needs*, "You don't learn to write by going through a series of preset writing exercises. You learn to write by grappling with a real subject that truly matters to you" (1993). Additionally, Zemellman and Daniels tell us that "writing comes closer to these kids' urgent personal concerns than any other school subject" (1998). How very true we find these statements to be in the upper grades!

Students who have had the Four-Blocks in the lower grades come to the upper grades ready and willing to write as soon as the time arrives. Others will soon be ready if teachers will demonstrate patience and offer many good models of writing.

On days when the students will be writing on their own self-selected topics, the teacher will model, as usual, whatever she wants students to know about writing, grammar, usage, or mechanics. The students might add whatever the mini-lesson was to their notebooks, knowing that this is something that will help them at some point as they compose—either today or on some future day.

Then, the class knows that it's time to get busy writing. Some students are beginning a new composition. Perhaps some idea has just occurred to them during the teacher's model lesson. Perhaps they've referred to the idea lists in their notebooks and found something appealing. Maybe something from the sharing time the day before stimulated their thoughts about a particular topic, or perhaps they've decided to work on some of their required writing. They immediately get organized to start writing.

Some students are continuing to work on an on-going piece that needs more work, elaboration, or storyline. These students may have been working for days or, occasionally, for a week or so on a piece that has enough potential for this investment of time and energy. The teacher usually knows which students need to be monitored to encourage them to keep a good pace and to stay focused or, occasionally, to bring closure to a piece that has grown beyond its potential! Sometimes less is definitely best!

Some students will be working with the teacher during this time, as the teacher guides them to make decisions that will strengthen their writing. And, still some students will be revising and editing their work towards proudly completing their final drafts.

Although rough drafts are considered "sloppy copies," students are still held accountable for spelling high-frequency words on the Word Wall correctly during their rough draft writing.

What Students Write: Focused Writing Pieces

In the upper grades there is more of a balance between self-selected writing and focused writing. What is called "writing on demand" is not necessarily such a bad thing. It's often like a real-world task where a boss will say to an employee, "I need a summary of the meeting on my desk first thing in the morning," or "Write a letter to this client telling him...." Likewise, a teacher's career is filled with numerous writing tasks—curriculum guides, applications, documentation for National Board Certification, letters to parents, and newsletters. Creative writing, unfortunately, is a small percentage of the writing in which adults engage.

As additional defense of more focused writing for the upper grades, some teachers find that they must prepare students to write on demand for a state assessment program. Students who have had free reign of writing topics, modes, and formats may find it difficult to deal with a sudden switch to the confines of a state assessment with defined topics, time frames, and requirements of the type of pre-writing, writing, and final draft that must be produced. Therefore, practice in preparation seems only fair.

Focused writing is not the only opportunity that teachers have to offer direct instruction in curricular items. Direct, explicit instruction occurs daily through mini-lessons. Even though teachers won't necessarily require that students employ the skill or strategy "de jour," they do expect students to absorb it, perhaps to record it in their notebooks, and, certainly, to apply it when it is appropriate in their writing. On the focused writing day, however, teachers will sometimes ask students to write on certain topics, to experiment with a new format, or to write in a certain genre so that the class can be offered more direct support throughout the steps involved. These are likely the lessons that must be taught to all of the students and that require some "hand-holding."

When the teacher determines that focused writing is necessary, he may announce that, "This week we're all going to work on report writing, so we'll be suspending your personal writing for now. We'll get back to the pieces you're working on next Monday." Maybe the teacher says, "In March you'll have the opportunity to show some of what you've learning about writing this year on our state assessment. Today, I want to give you a sample so that you'll know what to expect. We want to remember all the good things that you've been recording in your notebooks and practicing in your writing to show how you've developed your skills." Although students who are "into" their writing might be a bit upset by this, they generally understand the need to have some of their writing defined.

Students in the upper grades still appreciate as much freedom as possible during the focused writing days. For example, if the task is writing a research paper, the teacher might provide a broad topic. Perhaps in science the students have been studying rodents. For the research report writing, rodents might be the broad category and the students are allowed to choose any rodent they wish to find out more about. A student may find out that choosing beavers as a topic is still very broad and might need some guidance in further narrowing the topic. The customary assignment of a state or a country about which volumes and volumes are written is too broad for a student to tackle. Teachers should offer guidance in making topics more manageable for students and should guide them to conduct research that really interests them. The question "If you were going to visit Germany, what do you think you would want to know more about before your visit?" might be posed to students before they undertake defining their topics. Responses might be:

- "I'd want to know if their schools are like ours."
- "If I'm going to be driving while I'm there, I'll want to know about their traffic rules."
- "I would want to know the main attractions to make the best use of my time."
- "What do teenagers do in Germany? Do we have similar interests?"

These are the things about which students have natural curiosity, not the total population of the area, the color and design of the flag, or the natural resources. Teachers need to stimulate students' interest in their pursuit of information. It's not always the content that is the objective on the exercise. It's often more important that students learn the process of report writing: choosing a topic, defining and narrowing the topic, determining the questions that should guide the research, gathering the information concisely, and translating the research into an informative, well-organized written report.

Modeling all of the steps of what a teacher expects students to accomplish is critical. Although mini-lessons divided into small chunks may draw out the lesson over many days, teachers should consider the time well-spent. A typical research paper might be divided as follows:

Gathering the Information

Day 1

A seventh-grade teacher models by thinking aloud **how to narrow a topic** from a broad category to a manageable focus. A report topic that starts as *immigration*, which is a topic being covered in history, is whittled down to a report about the tests taken by immigrants at Ellis Island—far more manageable! The teacher uses the following process:

1. She picks a broad topic: immigration.

2. She lists things she wants to know about this topic:
   - Why did people come to America?
   - What were the different ways people came to America?
   - What were the dangers of the trip to America?
   - How did people come to Ellis Island?
   - What role did Ellis Island play?
   - What did people bring with them?
   - Was everyone allowed in the country?

3. She strikes items that might be difficult to locate information about and items that are less interesting to her than others. (Strikes all but "Was everyone allowed in the country?" and "What role did Ellis Island play?")

4. She arrives at one topic that both interests her and about which she thinks there would be adequate information for a report. "These two topics seem to be related. I know that people were inspected at Ellis Island and that not everyone was allowed to come into the U. S. I wonder what the test was that allowed some and not others? I think that would be a great topic since we worry so much about tests around here. What if our test scores determined whether we would be citizens of a country where we wanted to live? When you think about it, it makes our testing here at school seem pretty insignificant, doesn't it? I think that's what I'd like to title my report, "The Ultimate Test: Passing at Ellis Island."

5. On this day, students are expected to go through this same process about a history topic they're studying, sharing with a partner their process of elimination.

Day 2

The teacher models finding a further focus for her own report by **coming up with major questions** she wants to answer about the topic. She wants to prevent a presentation of too many facts and figures by answering approximately three good questions as she searches for information.

1. The teacher brainstorms a list of many questions that interest her about the topic.

2. She prioritizes her list to three items, offering her thinking about these choices.

3. She then folds a sheet of paper into three segments and transfers her items to the top of the paper, one onto the top of each segment of the sheet.

Kinds of inspections?	Who inspected immigrants?	How were people separated?

4. Students brainstorm questions that they want to try to answer about their topics and share with a buddy their process for selection.

Day 3

The teacher talks about **choosing appropriate resource materials** to find information about the topic.

1. She tells how she located resources on the library computer under the topic: Ellis Island. She found a short informational book, *If Your Name Was Changed at Ellis Island* by Ellen Levine (Scholastic, 1994), as well as several other resources.

2. She wants to find three different types of resources to be sure to get unbiased information and a broad base of information.

3. She folds the paper from the previous day in thirds lengthwise so that the paper has nine sections within the folds. She jots titles of her resources along the left margin, one resource in each of the three rows of the paper.

	Kinds of inspections?	Who did inspections?	How were people separated?
World Book			
Book: If Your Name...			
Internet			

4. Students have an opportunity to get started with their search for three different resources for their topics. They are to bring in their first resource on the following day.

Some Informational Sources for Students

Computer on-line catalog
Internet search
Non-fiction books
Periodicals (On-line and bound index)
Museums
Historical societies
Genealogical societies
Related organizations
Chambers of commerce
Library of Congress (on-line)
Libraries
Interviews

Day 4

On this day the teacher shows students how to **skim to find information** that answers the questions for the report, skipping information that is irrelevant. Additionally, she begins to teach them how to **paraphrase and make notes** on the information they find. The students are delighted to find that reading the whole text isn't always necessary, "Wow! You mean we don't have to read the whole book?" "No," the teacher responds, "only the part that pertains to what you're writing about. Of course, if you want to know more, feel free to read all that you'd like!"

1. The teacher first jots down a more thorough citation on the first resource she has chosen to use. The information is jotted on the back of her organizer.

2. She models how headings and subheadings can be used to pinpoint information easily.

3. She reads information under relevant sections and makes notes that help to answer only the questions she has determined will be included in her report.

4. She fills in information on her organizer with notes that she gathers from the text.

5. Students are expected to start searching for relevant information and filling in their writing organizers. Citations are to be written on the back with the exception of page numbers that are recorded where the information is written on the front.

Days 5–7

The teacher continues her modeling each day: taking her notes from different sources, recording the citations carefully, and skimming and paraphrasing the information. She has time after her brief modeling to assist students in their attempts to apply this process. After several days of teacher-modeling and practice, the teacher sets a deadline by which this part of the report process must be completed and the writing of the report can begin.

Turning the Notes into a Report

Day 1

Now that students have gathered all of their information, the teacher begins to model **turning the information into a well-organized report**. She'll start by **writing a good lead paragraph for a report**. She explains to the students that, "One of my college professors once gave me this tip that has remained with me over the years. He said that a research report simply follows this format: First, tell 'em what you're going to tell about; second, tell 'em about it; and third, tell 'em what you told them. That's a pretty easy way to remember what a report is all about. Today, we're going to gather our information across the top of our organizer and 'tell 'em what we're going to talk about'."

1. She deals first with the information across the top of the organizer on which she has taken notes. She captures the three questions on which her report is based into the lead paragraph.

2. Students are expected to write their lead paragraphs today.

3. For the concluding time, some students share with the whole class their lead paragraphs. Some are brave enough to ask for suggestions for improvement!

Day 2

Now that students have a lead paragraph, the teacher is ready to begin with how to move on to **the second paragraph or section of the report, turning paraphrased information into text**. "Yesterday we did the part of our report that was the 'Tell 'em what you're going to tell 'em' part. Now today we're going to move on to the 'tell 'em' part." I want to take my notes about the first question on my informational sheet and consolidate what I've found."

1. She folds her organizer so that the first column on her paper is revealed.

2. She begins to combine some of the responses she has found from the three informational resources.

3. She turns the notes into complete sentences, finding transitions to connect the information.

4. Students are expected to begin writing their second paragraph or section (for longer reports).

5. With the few minutes of sharing time at the end of the block, a few students read what they've written so far and talk about their process for translating notes into text.

Days 3–4

The teacher talks through the same **process for turning the next two sections of the organizer into paragraphs or sections of the report**. Students continue writing and sharing as on previous days. The teacher sets a due date for completion of the body of their report.

Day 5

The teacher models how to **write a concluding paragraph** for the report, "Now it's time to learn to 'tell what you've told 'em'. We're going to learn to summarize what the report has accomplished in our concluding paragraph."

1. She returns to the three basic questions on which the report is based and summaries those questions, ending with a thought-provoking line about the critical evaluation process at Ellis Island that sometimes meant life or death for people.

2. Students work on their conclusions with the help of the teacher who monitors their progress, stimulates their thinking, and guides their writing.

3. Students share their attempts at writing concluding paragraphs with a buddy nearby.

Days 6+

The teacher begins the process of re-reading portions of her model research paper to see what **revisions** might be necessary. She lets the students assist with this process as she asks guiding questions: "Is this lead paragraph interesting to my reader?" "Do my paragraphs flow smoothly, one to the next?" "Have I given enough information on this topic or have I left you with too many questions?" Students then work to revise their writing with the help of a peer.

Following Days

The teacher now begins to **edit the report carefully**, including as many items as possible from the mini-lessons they have covered during the year.

1. After a quick edit, she divides the mini-lessons they've covered and listed in their notebooks into quarters—to match the number of groups (four) she has in her classroom. Each group of students is responsible for looking over a quarter of the lessons to see if corrections need to be made.

2. They make their suggestions and she cleans up the writing as necessary.

3. Students then work on their own reports to revise and edit as appropriate.

This focused writing unit has taken a great deal of time from the class. However, it's time well-spent when students have learned through modeling and support the process of writing a report. Report writing is not something that students improve in through merely writing more and more assigned reports. They need some hand-holding through the process. It may only have to be done once to have them understand the process. After spending so much time absorbed in their reports, they will need to return to their own self-selected topics for a while!

*All boldfaced portions throughout the lessons above are the daily mini-lessons.

Some Focused Writing in the Upper Grades

Report writing/Exposition

☑ How to narrow a topic

☑ Resources that are appropriate for information

☑ Different ways to organize gathered information

☑ How to translate bits and pieces of information into exposition

Developing standards for quality writing

☑ Rubric development

☑ Applying rubrics

Letter writing

☑ Letters that persuade

☑ Business formats

☑ Friendly letters and forms that are appropriate

☑ Etiquette of letter writing

Writing various modes

☑ Elements of narrative writing

☑ Elements of descriptive writing

☑ Elements of persuasive writing

☑ Elements of expository writing

Addressing a prompt on a standardized test

☑ Rubrics used

☑ Stages of the writing process required

☑ Any limits and guidelines imposed

Rarely are the focused writing days used to emphasize any singular rule of punctuation, usage, capitalization, parts of speech—the mechanics, so to speak, of writing. Special days aren't designated for application of these grammar points since teachers expect students to use these mechanics in everything they write. Focused writing days are used for "putting it all together" in a larger context.

Segment Two: The Teacher's Role

There are two distinct opportunities for the teacher to offer direct, explicit instruction. The model writing in the beginning of the block, previously discussed in this chapter, is an opportunity to teach skills, strategies, and techniques that will help most or all students improve their writing. Another chance for direct instruction is the time the teacher takes to work individually with students while everyone is writing. When individual conferences are not occurring, the teacher is likely to work with students who need encouragement to write, those who need some help with revising their writing, and those who might need the teacher to respond to their writing in various ways.

Getting the Year Started through Encouragement

As the year begins, after teachers model writing and include the mini-lesson they will move around the room offering assistance, encouraging students, and monitoring students' attention to their tasks. Some students may need help finding ideas, others may need help organizing their materials, and still others may need assistance expressing an idea. The teacher is present to say, "Great lead sentence for your paragraph!" "The dialogue you're using really makes this piece come alive!" and "Do you think the reader will be able to picture your setting clearly?" The teacher causes students to be more thoughtful about their writing. As she moves from student to student, she sometimes has mini-conferences and sometimes offers encouraging words.

Within a few weeks, upper-grades students may be ready to begin turning their efforts towards publishing a gem among the many pieces they have written.

Conferences

In the upper grades, students still write several pieces before choosing to publish one that is good enough to carry through the whole writing process, one that shows potential as a published piece. Students should come to realize that all of their writing does not merit publishing. There will be the occasional piece that they will recognize as special and will be willing to work harder to refine.

Offering guidelines for publication allows the teacher to slow down the publication process to a manageable number of students, and lets students write enough pieces to be able to compare them to find the one suitable for publishing. Many teachers define the number of pieces students will write, usually between 3-5 good pieces, before choosing one to polish. Students should then sign up for a conference with the teacher. Teachers will likely want to see students at least once over the period of two weeks, even if just for brief contact to see how the student is coming along.

When teachers meet with students, they may accomplish a number of things:

☑ Look over all of the student's pieces since the last conference.

☑ Discuss whether the student appears to be spending time productively during the Writing Block as evidenced by his writing log.

☑ Work with the student to set personal goals for growth in writing. (See the reproducible form on page 230 of the Appendix.)

☑ Assess together whether the student is meeting the goals set.

☑ Choose a piece of writing for publication.

☑ Make choices about revising writing for improvement.

☑ Edit writing for publication.

When stressing legible handwriting to students, teachers may wish to share an amusing anecdote about consequences of poor penmanship. Mark Twain's first published article appeared with the byline 'Mike Swain' because the editor could not read his handwriting! (Krull, 1994)

The best conferences are those that show true collaboration between the student and the teacher. The teacher may never need to take the paper from the hands of the student. As he sits alongside the student, they can read the text together, or either the teacher or student can read sections of the paper to the other. The teacher carefully guides the student to reflect on what has been said, to make the choices writers need to consider, to be more objective about the writing, and to make changes that might make the writing better.

Teacher's Self-Evaluation for Writing Conferences

Have I...

☑ let the student retain ownership of the piece of writing?

☑ helped the student grow individually in at least one area?

☑ focused the conference narrowly enough so that growth can occur?

☑ asked questions that will allow the student to make choices, rather than making the choices for him?

☑ helped the student realize that correctness is not what good writing is?

☑ remained positive with the student to encourage his ideas and attempts?

How Instruction Is Determined in the Conference

The teacher usually has three major goals in his conference with a student: 1) to encourage the student to apply the mini-lessons that have been taught consistently throughout the year; 2) to support the student individually in his area of greatest potential growth by evaluating the student's writing; and 3) to build the confidence of the student as a writer. The skillful teacher includes all three goals in each and every conference.

> **Editing writing makes the writing cleaner and "prettier." Revising makes it better! Teachers should instruct and support both.**

As the teacher reviews the piece of writing that the student has chosen to discuss, she must carefully evaluate the writing, making note of the area where she could help this student grow—the area that would make the greatest impact in that student's writing. This is often difficult with struggling students, taking care not to overwhelm the student with too many changes that will make the piece a better one. Focusing on one or two areas will give that student the opportunity to play an active role in the revision process. If the student has kept a record of the daily mini-lessons, the teacher can ask that the student refer back to certain items that may not have been applied in his writing.

Comments during the conferences to stimulate students to think about their writing in a more focused way might be:

> "Let me read the first paragraph back to you. Let's decide whether it grabs readers and makes them want to read more."
>
> "Let me read this paragraph aloud to you, pausing only where you have punctuation marks. As I read, think about whether the message is clear or whether some additional punctuation might be necessary to clarify your meaning."
>
> "I really like the way you're putting the human interest in the story by having the character's dog portrayed. I'm having a little trouble picturing the dog, though. Let's read back through that part and see if there's an opportunity for you to describe more about the dog."
>
> "When we write, we try to find ways to help the reader know that our ideas are shifting. We don't want them to feel like they're being pulled in different directions without warning. Let's make sure that you've provided those transitions in your paper to let the reader know where he's headed."

The teacher may want to work with each student to set a personal goal for growth in some particular aspect of writing. That goal can be monitored throughout the reporting period, or for as long as necessary to see improvement before another goal is set. Students need and appreciate something specific to strive for in their writing.

> **Teachers may want to provide a resource area in the classroom to help students as they refine their writing. Materials could include the following:**
>
> Word Wall and/or Portable Word Wall   Thesauruses
> Dictionaries   Rhyming dictionaries
> Style handbooks   Grammar reference book
> Samples of writing   Editor's Checklist
> Computer with Internet access

Two Kinds of Conferences

Some teachers choose to orchestrate a dual system for their conferences that are intended to serve two different purposes. (This system is easier to implement for those teachers who have a generous amount of time for the Writing Block.)

Status Check

One of the conferences is a brief status check where teachers visit a certain number of predetermined students to see where they are in the writing cycle, whether they've encountered any stumbling blocks, if they're staying focused and producing a reasonable amount of writing, or just to encourage them. Status conferences are each done in a couple of minutes and usually include 3-4 students daily. The status conference allows teachers to touch base with all students over the course of the week. To increase the amount of time for these conferences and to limit the numbers of students seen, the teacher may eliminate the students she knows will be meeting with her for a more in-depth conference about publishing their work. Sometimes, however, she might include those students to prepare them for their upcoming conferences.

Publishing Conference

The second conference is the publishing conference during which teachers work in-depth with a student. Often they are ready to choose the one piece among the whole cycle of 3-5 pieces to revise and edit just one. This time is provided whether or not a student is ready to publish a piece. This is the conference that will require more time, more attention, and more focus. The teacher will help students to grow individually in their writing. All teachers will have this type of conference whether or not they are able to employ the dual system. Although the teacher will work individually with students, she may have all of the conferees seated together at her conference table. This way, once she helps one student pinpoint an area to revise, that student can proceed with working to improve that area while the teacher moves on to work with another student. Then, the teacher can recheck the work of the first student for further direction, encouragement, or approval.

Here's a sample two-week schedule for a class of 23 students where the dual system is operating well:

Day	Status Conference (about 10 minutes)	Publishing Conference (about 20 minutes)
	Goal: See every student in one week, except perhaps those scheduled for publishing if time does not allow.	Goal: See students who are ready to publish, usually about half the class
Monday	Students 1, 2, 3	Students 4, 5
Tuesday	Students 6, 7, 8	Students 9, 10
Wednesday	Students 11, 12, 13	Students 14, 15, 16
Thursday	Students 17, 18, 19	Students 20, 21, 22
Friday	Students 1, 2, 3 (These students are scheduled for a publishing conference on Monday. The teacher will check to see that they are prepared.)	Student 23 (Teacher may also revisit students who needed a second conference before publishing or those who may have been absent on their assigned day)
Monday	Students 4, 5, 9	Students 1, 2, 3
Tuesday	Students 10, 14, 15	Students 6, 7, 8
Wednesday	Students 16, 20, 21	Students 11, 12, 13
Thursday	Students 22, 23	Students 13, 17
Friday	Students (Teacher may see following week's Monday publishing students.)	Students 18, 19

Writing

Here is how a teacher may fill out a Teacher's Writing Conference Roster for the previously-listed schedule to ensure that adequate time is spent with each student and that they are all encouraged to continue to write and to grow as writers:

Teacher's Writing Conference Roster

S= Status Conference P= Publishing Conference

Date Student	2/14	2/15	2/16	2/17	2/18	2/21	2/22	2/23	2/24	2/25
1 (name)	S					P				
2	S					P				
3	S					P				
4	P					S				
5	P					S				
6		S					P			
7		S					P			
8		S					P			
9		P				S				
10		P					S			
11			S					P		
12			S					P		
13			S					P		
14			P				S			
15			P				S			
16			P					S		
17				S					P	
18				S						P
19				S						P
20				P				S		
21				P				S		
22				P				S		
23					P				S	

Some teachers find it helpful to require that students have a peer conference before the publishing conference occurs with the teacher. Peers can often help with some of the editing to "clean-up" the writing. (See the reproducible My Writing Log on page 231 of the Appendix.) That allows the teacher more time to work with more important aspects of the writing/revision process. (See page 232 of the Appendix for reproducible Teacher's Writing Conference Roster.)

Publishing in the Upper Grades

Publishing in the Upper Grades can take many different forms. Students generally will produce better work if they know that it will have an audience. Here are ways that teachers can provide the opportunity to showcase students' completed pieces:

Book Format

Students can produce handwritten or computer-generated pages to be bound or stapled with covers. Teachers should find appropriate places to display the books such as special racks in the room, baskets in the reading area, a designated place in the library (in collaboration with the media specialist), the lobby of the school, or the principal's office. Comment cards can be kept in these folders as well so that those who stop to read the composition can record supportive responses. (See page 233 of the Appendix for a reproducible Reader's Response Log.) Ideas for a publishing center are shared in Chapter Two.

Professional Publication Submittals

There are many avenues for students to be published professionals. Teachers may wish to peruse a reliable guide that gives specifications for what various companies solicit from young writers. Two examples: *To Be a Writer: A Guide for Young People Who Want To Write and Publish* by Barbara Seuling (Twenty-First Century Books, 1997) and *Online Kids: A Young Surfer's Guide to Cyberspace* by Preston Gralla (John Wiley & Sons, Inc., 1999).

Mounted Display Folders for All Types of Writing

Bulletin boards can provide space for a display of current work. Large food storage bags or plastic notebook sheaths can be stapled to the board. Each container may have the name of a student written on a small mailing label. Students can be responsible for keeping a current final draft on display at all times. (Parents are eager to see students' work on display in the room!) Comment cards can be kept in these folders as well, so that those who stop to read the composition can record responses.

Portfolios

Many teachers have students design a portfolio notebook to display their talents in various modes and styles of writing. Students gather samples of their work throughout the year to capture their growth in writing, according to the personal goals they have set and the criteria established by the teacher.

There are many different ways that students' work can be published for others, together with some of the sharing that is done during the concluding segment of this block.

Segment Three: Sharing To Motivate and Refine

In *A Community of Writers: Teaching Writing in the Junior and Senior High School*, (1998), Zemelman and Daniels share that, "... in learning to write, students are invited—compelled, really—to make sense of the world, to weigh ideas, to explore values, to find their own conventions, to invent voices, styles, personae on a page—and then to test everything out by communicating with others, sharing writing, and exchanging responses." Sharing and exchanging are so critical to the refinement and improvement of the writing and of the writer! The third segment of the Writing Block is where that occurs.

Certainly it is true that some writing can be written just for the pleasure and enjoyment of the writer, just as a song might be sung and enjoyed only for the ears of the singer. However, writing that continues in such a vacuum may eventually lose its appeal. For many people, the reaction of others to what has been written is what becomes truly fulfilling about the art of writing. Writing informs, brings pleasure and enjoyment, and helps us to recall and re-experience much of life. It can connect us to others.

In the primary grades, sharing occurs daily and is usually accomplished with a child or two coming before the class to sit in the Author's Chair to read what they've written or to tell about what they've attempted to write (some are still in the picture drawing stage of writing). In the upper grades, sharing occurs as often as seems necessary to inspire these young writers. In some classes, this is daily, in others every other day, and in others once a week. So many purposes are served by the sharing that teachers would certainly not want to eliminate this time from the Writing Block, even when they are severely limited in their total workshop time frame.

Ways for Students To Share Their Writing

There are so many ways for students to share their writing, and it is the variety that keeps the classroom motivated and engaged. Here are a few ways that teachers at the upper grades have students share:

Author's Chair/Stool

Students may come before the class to sit in a special place—a stool or chair—reserved for this sharing experience. They may read or discuss something they have published or something that is being written currently. There may be time for only a couple of students per sharing period to do this.

Podium

Students may stand behind a podium (just a tall box in some classes) to share their writing. The podium may give some added confidence to many students who dread standing in front of the class. Again, it's likely that there would only be time for a couple of students per sharing period.

Peer Sharing

Students may meet with a peer so that they can share with each other what they've written. They may exchange pieces or may read aloud their own writing to the other student.

Peer Group Sharing

Students may occasionally have time to share with their cooperative group what they're working on and ask for recommendations. All students can share very briefly what they're working on and whether they need help, or one student in each group can share and get assistance.

Directed Peer/Peer Group Sharing

In this format, students join with a peer or sit with a group of peers. The teacher directs the sharing with questions such as, "Today I would like for everyone to share the purpose behind your writing," "Today I want everyone to share the characteristics of your writing that define its genre," or "Today let's all share our lead paragraphs and get some feedback as to what you hoped to achieve with that lead and whether your peers feel that you accomplished that."

Display Sharing

During the sharing time, the teacher may instruct students to go to the display bulletin board where all students have a sample of their current writing on display to bring a composition back to their desks to read. Often there is a response form at the end of the piece for the reader to record some response (a kind, constructive one, of course!), which will be available for the writer of the composition.

Adult Response

Occasionally, the teacher might require that students share one of their pieces with a trusted adult—parent, another teacher, the principal, employer—for a response. Some students may be willing to share the response they received with the class. Teachers may want to recruit some volunteers from the staff who would be willing to serve as the adult critic for some students who have difficulty locating someone for this role.

As students learn more about writing and as they become more confident in their ability to write, this sharing time will become more and more critical to their development. They will rely upon their teachers, their peers, and themselves to refine and encourage good writing. They will develop a critical eye for writing, both from the standpoint of a writer and from the standpoint of a reader.

Favorite Teacher Resources for the Writing Block:

☑ *In the Middle: New Understandings about Writing, Reading, and Learning* by Nancie Atwell (Boynton/Cook, 1998)

☑ *Teaching Genre: Exploring 9 Types of Literature To Develop Lifelong Readers and Writers* by Tara McCarthy (Scholastic, 1996)

☑ *Dynamite Writing Ideas: Empowering Students To Become Authors!* by Melissa Forney (Maupin House, 1996)

☑ *Craft Lessons: Teaching Writing K–8* by Ralph Fletcher and Joann Portalupi (Stenhouse Publishers, 1998)

Summary of the Writing Block

The purposes of this block:

☑ To help students become effective communicators of written language for varied purposes and audiences

☑ To allow students the opportunity to apply their knowledge of phonics, spelling, and decoding in an authentic context

☑ To allow students to see reading from the writer's point of view

Segment One (10–15 minutes)

The teacher provides a model of writing to the whole group and includes the following:

1. A mini-lesson

2. A self-check using an Editor's Checklist

Segment Two (20–30 minutes)

1. Students write.

2. The teacher holds conferences with students for status check and/or publishing.

Segment Three (5–10 minutes)

The teacher brings closure by having students share.

A Typical Week in an Upper Grades Writing Block

Monday

Segment 1 (Mini-Lesson: Business Letter Format)

The teacher sits alongside his overhead projector and shares, "Writing has many uses in your lives beyond school. One real-world kind of writing is writing letters—business, friendly, thank-you notes, invitations, responses, and memos—just to name a few types. I thought today I would 'kill two birds with one stone,' so to speak. I need to write a business letter, and I thought I would share mine with you. It's one of those things that's on our list to learn this year!" He continues by explaining that he needs to write to the teacher licensure office to request an update of his credentials. He writes his letter on a transparency, thinking aloud about where the date and address go, what punctuation is needed for a formal business letter, the appropriate word choices, and the brevity expected. After he has his rough draft prepared, he asks the students to help him use the Editor's Checklist as a quick check of his work. He asks for the students' suggestions for any revisions that they feel would offer more clarity to the letter. The students give their "approval" of what he has written. "I'll copy this over on the computer at home tonight, and it'll be in the morning's mail! Thanks for your help! We will all have an opportunity to write a business letter next month as part of our social studies unit. We'll practice again, though, between now and then."

Segment 2 (Student Writing—Self-Selected Topics)

On this day, the students have the opportunity to continue with their own writing projects. Some are starting first drafts of pieces; some are continuing their work on pieces begun days before; and still others have scheduled publishing conferences or are working on their revisions for publishing a piece. The teacher has a quick status conference with three students at their desks before settling in the area designated for publishing conferences. Today, three students are scheduled for conferences. All three join the teacher at the same time. While two do some final peer editing together, the teacher starts with one student to polish a piece of her writing. After he has guided this student to make decisions about her selection, he works with another of the three students, while the other two continue working individually on their pieces. The teacher continues to rotate among the three students, assisting them with the writing process. At the end of the 20 minutes allocated for conferencing, the teacher calls for all students to bring their writing to closure.

Segment 3 (Sharing)

With the 10 minutes remaining in the block, the teacher asks for volunteers who may want to share the topic they're writing about and their beginning paragraphs. This is a good sampling to give other students ideas about getting started with their writing. Many of the students have expressed that they often have difficulty with their first paragraphs. After the first student shares his beginning paragraph, the teacher says, "Now, tell us what you hope to accomplish with your beginning. Did you hope to catch the reader's attention? Did you hope to establish the main character, the setting, the mood, or some other literary element?" The student responds that he had hoped it would catch the attention of his readers and make them want to read more. The teacher may ask the class whether they feel that the paragraph has, in fact, accomplished what the writer intended. Sometimes students are reluctant to receive input openly; however, the teacher continues to work hard to create an atmosphere in which students will feel confident in asking for others' input and will actually appreciate it.

Today, three students share their first paragraphs with the class and their reasons for using their particular starting line.

Tuesday

Segment 1 (Mini-Lesson: Pronoun-Antecedent Agreement)

Today, the teacher announces that he has been thinking of recording some of his family's traditions and memories. "It's such a shame when families don't record these important things about their lives for their descendents to enjoy. I think I'll begin to use some of my model lessons to record my family history and traditions. I guess the holidays that are fast-approaching have reminded me of the importance of this kind of writing. If the samples I write turn out to be pretty good, I might put together a little book for my children. We'll see how it goes!" He begins to write about a tradition that began with his grandparents. After their Thanksgiving dinner each year, they always celebrated the official Christmas season by giving each of their children a small tree ornament and explaining what that ornament symbolized for that child. This tradition had continued with his parents, and he recalled how special he felt each year as his parents honored him and his siblings with their ornaments. With a good beginning about how the tradition started, he concluded his model with, "Now, tomorrow I want to add to this piece by recalling some of the ornaments my parents gave to me. I'm going to stop now, though, and read what I've written so far." He reads it aloud and remarks that because of all the family members involved, he has had to use many pronouns to refer to them. "Maybe I need to double-check to be sure that it's clear to whom these pronouns refer. Sometimes writing can be so confusing when the pronouns and their antecedents aren't clear." He reads over the piece and underlines the pronouns as he comes to them. "Yes, I think that one might be ambiguous—meaning that it's unclear whether it refers to my mother or to my sister. Let's see if I can clarify it." He makes a change, and the students agree that it's clearer to them. "Okay, now it's your turn," he says, as he turns off the overhead projector and ends his model lesson.

Segment 2 (Student Writing—Self-Selected Topics)

The students continue to write in their notebooks at different stages just as they did yesterday. The teacher checks his roster to see which students are due for a status check, then goes to their individual desks to see where they are with their writing. "Will you be ready for a conference next week?" "If you're having trouble with that ending, why don't you see if Mark will work with you. The two of you work well together." He visits three students quickly and then settles down at the conference area where four students have gathered to meet with him. The teacher works with them individually and as a group to address a few problems.

Segment 3 (Sharing)

The teacher decides that since his model lesson was a bit longer than usual, and because his students seem so engrossed in their own writing, he will not interrupt them for sharing today. Surely, there will be time tomorrow!

Wednesday

Segment 1 (Mini-Lesson: Details/Imaging)

The teacher returns to his composition from the previous day. He models for students how to reconnect to pieces that are being composed over several days. He reads over it and makes a decision about where he'll go from here. "It occurs to me that I've been telling about the idea of the tradition without sharing with you the atmosphere of those celebrations. I think I'll go back today and see where it might be appropriate to insert something about the sights, sounds, and smells of those occasions that I recall so clearly." He reads back over the composition and interjects phrases like, "the lingering smell of cinnamon from the homemade apple pie," "the shining foil of the tiny packages that held each ornament," and other details that help to bring the experience alive for the reader. The students agree at the conclusion of his revisions that the piece is much easier to visualize now. The teacher does a quick edit with the help of the students and the Editor's Checklist. He now announces that it's time for the students to write.

Segment 2 (Student Writing—Self-Selected Topics)

This segment proceeds just as on Monday and Tuesday, with the teacher holding status conferences with a few students to keep them focused, and then meeting with three students for more in-depth conferences.

Segment 3 (Sharing)

The teacher has made a note of several students whom he would like to have share with the class for various reasons. He has asked these students, either during their status conferences or their publishing conferences, if they would share from certain things from their pieces that he thinks might help other students. "Kirk has a topic that might interest you, and I've asked if he would share his first page." "Maria, would you read the paragraph that I marked on your paper? It has a metaphor that is a super description of an aging person." "Marcus has used a couple of transition words well in his informational piece that I'd like for you to hear." These students share with the class, and the teacher elicits positive responses from the class.

Thursday

Segment 1 (Mini-Lesson: Addressing a Prompt)

"Students, I'm going to continue to work on the piece I've been writing about my family's tradition, but today I need to work with you all on a special kind of writing that we all must learn more about. This spring, as you know, you're going to have the opportunity to show the school district what you've learned about writing. Every few weeks, I want to teach you something about that kind of writing because it's a bit different from what you normally write in our class. So, I want you to feel comfortable with it and to know exactly how the district will score your papers. You've been using rubrics in our class, so that won't be new to you. Their rubric, however, is a little different from the one we use so often. Today, I want to share with you the process you'll go through when you're taking this writing test, and do a little pre-writing to get organized. Tomorrow, we'll talk about the rubric, so that you'll know what to include in your writing and you'll start writing your piece. We'll probably take several days to write the composition and apply the rubric."

The teacher then starts by sharing the design of the test and that the district wants all students to show some pre-planning of their writing on a sheet that is provided for that purpose. "Let's consider the prompt, 'Describe the perfect school.'" He brainstorms with the students the variety of ways that they have already learned that they might organize their thoughts for writing: webbing, outlines, jot lists, etc. He then chooses one of those—webbing—and begins to sketch a topic web on his transparency. He writes the words "perfect school" in the center circle and then fills in the satellite circles with key words for the ideas he might use in his description, such as "teachers," "administrators," "students," "environment," "goals," and "schedule." He begins to sketch in ideas that branch out from one of these as he thinks aloud. "Okay, let's give you a chance to use this same method to develop this same topic today. We'll only have time today for you to work on your pre-writing organization, and I'd like for you to use this same type of organization using a web as I've modeled for you today. You certainly may use some of the same words I've used in the branches of your map, although I'll want you to add a great deal more detail under more of the branches than I did. I'll come around and check on your progress as you begin to work."

Segment 2 (Student Writing—Focused Topic)

The teacher visits students at their desks as they work, answering questions and stimulating their thoughts. After about 20 minutes, he tells the students to bring their work to closure.

Segment 3 (Sharing)

There is time remaining for a couple of students to share some new ideas they've come up with for the perfect school. The students enjoy hearing from their peers.

Friday

Segment 1 (Mini-Lesson: Writing to a Prompt)

The teacher begins the mini-lesson by sharing a transparency of the rubric the district uses to evaluate the compositions for the district writing test. Each item is discussed briefly, and the students find that they are familiar with all of the terminology. The teacher explains how much weight is given to the different items. The teacher then moves along and models how to go from the planning sheet to the actual writing. He writes a beginning paragraph that shows a clear direction for combining the main points in his graphic organizer. Next, he begins to construct a second paragraph using one of the subheadings from his graph and expanding on the key words he has attributed to that subheading. He composes two complete paragraphs of his composition before stopping to do a quick-edit using the Editor's Checklist. "Now, it's time for you to begin your compositions. I want you to try to draft at least two paragraphs today before we have some time to share. I'm hoping that several of you will share your first paragraphs with us as we end our workshop time."

Segment 2 (Student Writing—Focused Topic)

The teacher visits students again to see that they are focused and progressing with their work. Occasionally, students ask for technical help with their work, and the teacher lends assistance.

Segment 3 (Sharing)

Several students volunteer to share their first paragraphs with the class. The teacher offers encouragement and feedback to those who have shared. "Tomorrow, we'll continue with these compositions. We'll also begin to apply the rubric that we've talked about to your papers."

Chapter 6

Working with Words Block

The Working with Words Block is the time that students will collect, analyze, explore, discuss, and appreciate words. Some words will be interesting to students because of their histories, some because of their sounds, some for their precision, some for their familiarity, and some for their novelty. This basic element of our spoken and written language is worthy of a time—even in the upper grades—devoted to learning more about the power of words in our lives.

So many of today's adolescents seem to lack the ability to express themselves clearly and precisely—or, often, even coherently. Fads have produced awkward speech patterns, poor grammar and usage, and fragmented sentences: "Duhhhh!!!" "He was, like, tired after the game." "You know…we were like…you know…ready to leave the movies…you know." Yikes! Fads have created a diction disaster, verbal vandalization, and a literacy landslide! What can we do to reverse the trend?

> In February of 2000, *Time* reported this trend in the vocabularies of typical 14-year-olds:
>
> 1950–Vocabulary of 25,000 words
>
> 1999–Vocabulary of 10,000 words

During each of the blocks, we will help students develop their knowledge of vocabulary and will provide them with ample opportunities to apply their knowledge in a rich context—real reading, writing, speaking, and listening. The structure of the Working with Words Block alone not only will teach students much about basic spelling and decoding patterns but also will go far beyond the word level of literacy. In this block, students will learn about how malleable words can be used in communicating with clarity, precision, and expression. They will learn how words will empower them in their everyday lives.

The creators of the Four-Blocks™ framework, Dr. Patricia Cunningham and Dr. Dorothy Hall, have shared in *Month-by-Month Phonics for Upper Grades* (Carson-Dellosa, 1999) how the basic goals for teaching children about high-frequency words, spelling, and decoding in grades one to three expand to five goals appropriate for the grades beyond. Cunningham and Hall share that the book, "is intended to help teach struggling readers—whether they are fourth graders or tenth graders—become fluent decoders and spellers. It also provides activities through which students who are learning English can learn to use our English spelling system."

The five goals that Cunningham and Hall share for meeting critical word fluency are below with a brief explanation of each:

1. Learning high-frequency, commonly misspelled words

High-frequency words are those that students will encounter often in their reading and that they will **need** (not just **want**) to use often in their writing. These words often have irregular patterns. In the upper grades, students commonly confuse "through" and "though," and they still misspell simple words like "said" and "they." Teaching students interesting facts about word derivations (once upon a time, "said" had the same sound pattern as "braid"!) and concentrating on the letters with activities where students are rhythmically involved in snapping, clapping, stomping, or tapping each letter along with the class, will help students commit these letters to their long-term memories.

2. Learning one- and two-syllable words that follow a pattern, but are used less frequently

Guided by the research that says that our brains work as pattern detectors when we decode new words, teachers will instruct students to recognize and process word chunks, also known as "onsets" (the beginning chunk of a word, up to the first vowel) and "rimes" (the first vowel and thereafter) to increase their ability to decode words. Once the word chunks are learned, students can apply their phonemic knowledge to manipulate the sounds at the beginnings and ends of words to change them to new words, such as learning the word "best" and then using it when they write a story about a cowboy out "west" who wears a "vest."

Cunningham and Hall give teachers a wonderful activity called Brand Name Phonics to appeal to upper-grade students as they apply this simple concept to spell and decode words that are used less frequently, such as using Sprite® to spell and decode *bite, quite, spite, ignite, unite, polite,* and *campsite.* What a fun activity for students of all ages, and what a lasting impression this activity makes!

3. Spelling words with two or more possible patterns

Many activities in Four-Blocks teach students to rely upon words that have the same sound pattern (rhyme) to spell words by also using their spelling pattern (rime). It would be logical for a student who's writing a story about the plight of the Native Americans of the 19th century to spell "plight" as "plite" if he hears the same sound pattern as "bite," or "kite." In the lower grades, we encourage students to use that system of "what has the same sound as another word" so that they'll put words on paper more fluently as they're writing, rather than running to a dictionary or changing to another word they're sure of. In the upper grades, we teach students that there could be several spelling patterns (rimes) that have the same sound pattern (rhyme). We want these students to develop their visual cueing systems to be able to detect what looks right as they see a word. Hence, an activity like What Looks Right? in the book *Month-by-Month Phonics for Upper Grades,* is a great way for kids to explore with the teacher when rhyming words don't have the same rime!

4. Decoding and spelling polysyllabic words

So much of the instruction in spelling and decoding in the lower grades deals with one- and two-syllable words; however, students in the upper grades, obviously, will begin to deal with more and more words with more and more syllables. *Month-by-Month Phonics for Upper Grades* shares a list of 50 words that contain examples for all common prefixes and suffixes, as well as common spelling changes involved in adding these morphemic units to words. The Nifty Thrifty Fifty (try saying that quickly five times!) are introduced gradually, eight per month, so that students will know how word parts will help them figure out many other words.

5. Applying strategies while reading and writing

Far beyond memorization of word lists and spelling rules is the application of what a student knows about words and rules. Often this higher level of knowledge was not included during the time of the day when we taught traditional spelling lessons. When we didn't help students apply what they had learned to their everyday reading and writing, they often didn't make the transfer on their own. So what if a student memorizes a list of words and makes 100 on the weekly spelling test? Did he ever necessarily use those words again correctly in his *real* writing? So what if students can complete a worksheet of when to add -es or -ies to words with accuracy? Did they know how to do it correctly when they wrote those same words in their own compositions? Cunningham and Hall help teachers take students to a higher level of the learning taxonomy where students will actually apply their knowledge about words. Through activities such as Guess the Covered Word and even through dictation, students gain an understanding of how what they've learned will actually be useful to them.

This book will not attempt to recreate for the reader Cunningham and Hall's wonderful *Month-by-Month Phonics for Upper Grades.* At the request of teachers who have been guided by the *Month-by-Month* publication, we will explore how teachers can use that book—not as an exact recipe for the classroom—but as a template to plug in other lessons and activities; how teachers can organize their day using the *Month-by-Month* lessons; and how teachers can move students beyond the five basic fluency-building goals, once those objectives have been met.

Building a Template from a Recipe

Although *Month-by-Month Phonics for Upper Grades* has words and lessons desig-nated for each month of the year, teachers from grades four and above realize that they can't all teach the exact same words and activities yearly to students. They must use the book as a template in which they learn to plug words and activities that they feel are appropriate for their students at their grade level. Let's take a look at each of the goals to find ways that teachers can move beyond the book to plan their own lessons from scratch.

Goal I: Learning High-Frequency, Commonly Misspelled Words

There are 100 high-frequency words that make up half of all written material (Fry, Kress, and Fountoukidis, 1993)! In schools where Four-Blocks has been taught at the lower grades, these 100 words have been learned by children who have now reached the upper grades with greater fluency because they have developed automaticity with these words and other high-frequency words.

Teachers in the upper grades should now spend time teaching students the words that they are commonly misspelling in their own writing. No published lists can determine for a teacher exactly which words will be of greatest ben-efit, although the lists might be a good start-ing point. Teachers may want to spend one a day a week (or a month, as time allows) to randomly read through students' rough drafts, paying attention to commonly misspelled words and listing them on paper. Using stu-dents' rough drafts is particularly important, as this is the writing that reveals whether stu-dents have developed automaticity with the high-frequency words. Teachers will usually find that some of the words misspelled and misused by their students are those words that appear on published lists. However, some of the words are special needs for just that class and just those students.

The Mysterious intruder

Babysitting is usually such an easy job, especially when you're sitting for a young child with an early bedtime. The other night though, I really earned my money! The night started out as a quiet, uneventful evening, but ended up as anything but quiet and uneventful!

I checked on Toby, the five-year-old boy I was sitting for, and found him nestled in his bed fast asleep. That was great because I was counting on time to work on alot of homework I had for the next day. I turned on the television-just for background noise, of course-and spread all of my books, my notebooks, my pencils and my calculator across the sofa. Propping up against a mountain of pillows, I settled comfortably and began my homework.

Not five minutes into my first page of algebra problems, I heard a door creak in the kitchen. I grew still and reached for the television remote.

Misspelled/Misused Words Second Period Block Writing	
Word	**Times Noticed**
especially (especialy)	II
a lot (alot)	THL
usually (useally, usully)	I
because (becase)	I
through (threw, though)	II
accept (except)	I
truly (truely)	II
sincerely (sincerly)	II
achieve (acheive)	III
believe (beleive)	IIII

What Should You Do with the High-Frequency Words?

Once teachers have determined the words that would be most valuable for students to learn—or re-learn, as the case may be!—then there are some do's and don'ts in dealing with the words:

With the High-Frequency Words, We Do...

☑ Let students experience the words.

There are a number of quick ways to have students tactually and kinesthetically engaged in learning these words.

Some ideas are:

- ☑ Touch, Tap, and Talk–Taking each word separately, have students touch-and-spell the word by pointing their pencils at each letter as they spell along with a buddy or with the whole class together. The pencil will help them focus on each individual letter and will ensure them that they haven't inadvertently omitted any letters from their writing of the word. They may practice this two to three times. Then, have students look away from the word and tap rhythmically to each letter as they spell the word again, two to three times. Then, they may verbalize to their partners what will help them to remember the word correctly.

- ☑ Mary Mack Spelling–In classes where it might still be considered "cool," have students review their high-frequency words by turning to a partner and clapping together—Mary Mack style—each of the letters in the words. Repeating each word three times will help students commit the words to memory.

- ☑ Snap, Clap, Stomp (or whatever movements you determine)–Along with the "if-it's-still-cool" caveat, have students devise some movement to the words being reviewed. In some classes, teachers and students have been very creative, relating their movements to sports, dance movements, and other activities popular to the age of students. For example, during a big basketball play-off in one district, students were making the motion of a free throw to each letter, dribbling to each letter of the words, and then turning to a partner and doing a "high five" to the letters. Just be sure that the action isn't getting all the attention—that kids are still concentrating on the spelling!

☑ Have students write the words, paying attention to the spelling as they write.

Cunningham and Hall suggest that students will pay closer attention to the spelling of the words if they are writing in response to clues about the words. Rather than saying, "Write the word *conscience*," the teacher says, "Write the word from our list that has 10 letters and means, 'having a sense of what is right or wrong.' It also has one of your favorite school subjects hiding in it!"

☑ **Expose students to the commonly misspelled words through a Word Wall that is ever-present in the classroom.**

Teachers usually reserve space on a wall in their rooms to display the words for which students need easy access. All of the letters of the alphabet are displayed, and under each letter are the words that start with that letter. The Word Wall is blank at the beginning of the year, and the words are added gradually, usually with approximately 8 to 10 words added per month. **(In the lower grades, students learn five new words per week; however, the upper grades students are addressing more goals and also, hopefully, have fewer high-frequency words to learn.)**

If an upper grades teacher has several classes at different grades, she may rely solely on the portable Word Wall idea below so that every class uses their own appropriate word list. Some teachers have more than one Word Wall displayed in the classroom as resources for different classes. This, of course, would require a great deal of wall space, which is often not an option for many teachers.

Features to consider for words that are included on the Word Wall:

☑ Large and legible (Sit in the students' desks in various areas of the room to be sure they all can see the words.)

☑ Accessible to everyone in the class (without having to get up!)

☑ Usually in lower-case letters (unless the word is a proper noun which usually isn't a high frequency word)

☑ Cut into configurations (may aid students who are highly visual)

☑ Written on, or backed with, colored paper (again, to aid students who are visual learners and to help some students differentiate words that have similar characteristics)

☑ Designate words with valuable spelling patterns (Place an asterisk, a sticker, or a checkmark beside these words and constantly remind students that these spelling patterns will help them spelling many other words.)

☑ **Hold students accountable for the words once they've been taught.**

In an effort, again, to help develop automaticity with these words, students should use these words correctly even in their rough draft writing. When teachers see students misspelling the words that have been taught and reviewed, simply marking a "WW" and asking that students pay attention to the spelling will help them.

☑ **Ask the students to remain accountable, even after they leave the classroom.**

Students can carry lists of the Word Wall words with them to other classes and home as well. A portable Word Wall will provide a quick resource for students. Some students enjoy having them for use during the Writing Block, especially students who may have difficulty seeing words at a distance on the walls. A portable Word Wall is included in the back of *Month-by-Month Phonics for Upper Grades*, using the words taught in the lessons of that book. However, teachers can have students create their own. (See page 234-235 of the Appendix for reproducible Portable Word Wall.) Be sure that if students are adding the new words weekly to the portable Word Wall, they spell the words correctly—or else they will surely learn the words incorrectly. This can be solved by giving the students one minute after writing the words on their portable Word Wall to exchange folders with another student for a quick check. Students are far more critical of their classmates' work than of their own!

☑ **Teach students specifics and interesting tidbits about words that will help them to retain the words.**

A great resource for these lessons would be *The Reading Teacher's Book of Lists* by Edward Fry, Jacqueline Kress, and Dona Lee Fountoukidis (Prentice Hall, 1993) that contains lists of every description. Categories of words that might be used to construct lessons for upper grades to address this first goal would be:

☑ **Close Calls**—Words or phrases that sound similar or have other confusing characteristics although they have different meanings.

Examples:

access (n.) admittance	or	**excess** (n., adj.) surplus
any way (adj., and n.) in whatever manner	or	**anyway** (adv.) regardless
conscience (n.) sense of right and wrong	or	**conscious** (adj.) aware

☑ **Homographs and Heteronyms**—Homographs are spelled the same but have different meanings and different origins. Heteronyms are spelled the same but have a different pronunciation.

Examples:

affect (v.) to influence	or	**affect** (v.) to pretend
content (n.) something contained	or	**content** (adj.) satisfied
converse (v.) to engage in conversation	or	**converse** (adj.) opposite

Even the word **spell** is in this category!

spell (v.) to name the letters of a word; or **spell** (n.) like magic; or **spell** (n.) period of time

☑ **Homophones**—These words usually sound the same but have different meanings and, usually, different spellings.

Examples:

band (n.) group of musicians	and	**banned** (v.) prohibited
forth (adv.) forward	and	**fourth** (n.) after third
fair (adj.) honest	and	**fare** (n.) cost of transportation
complement (n.) complete set	and	**compliment** (n.) flattering remark

When similar words are placed on the Word Wall, a clue may be placed alongside them to aide the students. For example, the word *conscience* might have a little angel or halo beside it to distinguish it from *conscious*. Teachers will surely want to back these words with different colors. It will be so much easier for the teacher to refer to similar words by pointing out their colors, such as, "*Through* is the blue word on the Word Wall," when the student has confused it with *though*, which is a red word.

The categories above are especially important in the age of technology with the frequent reliance on "spellcheckers" and other such spelling aides that won't catch these kinds of errors made in writing. The confusion of some of these words could certainly prove to be embarrassing! By the way, it is not at all important that students be able to label which pairs of words are homophones, which are homonyms, or which are heteronyms. It's important that they know that confusion with words exists, and that the more they know about words, the better off they'll be!

☑ **Continue to review the words that are placed on the Word Wall. Everyone becomes immune to common, everyday items in the environment.**

If words are placed on the Word Wall and never reviewed, students will forget about the words and won't use them correctly. Two review activities are loved by upper- and lower-grades students alike:

☑ **Be a Mind Reader:** As a quick review of words that are already on the Word Wall, have students number their papers from 1 to 5. Give them clues towards finding a word that you have "on your mind." The first clue is always, "It's a word on the Word Wall." This gives the students a chance, without specifics, to see if they can read your mind. The next real clue might be, "It's a blue word." The following clue might be, "It's a seven-letter word." Each time a clue is given, students respond by making a guess on their papers. They write a word for each clue, either writing their previous guess again or revising their guess to a new word. The fourth clue might be, "It's often written incorrectly as a two-letter word." And, the fifth clue might be, "It fits in the sentence, 'Although we had _____ seen the movie, we wanted to see it again." After all the students have written five words, the answer is revealed, and a quick check is done to see how many students had the word on the fourth clue, the third clue, the second clue, and who may have actually "read the teacher's mind" by getting it right on the very first clue!

☑ **Wordo**–This is an activity that takes a bit more time—though no particular planning—and yet is fun and engaging for all students. All students are given a playing card (See page 236 of the Appendix for reproducible Wordo Card.) that looks similar to a bingo card. The card (or sheet of paper on which the grid has been copied) has space large enough for words to be written. There are two options for filling in the playing card. One is more controlled, giving students the opportunity to review the same 16 to 25 words.

Option 1–The teacher calls on one student to start the game by calling out any word on the Word Wall. As that student responds with a word, all students choose a space anywhere on their cards to write the word. (Some teachers have students spell the words as they write them to ensure that they'll spell them correctly.) Then, the student who gave the first word calls on another classmate to give a second word that all students write in one of the grids. As the students each select a word from the wall, the teacher writes that word on a small piece of scrap paper, folds it and puts it in a pile. This process continues until the students have all the spaces on their grids filled. Then, the teacher begins to draw words from the pile. Students will mark the words in some way (with check marks or with objects) until someone marks all words as in bingo and calls, "Wordo!"

Option 2–Instead of having everyone add the same words to their grids, a variation is to allow all students to fill their grids with any words from the wall, so that everyone has different words on their cards. Then, either the teacher calls words randomly from the wall until a winner is declared, or the teacher allows each student to call out a word from their cards that is marked only by students who have included that word on their own cards. This version may take a bit longer than the more controlled version, but is nevertheless fun for students!

On the Other Hand, with the High-Frequency Words, We …

☑ Don't have students write the words a certain number of times.

Teachers have found that having students write each word five to ten times does not help students learn to spell words. The students write mechanically, with little regard to the actual spellings.

☑ Don't crowd the Word Wall with words other than the high-frequency, commonly misspelled words.

There can be other places in the classroom to display words that students may want to access for their writing—science words, math words, theme words, etc. The expectations of students' use of these words are different. It's wonderful if they use those words correctly—but not required.

☑ Don't get too picky about the construction of the Word Wall.

Great debates rage about whether the words under each letter of the alphabet are to be rearranged weekly in alphabetical order after new words are added, whether words are to be in cursive or manuscript, whether to configure the lowercase *i* as an upper-case letter around the dot, and other such trivia. Let's just include the basics and give students the support they need.

> The issue of whether upper-grades Word Walls should be written in cursive or manuscript can be defended both ways. Students will read these words in book print, which is manuscript. Students are often required to write the words in cursive. This debate is left to the best judgment of the individual teacher constructing the wall.

Goal 2: Learning One-Syllable and Two-Syllable Words That Follow a Pattern, But Are Used Less Frequently

Writers need to acquire the ability to decode and spell words never seen or used before. Rather than memorizing and applying dozens of rules, writers are far more apt to use known patterns to help them figure out new words (Caine and Caine, 1994). This is why, so often, students memorize the rules and apply them to do well on Friday's test, but don't seem to apply the rules in the context of their "real" reading and writing.

Towards making a difference where it really counts, students must depend upon their visual and auditory cueing systems either to decide that, "Oh, that sounds like the word ___," or "Yes, that looks like the word ___."

Two popular activities to provide the practice and application for this goal, according to *Month-by-Month Phonics for Upper Grades,* are Brand Name Phonics and Making Words. A brief description of these activities follows:

Brand Name Phonics

The teacher presents two to three products that are present in the environment of the students, often using their brand names. The students write those words on a sheet of paper, forming columns by drawing lines between the words. Then, the teacher either shows an index card with a word written on it, or says some words that have the same spelling patterns and likely the same sound patterns. Students match the new words with a pattern in the words of one of the products.

For example, one lesson in *Month-by-Month Phonics for Upper Grades* is:

Products shown and discussed: Kit Kat® and Goldfish®

☑ Teacher reads these one-syllable words: spit, split, that, grit, flat, dish, bold, spat, mold, rat

☑ Teacher shows these one-syllable words: slit, old, hold, wish, swish, quit, chat, hat, hit, brat

☑ Teacher reads these longer words: admit, profit, misfit, wildcat, credit, democrat, selfish, unselfish, acrobat, blindfold

☑ Teacher shows these longer words: permit, visit, combat, outfit, nonfat, catfish, starfish, billfold, doormat

Students will write the words that the teacher has shared in one of the columns underneath the word that they recognize with the same spelling/sound pattern. The teacher helps the students verbalize how they figured out the patterns and how this will help them in their day-to-day reading and writing.

Making Words

For this activity, the teacher gives each student all of the letters that will create a big word. The teacher usually refers to this word as the secret word, which may be a word that connects to a theme or topic being studied, or which might just be a word that provides exposure to patterns that need to be taught. The teacher has these same letters in a pocket chart in the room where she will guide this activity.

☑ **Step One**–The activity starts with the teacher instructing students to make a small word, usually a two- or three-letter word. Even though these are words that most of the upper-grades kids know, these are often the words that contain the basic spelling patterns of the more difficult words that they will learn to spell. The teacher guides the students through building 10 to 12 words, adding and deleting the fewest letters possible to allow students to see the possibilities for manipulating sounds and letters to make new words from words they know. Finally, the secret word is revealed that has all of the letters given to the students.

☑ **Step Two**–In the second step of this activity, after the secret word is discovered, the teacher leads the students in a sorting activity, giving the students an opportunity to share what the 10 to 12 words they've made have in common—spelling patterns, sound patterns, plurals, certain parts of speech, etc. The words that the teacher has used in the sorting activity are all written on index cards that are arranged vertically in the pocket chart, accentuating their patterns.

☑ **Step Three**–In the final step, the teacher allows the students to apply their knowledge of the patterns they've been exploring. With the index cards in the pocket chart still

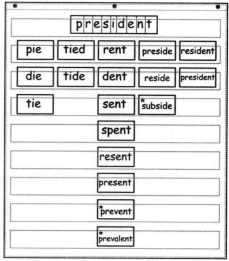

* mystery word

sorted, especially for the rhyming and spelling patterns, the teacher calls out some new words, usually going beyond those that are limited to the use of the letters in the mystery word.

Going Beyond *Month-by-Month Phonics for Upper Grades*

Teachers who need to go beyond *Month-by-Month Phonics for Upper Grades* can certainly venture out, creating their own lessons and activities. Here are some alternatives that might provide variety:

Brand or Bland?

This activity mimics Brand Name Phonics, but isn't limited to brand names and doesn't use the word "phonics," which sometimes has negative connotations with upper-grades students who consider that phonics is for primary kids. It also can give students the responsibility for thinking through constructing the rhymes. If students take one block period per month to plan this activity, then the teacher has a month of weekly activities. Here is the basic set-up for upper-grades students:

1. Working with partners or small groups, students produce a list of two or three brand names (teacher may need to determine how many according to the amount of time available) and the words that tell what their categories are (the "bland" or generic words). For example: *Cascade*™ and *detergent*; *Coke*® and *drink*; *Listerine*® and *mouthwash*.

2. Students use their rhyming dictionaries to help find three to four words that use the spelling patterns of each of their words. Students should try to think up or find words that are somewhat familiar to their classmates—not totally obscure—but that provide a challenge! Students write their words on a sheet of paper under the correct lead word that has that rhyme. (Teachers will need to work with students to understand the rime patterns that can be used.)

3. Students write the words they come up with clearly on index cards, one per card.

4. Students turn in their master lists and note cards to the teacher. Now the teacher checks over the cards to be sure that the rhymes are correct. When that is determined, she packages the cards and the guide list in an envelope for future use.

5. On the day of the Brand or Bland activity, the teacher can guide the activity or can allow one of the students that prepared the activity to call out the words. Classmates are instructed to make the appropriate number of columns on their papers, placing the brand and bland words across the top. Then, the person calling out the words (teacher or student) arranges the cards in order of ascending level of difficulty. The words are shared by showing half the words on the cards (tapping students' visual cueing systems) and by saying half the words (tapping students' auditory cueing systems). Alternating every other word by saying or showing the word might do this best. As the words are shared, the students are to write the word under the column of the brand or bland word they have as headers on their papers, using the patterns to help them spell the words correctly.

Of course the teacher can construct these lessons, too, especially if the students struggle over creating the activity; however, having the students involved to that degree usually causes them to think harder about the patterns. Students who have had Four-Blocks in the lower grades should have a good understanding of the rime patterns necessary for success with this activity.

Riming Relay

Students participate in this activity in cooperative groups or teams. The teacher gives the whole class a category, such as music, cars, sports, or rock stars. Then, the teams must come up with a word in that category that has a rime pattern that can be used to construct other words. Within a specified amount of time, they brainstorm, in their small groups, a list of words that have the same rime as the lead word. (The teacher should determine if the groups can use a rhyming dictionary.) They write their words on a transparency. At the end of the time, all groups stop writing. Each group individually presents the list they have constructed by placing it on the overhead projector. Other groups can challenge whether certain words on the list are legitimate. Words that are found not to be legitimate are stricken from the transparency. A point is given for each word that does have the same rime (spelling pattern). After each group has presented their list, the group with the most points is designated as the winner.

Working with Words Block

The teacher gives the category, *sports*. Different teams come up with these lists, based on the lead words *ball*, *club*, *kickoff*, and *hit*:

Group 1	Group 2	Group 3	Group 4
ball	club	kickoff	hit
fall	cub	scoff	fit
tall	pub	cast-off	kit
y'all	snub	tip-off	skit
mall	bathtub	trade-off	pit
call	nightclub	shutoff	pinch-hit
football	washtub	standoff	outfit
baseball	dub	Stroganoff	knit
shortfall	hubbub	payoff	transmit
volleyball	rub	blast-off	snakebit
cannonball	tub	play-off	permit
downfall	flub	takeoff	counterfeit*
eyeball	grub	rip-off	misfit
hardball		well-off	candlelit
rainfall		write-off	benefit
stonewall			unfit
waterfall			submit
whitewall			pulpit
windfall			moonlit
overhaul *			

*challenged

Other categories could be cars, movie stars, rock stars, female singers, male singers, rap singers, TV shows, baseball, football, sports teams, children, racing, movies, songs, careers, novels, colleges/universities—the list is endless!

Making Words

This activity can be used at all grade levels. Four books are currently available to support teachers by providing ready-made lessons. Two of these books were written expressly for the upper grades—*Making Big Words* (Cunningham and Hall, Good Apple, 1994) and *Making More Big Words* (Cunningham and Hall, Good Apple, 1997). These are wonderful aides for teachers, especially those who wish to connect the mystery word to a theme being studied. The indices in both books make it easy for teachers to check for these thematic connections. In addition, teachers can always construct their own lessons. There are several resources to help teachers do this. A handy hand-held gadget such as a Franklin Spelling Ace® with an anagram function can be used by the teacher to input whatever word is being considered for the mystery word. Once the word is given to the gadget, the Spelling Ace® will give all of the words that can be made with these same letters, down to the small two-and three-letter words. The teacher can then arrange all of those words on a self-made chart sorting by the number of letters in each word. Additionally, there are some Web sites that perform this same anagram function, allowing the user to enter a word and then giving them the words that can be made from those letters. Below is an example:

Social studies topic: *immigration* (secret word)
Words that can be made with these letters:

3	4	5	6	7	8	9
art	rain	train	margin	ingrain	trimming	immigrant
air	mint	grain	aiming	migrant		migration
aim	tram	taming	airing			
arm	maim	rating	arming			
ant	mart	mating	miming			
	rant	ration	miring			
	grit	gamin	timing			
	gain	giant				
	gait	grain				
	gnat	grant				
	grin					
	mart					
	rang					
	ring					
	trim					
	trig					

Then, the teacher will plot how he should move from word to word, removing the fewest and adding the fewest letters to help retain basic word patterns. These will be the rime patterns the class will sort for during this activity. Only about a dozen words will be chosen.

Next the teacher will study the patterns and determine three to four transfer words—words that use the basic patterns the students will build to make other words. In this activity, the transfer words might be: expl<u>ain</u>, expect<u>ant</u>, and educa<u>tion</u>.

The activity must be briskly paced to hold the interest of all students. They will (1) build 10 to 12 words at the direction of the teacher; (2) sort words for what they have in common, emphasizing the rime patterns; and (3) use the patterns they've sorted for to write new words (explain, expectant, education).

The mystery word choices are infinite! Remember that the words for this activity should be words with which many students are familiar. It's the patterns and attention to the spelling that is important—not so much the vocabulary building.

Goal 3: Spelling Words with Two or More Possible Patterns

In the lower grades, teachers work long and hard with students to get them to rely upon a similar sound or spelling pattern to spell or decode words. We want students to say to themselves, "If I want to use the word *blame* in my writing and it sounds like the Word Wall word *same*, then I'll write the word using that same pattern—b-l-a-m-e." Easy enough! And, that works well to a point. It works well to get words on paper when students are writing rough drafts. Sometimes students are surprised in the writing conference to find that some words are misspelled because the sound-alike pattern didn't match the spell-alike pattern, or vice versa. So, what's a student to do? Teachers need to reassure students that it's fine to make those guesses based on the sound pattern, but they must also be aware of these different spelling patterns and must develop a critical eye to know when something "looks" right.

A standard activity in *Month-by-Month Phonics for Upper Grades* is called, not surprisingly, What Looks Right? This simple, but high-impact, activity allows students to use their visual cueing systems to choose the correct spelling pattern among two or three possible patterns. The teacher directs the students to write guide words at the tops of their papers, which are divided lengthwise by lines. The guide words are words that have different spelling patterns for the same sounds, such as *air*, *care*, and *wear*. The teacher then begins to use each of those spelling patterns to write a word that uses that sound pattern. For example, the teacher writes *compair*, *compare*, and *compear* under the appropriate guide words. The students are to decide what looks right, and are to write it in the column they feel is correct. After a designated number of words, the students check their guesses by using a dictionary, and then the whole class agrees on the correct spellings.

Although *Month-by-Month Phonics for Upper Grades* provides weekly What Looks Right? activities, teachers are not limited to these examples and are free to design their own lessons. Rhyming dictionaries are helpful again in constructing lessons. Teachers can look up an ending sound such as -ow (long o sound) and will find perhaps a hundred words that make that ending sound, but which have several different spellings. For example, all of these words, though spelled differently, make the same long "o" sound: *beau, blow, toe, no,* and *merlot.* If a teacher wishes to raise the difficulty level of the exercise, she merely adds more guidewords. With this exercise, she could use two or all five patterns. She would direct students to write the guide words on their papers, and then would call out words she has prepared for students to decide under which column (pattern) the word should be written. Here are some sample words:

beau	blow	toe	no	merlot
elbeau	elbow	elboe	elbo	elbot
threau	throw	throe	thro	throt
chateau	chatow	chatoe	chato	chatot
crossbeau	crossbow	crossboe	crossbo	crossbot
braveau	bravow	bravoe	bravo	bravot
kneau	know	knoe	kno	knot
besteau	bestow	bestoe	besto	bestot
macheau	machow	machoe	macho	machot
scarecreau	scarecrow	scarecroe	scarecro	scarecrot
escargeau	escargow	escargoe	escargo	escargot

Rhyming dictionaries will make designing these activities so easy!

Rhyming Relay

Another version of the Riming Relay that addresses Goal 2 above allows students points for words with the same rime (spelling) pattern or points for words that rhyme (have the same sound pattern). The teacher gives the whole class a category again, such as *music, cars, sports,* or *rock stars.* Then, the teams must come up with a word in that category that has a rime pattern and/or rhyme pattern that can be used to construct other words. Within a specified amount of time, they brainstorm in their small groups a list of words that rime with that lead word. The challenges will come when students use the incorrect spellings for words that sound alike.

Working with Words Block

The teacher gives the category, *music*. Different teams come up with these lists, based on the lead words *sing*, *band*, *rock*, and *drum*:

Group 1	Group 2	Group 3	Group 4
sing	band	rock	drum
spring	brand	Bach*	bum
sling	gland	block	chum
fling	canned*	sock	some*
king	sand	lock	dumb*
Ming	land	clock	plum
downswing	manned*	flock	plumb*
offspring	stand	mock	thumb*
earring	strand	Bangkok*	become*
first-string	fanned*	smock	sum
hamstring	nightstand	Woodstock	crumb*
everything	quicksand	headlock	hum
innerspring	reprimand		strum
heartstring	swampland		gum
	contraband		overcome
	Thailand		numb

*Words that rhyme, but are spelled in a different way from the pattern.

The winner is determined by how many points the teachers allocates for *rhyme* patterns and how many for *rime* patterns.

All of these activities provide an engaging opportunity for students to explore the multiple spellings for sounds.

Goal 4: Decoding and Spelling Polysyllabic Words

Many, if not most, of the students in the upper grades have learned the basic language/word patterns by the time they reach fourth grade, especially if they have been exposed to them constantly since Building Blocks™ in kindergarten and Four-Blocks™ in first, second, and third grades. Now they are ready to explore, beyond the basics, the structural meanings of words, and the derivations of words and word parts that will help them to figure out many other big words—also known as polysyllabic words. This is when word study really begins to elevate!

Even though some of this section deals with what we might term vocabulary, we include words in this block that deal with the word level of reading and writing. We study the interesting relationships and links that these words provide to other words. It's all about figuring out how to understand and control our language and to understand and to be understood in communication.

We still want to present our word study in an engaging manner. Word study can be as dull and boring as any subject possibly can be, or it can be the spark that kindles a student's interest and imagination in reading and writing. We'll explore some exercises that might provide that stimulation for your students.

Nifty Thrifty Fifty

The onsets and rimes that help us to figure out one- and two-syllable words are not the keys to figuring out big words that we read. Big words are formed from chunks, or morphemic units, called prefixes, roots, and suffixes. Where the onsets such as *ch*, *scr*, *p*, and *tr* don't hold any particular meaning for us, the prefixes, roots, and suffixes do have meaning attached that will provide a clue to understanding what is being said. Understanding the smaller units in one word can also help us to decipher many other words. In fact, linguists tell us that for every word we know, we can figure out how to spell, decode, and build meaning for six or seven additional words (Nagy and Anderson, 1984).

Cunningham and Hall, in *Month-by-Month Phonics for Upper Grades*, share a list of 50 key words that are formed from most of the useful morphemic units of our language. The book provides weekly exercises to help students learn what all of these word parts mean. The 50 words are referred to as the Nifty Thrifty Fifty and truly are nifty in enabling older students to have a better understanding and control of our language. In learning more about spelling, these exercises will teach students how the spelling might change when suffixes and prefixes are added to the base, or root, of the word.

Here is a Nifty Thrifty Fifty word from *Month-by-Month Phonics for Upper Grades*:

Discovery	A **discovery** is something you **discover**. The prefix **dis** often changes a word to an opposite form. To cover something can mean to hide it. When you discover it, it is no longer hidden. **Discovery** is the root word **cover** with the added prefix **dis** and suffix **y**. There are no spelling changes.

Students will learn these interesting things about word parts and that the addition of the "y" even changes the word magically from a verb to a noun—abracadabra!

Latin and Greek Base Words

Several years of fascinating word exploration courses can be gleaned from a good, long list of Latin and Greek base words. Through such a study, students will come to realize that much of our English language originated in other languages, and, again, just as with Nifty Thrifty Fifty, this word study can lead to a greater reading and writing vocabulary.

Here are several approaches to using a list of Greek and Latin base words to teach older students:

☑ Deductive Word Play

Give the students three to five examples of familiar words that contain one particular base word. Have them work as partners or small groups to identify what they think is the base word and, most importantly, to deduce the meaning of the base word. Here is an example:

Teacher gives: Students respond:

Words	Base	Meaning
abbreviation, brevity, breve	brev	short
audience, auditorium, audible, audition	aud	hear
annual, anniversary, annuity	ann	year

After students have had a chance to work together on identifying the bases and figuring out the meanings, they can come back together as a whole group to check their work with the teacher. The class members might also be able to think of additional words that use that same base and meaning.

☑ Graphic Word Study

A graphic might be used to have students see the relationships between words using the same base and to figure out the meanings. The teacher can choose these options: (1) give students the words and ask them to fill in the base word and its meaning; (2) give students the base word and its meaning and let students fill in the words they can think of that use that base word and meaning; or (3) give students a couple of words and let them figure out the base and its meaning, then come up with a couple of additional words that use that base.

Example 1:

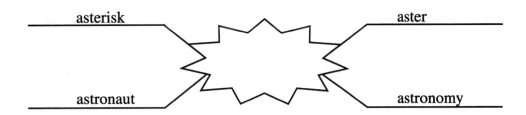

Example 2:

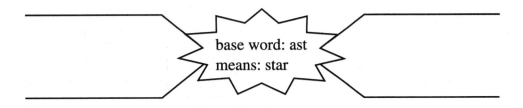

Example 3:

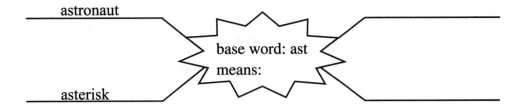

Working with Words Block

Here are some words, bases, and meanings to get you started. Then, all you'll need to do is to consult a Greek and Latin dictionary, your collegiate dictionary (note the etymology given), or some word list such as provided in *The Reading Teacher's Book of Lists*.

Base	Meaning	Words Using that Base and Meaning
cap	head	cap, captain, capital, capitol, caption, decapitate
aero	air	aerobics, aerate, aeronautics
aqua	water	aquarium, aquatic, aquamarine
ambul	walk/go	ambulance, amble, ambulatory
belli	war	antebellum, belligerent, rebellion
cam	field	camp, campus, campaign
bio	life	biography, autobiography, biology, biochemistry
div	divide	divide, divorce, division, dividend
don	give	donate, donor, pardon, donate
form	shape	form, uniform, transform, reform, conform
grad	step/stage	grade, gradual, graduate, graduation
hydr	water	hydroelectric, hydrogen, hydrant, dehydrate
integ	whole	integrate, integral, integrity, integer
lab	work	labor, laboratory, collaborate, eleborate
man	hand	manual, manufacture, manuscript, manipulate
migr	move/change	migrate, immigrant, emigrate, migratory, migrant
orig	begin	origin, original, originate, aborigine
pend	hang	pendulum, suspend, appendage, appendix
pul	urge	compulsion, compulsory, expulsion, repulse
rid	laugh	ridiculous, ridicule, derisive
terr	land	territory, terrain, terrestrial, terrace
turb	confusion	disturb, turbulent, perturb, turbine
vict	conquer	victory, victim, victimize, convict, conviction

Occasionally students will find that the Latin and Greek bases differ in their meanings for the same base spelling. For example, the Latin *ped* means *foot*, hence, the words *pedal*, *pedestrian*, and *pedestal*; whereas, the Greek *ped* means *child*, explaining the word *pediatrician*. Teachers could have students explore some of these differences in word derivations by throwing out a question and letting students use dictionaries to figure out the answers:

> How do base words help these doctors know what they'll do for
>
> you: pediatrics and orthopedic specialists? How are they alike and
>
> how are they different?

Exploring Words and Word Parts

Just as with activities such as Nifty Thrifty Fifty, we learn that it's not only the meanings of Latin and Greek bases that will facilitate our understanding of words. Our common suffixes and prefixes also have meanings that will aid us. We can use the same types of exercises with deductive or inductive reasoning to explore these word parts.

A teacher gives this graphic and students are to figure out what the two given words have in common as the meaning of the prefix, and then are to try to think of two words that use that prefix to fit the meaning. A dictionary could be used if the activity is too difficult for the students on their own.

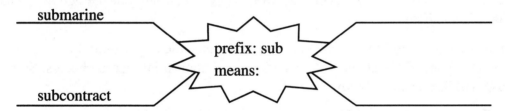

Another version might be to give students words with the same prefixes and have them figure out the prefix and meaning.

Or, teachers might give the prefix and its meaning and let students find words that use this prefix and this meaning. Again, dictionaries might be helpful in this activity.

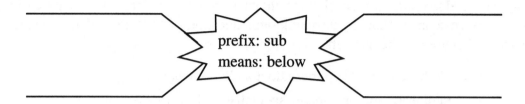

prefix: sub
means: below

The same activity can be done for exploring suffixes, though it gets tougher to use a dictionary to assist students. (See page 237 of the Appendix for reproducible Word Maps.)

Goal 5: Applying Strategies While Reading and Writing

Once again, why do we spend so much time on learning about spelling, decoding, patterns, syllables, prefixes, suffixes, bases, and word etymology? It's because we want to be better readers, writers, and communicators of the language. Although students may have a super time with activities like Making Words, Riming Relay, and Brand or Bland, unless they understand how to apply what these activities have taught them, they're no better off than they would have been without the activity! That's what it's all about.

There are many ways that teachers can give students the opportunity to apply all that they have learned about spelling, decoding, and appropriate word choices. Some of those will be discussed below.

☑ Guess the Covered Word (advanced)

An activity shared in all of the Four-Blocks publications that helps students recall and apply decoding strategies in their reading is the activity called Guess the Covered Word. At the primary level, and as the activity is introduced, the teacher presents isolated sentences or a few thematically related sentences with strategic words covered. The words covered are those words about which students can make reasonable guesses because of context clues they gather as they read the sentences. Students make guesses about the covered word, and those guesses are recorded. Then, consistent with the theory of using onsets and rimes to decode words, the first chunk of the word up to the first vowel is revealed. The students strike words they've previously guessed, but which now don't fit with the onset provided. They make new guesses based on this graphophonemic clue. The new guesses are recorded, and then the rest of the word is revealed. Through the use of this simple activity, the teacher draws attention to the fact that this is a real reading strategy, and that in your reading, when you come across a word you don't know you should: 1) ask yourself what makes sense in this context; 2) then, ask yourself what makes sense and starts with this beginning chunk (one, two, or three letters); 3) finally, ask yourself what makes sense, starts with this chunk, has these other letters, and is this length.

Month-by-Month Phonics for Upper Grades suggests weekly paragraphs that can help students recall some of the decoding strategies that they'll use while reading. This activity can be as sophisticated as a teacher feels is necessary to have students apply these strategies. What might be most useful is to use the text that students are reading in their literature books, their science books, their social studies books, and in newspapers—whatever reading is relevant to students. There are at least three options for presenting this activity to the class:

1. What the teacher might do to make life a little easier, rather than retyping or handwriting the text to be used, is to take the book to the copy machine, enlarge the text a bit using the enlargement function, and reproduce the page of text onto a transparency. Then, the teacher should cover some few words with small pieces of sticky notes. A strategically placed snip in the sticky note will allow the onset to be revealed easily. Then, the teacher positions the transparency on the overhead machine and walks through the text with the class word-by-word, recording the reasonable guesses in the margin of the transparency, revealing the beginning chunk, revising the guesses, and then revealing the rest of the word.

2. Another option for this activity might be for the teacher to make a copy of the page on which several words will be explored. Then, the teacher will completely black out the words that would ordinarily be covered, and will run enough copies for the students to use at their desks. The students will work with partners or small groups to make reasonable guesses for each blacked out word. After this, the activity can be completed as a whole group with the teacher using a transparency. As the teacher reveals the beginning chunks of each word, the groups will strike their guesses that now don't fit. The teacher will record in the margin of his transparency remaining words offered by different groups and, then, will reveal the actual words. If groups had that word on their paper, they circle it. If the teacher wishes to make this competitive, points can be awarded to groups for each word they were able to guess correctly.

3. A slight variation of #2 is for the teacher to give groups one copied sheet of totally blacked out words to make reasonable guesses. After three to five guesses have been made for each blackened word, then another sheet is passed out to the groups on which the teacher has blackened only the first vowel and thereafter to reveal the beginning chunk. Partners or small groups will work again to revise their guesses from the first page. To conclude, the teacher will give out the answers.

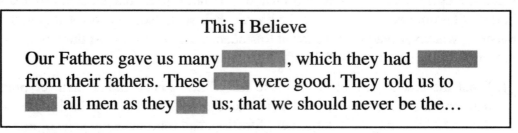

This I Believe

Our Fathers gave us many ████, which they had ████ from their fathers. These ███ were good. They told us to ███ all men as they ███ us; that we should never be the...

"Chief Joseph Inmutooyablatlat's Address to Congress, 1879" (*In a Sacred Manner I Live: Native American Wisdom* edited by Neil Philip, Houghton Mifflin Co., 1997)

Appropriate Materials Used by Upper-Grades Teachers for Guess the Covered Word

Newspaper articles (feature, news, sports, and even comics)

Magazine articles

Literature anthology pages

Speeches (i.e., Martin Luther King, Jr.'s "I Have a Dream"; John Kennedy's inaugural address, etc.)

Content area material (any text pages from social studies, health, science, math; the Constitution of the United States; etc.)

Teacher's or Students' writing samples (Get permission from students!)

Student Handbook

Driver's Manual

Even though Guess the Covered Word is a simple activity, it can provide an opportunity for students to apply what they've learned about decoding strategies to such a wide range of materials and for varied purposes. It's not just about decoding. It's also about diction, word choices, and synonyms.

☑ Clozing In on Words

Similar to the Guess the Covered Word activity is a Cloze exercise in which text is constructed so that students will need to apply much of what they've learned in a little different context. Again, text can be taken from content materials, from newspapers, or from something the teacher has made-up. Instead of blacking out the words in the passage, there are blanks to be filled in. If text is copied on a copier, certain words can be removed using correction fluid or something similar, and then that copy can be used to duplicate others. Students are given a certain amount of time to read the text and supply words in the blanks that are appropriate to the meaning of the text. The teacher should not hold students accountable for divining the exact word that is missing; however, teachers should expect that students would use contextually suitable words. If points are allocated for this exercise, then, perhaps, teachers will give bonus points when students do supply an exact word. Sometimes we may be surprised that we, in fact, like some words that the students have offered even better than the author's exact words!

☑ Editing As an Opportunity for Application

Quite often teachers may give students the opportunity to be the editor of a piece of text. This is, of course, a real-life, useful skill for students and adults. When the boss says, "Look over this letter and check it for errors for me," we'll hope we've developed our editing skills to do a good job. And, so, a teacher might prepare a piece of text—a letter, an excerpt from a story, or a summary of something that has been studied in class—in which he'll make some spelling errors. These errors are likely to be old and new Word Wall words, pattern words, Nifty Thrifty Fifty words, or any other words or patterns that have been studied adequately. This helpful draft might be framed at the top with, "Please help this writer to edit the rough draft of his letter." At the beginning of the year or for necessary support, the teacher might want to give clues, "You'll find 15 spelling errors." Some errors of other types—grammar, punctuation, usage—might be included occasionally as well to sharpen their skills in catching elements that have been included on the editor's checklist.

☑ Dictation As an Opportunity for Application

In an effort to get closer to the most realistic, authentic application of what we want students to know and be able to do, teachers may often dictate to students some carefully constructed text to be written by the students. The teacher designs a paragraph using old and new Word Wall words, Nifty Thrifty Fifty Words, words from patterns that have been taught, and words with word parts (suffixes, prefixes, bases) that have been studied. The paragraph is shared with students as they rapidly process what they've heard and make commitments on paper of their understanding. There's no need to worry about support students might find from around the room—the Word Wall or the cluster charts—since the dictation is probably too rapid to allow for lots of searching.

☑ Using Students' Real Writing Samples As Evidence of Understanding

The best, most authentic way of gauging where students are in their development with spelling and word usage is for teachers to look at the actual rough draft writing samples of their students. A teacher may find it helpful to create a rubric or checklist to use as she reads the student's rough draft to focus on exactly how or if the student is employing what has been taught during the Working with Words Block.

Moving Beyond the Five Goals

Goal 6: Analyzing, Evaluating, and Appreciating Words

There are populations of upper-grades students in schools or in individual classrooms that no longer need to focus on all five goals during the Working with Words Block. If the students are high achieving and have had a foundation in Building Blocks™ and Four-Blocks for three to four years, they readily identify basic patterns, and it is likely that they use most high-frequency words correctly with few exceptions. So, by the middle grades, at least, some teachers begin to eliminate formal, whole group instruction in Goal 1 and Goal 2, or at least don't devote a great deal of time to those instructional areas. They do continue to hold students accountable for basic words and sometimes individualize practice of some commonly misspelled with several students. However, with limited time for delivery of the blocks and in an attempt to add more time to reading and writing, teachers often choose to shorten the Working with Words Block, but still wish to encourage students to grow in their knowledge about words.

Higher on the learning taxonomy, even beyond the "application" level of Goal 5 are the levels of analyzing, synthesizing, and evaluating (Bloom, 1984). When students are given a chance for working with words at these levels in a constructivist setting, then appreciation for words is most certainly the outcome to be expected. And, when children begin to appreciate the words of their language, to understand their beauty, their malleability, and their power, then they have control over communication and better control over their lives.

Goal 6 for the Working with Words Block encourages just that—analyzing words, understanding relationships between and among words, evaluating word choices, and collecting words for their own use. Below are some activities that lead students in this direction.

☑ Word Relationships Through Analogies

An advanced skill that many psychologists say is an indicator of intelligence is the ability of people to infer the relationships between pairs of words. Any teacher who has taken the Miller Analogy test can attest to the level of difficulty posed by the seemingly innocuous, isolated words and symbols (colons) used in such testing programs. Here, students not only must decode and read words, but must evaluate the associations between the first pair of words, and then apply that to the second pair of words to determine a similar association.

Some easy examples:

Synonyms (small : little :: big : large)

Object/Category (red : color :: carrot : vegetable)

Part to Whole (page : book :: door : room)

Some analogous relationships that can be studied:

Opposites (young : old :: funny : sad)

Synonyms (receive : get :: fix : mend)

Object/Action (hand : wave :: foot : walk)

Part/Whole (classroom : school :: state : country)

Object/Function (stove : cook :: cup : hold)

Cause and Effect (downpour : flood :: hungry : eat)

Numerical Relationships (two : four :: eight : sixteen)

Sequence (hurt : cry :: read : understand)

Degree (private : captain :: warm : hot)

Object and Its Description (tundra : barren :: winter : cold)

Grammatical Relationships (relate : relative :: explain : explanation)

Place (city : state :: province : country)

Object and Classification (bus : transportation :: shovel : tool)

Member to Group (alligator : reptile :: Native American : tribe)

Object to User (plane : pilot :: plow : farmer)

The Working with Words Block can be a time to analyze the relationship between and among words through the use of analogies. We must explain to students the use of the symbols and a plain and simple way of explaining what the equation is saying. The single colon in testing terms refers, of course, to "is to," and the double colon to "as" or "like." Sometimes using more familiar, common language could help students make sense of this complex construction. Substituting "relates to" for the single colon and "in the same way that" for the double colon might be the key to getting students to understand the other fairly vague references.

"So, *small* relates to *little* in the same way that *big* relates to *large*. Okay, I get it! *Small* and *little* share the same meanings, and so *big* and *large* do, too!"

Sometimes it's just a matter of semantics! Some students might see the relationships clearer if a graphic is used, such as:

	=	

just like

	=	

Working as partners or in small groups makes this kind of detective word fun for students of all ages.

☑ Analyzing Words with Graphics

Time can be constructively spent by students using a graphic organizer to explore and analyze words as in the graphics below. Reproducibles of these activities can be found in the Appendix on pages 238 and 239.

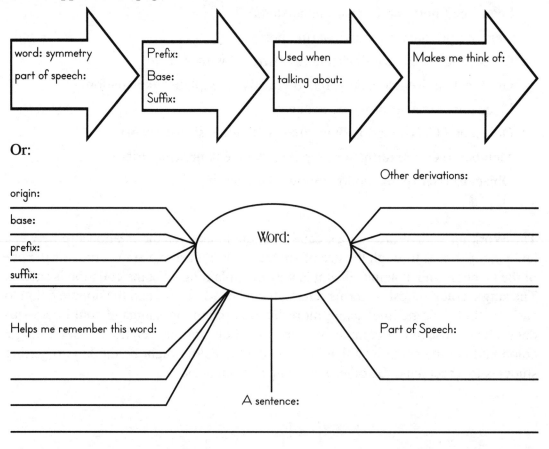

word: symmetry
part of speech:

Prefix:
Base:
Suffix:

Used when talking about:

Makes me think of:

Or:

origin:

base:

prefix:

suffix:

Word:

Other derivations:

Helps me remember this word:

Part of Speech:

A sentence:

☑ Words Connected by Themes

Teachers can continue to show students relationships by presenting words in topical or thematic clusters. Some clusters in the upper grades particularly relevant to writing, reading, and content might be the following:

Words that show sequence: first, next, last, second, third, since, later, now

Words that show transition: thus, therefore, furthermore, subsequently

Words that tell time: later, now, when, immediately, during, until, while, lately

Words that show spatial relationships: above, beside, behind, below

Words that describe size: enormous, minuscule, minute, microscopic, monstrous

Words that compare and contrast: and, or, either, neither, nevertheless, consequently

Words that describe emotions: hostile, belligerent, obnoxious, discouraged, exuberant

Words that describe motives: altruistic, benevolent, calculating, vindictive

Geometry words: symmetry, segment, vertex, axis, perpendicular, radius, isosceles

Algebra words: equation, fraction, postulate, theorem, numerator, factoring

Biology words: amoeba, backbone, crustacean, cartilage, extinct, hibernate, organism

Geography words: agriculture, boundary, community, domestic, equinox, erosion

Social studies words: authority, civilization, parliament, settlement, voyage, culture

Career words: doctor, dentist, chemist, clerk, retailer, teacher, politician

Computer words: byte, megabyte, ram, bit, diskette, cursor, hypertext, link, virus

Measurement words: centimeter, foot, gram, inch, kilometer, mile, pound

Test words: blank, column, estimate, incorrect, example, paragraph, passage, provide

The topics and themes are infinite and the ways to engage students is also limitless. Some suggestions might be:

☑ Vocabulary Charades

Give each small group of students one of the words within a cluster to act out impromptu for the class. The team captain of one of the other teams that raises his hand first and gives the correct word, gets a point for that team. The team that acted out the word also gets a point for their portrayal of the word. (Furnish dictionaries if students need to check the meanings.)

☑ Round-Robin Vocabulary

Give the students the topic or theme and let them brainstorm, with partners or in small groups the words that relate. At the end of a stipulated amount of time, let each team or partner group give a word to add to a master list. Rotate among the teams an equal number of times. Teams are eliminated as they fail to give a word that has not yet been used. The winning team is the last one to give a new word.

☑ Get Organized

Give students a graphic organizer similar to the one pictured, requiring that they write words in the circles that fit in that category, and then draw a quick illustration that represents each of the words.

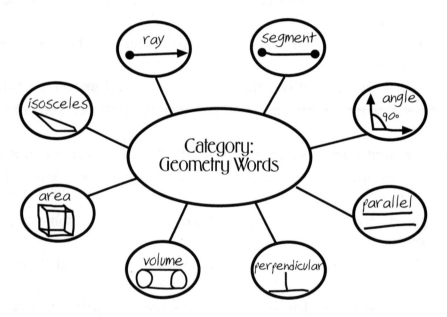

☑ The Origin of Words

Have students research the etymologies of the individual words within a category. They might also make cluster or theme vocabulary books with illustrations and the word origins. Alphabet books of these words are interesting to research and design.

☑ Student Organizers

Let students design graphic organizers that depict relationships among the cluster words.

☑ Group/Partner Discussions

Let students discuss the words and the uses for them. Especially interesting is a conversation among students about words that describe emotions. (How wonderful for students to learn to express their emotions—especially their angry ones—in words that are precise, intelligent descriptions of their feelings, rather than obscenities!)

☑ In Order

Allow students to decide a rank order of words from a cluster of words. They might put words in order of most to least importance, of relevance to their lives, of relevance to the lives of their parents, of strongest to weakest connotations, etc., depending, of course, on what the words pertain to.

☑ Word Collections

As students become more and more aware of interesting words in their environment, they may want to begin to collect words that they might want to remember and might want to use in their written or spoken communication. A wonderfully clever book that illustrates the concept of word awareness is Monalisa DeGross's *Donovan's Word Jar* (HarperTrophy, 1994). A young boy named Donovan begins to notice words in his environment—words on cereal boxes, words he hears adults say—and he even discovers some words that "slide down his tongue and roll off his lips" that appeal to him. Where some of his friends collect stamps, baseball cards, or coins, he begins to collect words and keeps them in a word jar. When the jar fills, he is perplexed about what to do with his collection. The book ends with a most interesting solution to his dilemma!

Reading this short novel to the class might be a way of getting students started with their own collection of words—words they can collect from what they read, what is read to them, conversations, advertisements, TV shows, and anything else in their environment. Now, what will be done with the words that the students collect?

Ideas for Word Collections:

☑ Bring a big jar into the classroom to simulate Donovan's jar. Invite the students to collect words to add to the jar. They should write the word and its context, if possible, and sign their names or initial the papers they use so that they can take credit for the words. Choose new words daily from the jar as a way of getting the Word Block started. This gets students' attention right away since they have ownership into the activity. Just a minute or two should be spent on discussing the word.

☑ Students can devote a section of their writing notebooks to a word collection. They should record words they think they may want to use in their writing.

☑ At specified times throughout the day, the teacher can call on students randomly to share a word from their recorded word collection. After briefly discussing the word and its possible uses, the word can be added to an "Interesting Words" chart in the classroom (perhaps in the shape of a large jar). Placing the initials of the contributing student beside the word might encourage the students to choose more appropriate, useful words.

☑ Even older students might enjoy keeping their new words in pictionary-style, writing the word and drawing a picture along with it to remind them of its meaning.

Organizing the Block for the Week

Depending upon how many goals a teacher chooses to address, how much time is available, and how often a teacher will address the chosen goals, teachers will want to design a lesson plan that will allow them to 1) offer variety; 2) be efficient with their time; and 3) teach what will help those students grow. Here are some plans that consider these objectives:

Susan Jenkinson, a fourth-grade teacher at Springdale Elementary School in South Carolina, offers this five-day plan for working with five goals, given 30 minutes per block:

Monday	Goal 1: Five new Word Wall words (discuss, rhythm, write, trace, check)
	Goal 4: Three Nifty Thrifty Fifty words (review all word parts)
	Handwriting practice included
Tuesday	Goal 1: Review five Word Wall words with Be A Mind Reader
	Goal 4: Nifty Thrifty Fifty words (concentrate on roots)
	Goals 2/3/5: Choose one activity from one of these goals
	Handwriting practice included
Wednesday	Goal 1: Quick routine with five new Word Wall Words
	Goal 4: Nifty Thrifty Fifty words (concentrate on prefixes)
	Goals 2/3/5: Choose one activity from one of these goals
	Handwriting practice included
Thursday	Goal 1: Word Wall words (students write words in response to clues given by teacher); Quick routine with all five new words (optional)
	Goal 4: Nifty Thrifty Fifty words (concentrate on suffixes)
	Goals 2/3/5: Choose one activity from one of these goals
	Handwriting practice included

Friday	Goal 1: Review 5 Word Wall words
	Goal 4: Nifty Thrifty Fifty words (make new words from this week's word parts)
	Goals 2/3/5: Choose 1 activity from one of these goals
	Goal 5: Application/Assessment (Dictation, Editing)
	Handwriting practice included

A plan for integrating all six goals into a five-day instructional week with 30 minute blocks

Monday	Goal 1: Two old and two new Word Wall words (choose: discuss/quick routine/On the Back Activity/Be a Mind Reader/Wordo)
	Goal 2 activity (Making Words, Brand Name Phonics, Brand or Bland, Riming Relay, etc.)
Tuesday	Goal 1: Two old and two new Word Wall words
	Goal 3 activity (What Looks Right?, Rhyming Relay)
Wednesday	Goal 1: Two old and two new Word Wall words (quick routine and On the Back activity)
	Goal 4 activity (Nifty Thrifty Fifty, Latin and Greek Base Words)
Thursday	Goal 1: Two old and two new Word Wall words
	Goal 6 activity (Word Collection, Theme Words, Analogies, etc.)
Friday	Goal 1: review Word Wall words
	Goal 5: Application/Assessment (Guess Covered Word, Clozing In, Dictation, Editing, etc.)

A plan for integrating all six goals into a five-day instructional week, given 20 minute Word Blocks where students need less time on Goals 1 and 2.

Monday	Goal 1: Five new Word Wall words (regular routine and On the Back)
	Goal 3: Choose one activity (What Looks Right?, Rhyming Relay)
Tuesday	Goal 2: Choose one activity (Making Words, Brand Name, Brand or Bland?)
	Goal 6 activity (Word Collection, Theme Words, Analogies, etc.)
Wednesday	Goal 1: Review Word Wall words (Be A Mind Reader, On the Back, Wordo)
	Goal 4: Choose one activity (Nifty Thrifty Fifty, Latin and Greek Base Words)
Thursday	Goal 4: Choose one activity (Nifty Thrifty Fifty, Latin and Greek Base Words)
	Goal 6 activity (Word Collection, Theme Words, Analogies, etc.)
Friday	Goal 1: Review Word Wall words
	Goal 5: Application/Assessment (Guess Covered Word, Clozing In, Dictation, Editing, etc.)

Moving Beyond the Classroom

Teachers and administrators should take every opportunity to encourage students' growth in word and vocabulary acquisition. Students—actually, people, in general—are never too old or too smart for instruction in and exposure to new words. At the middle and high school levels, additional support is often given as students are preparing for SAT or ACT tests for college entrance. The activities mentioned in this chapter will better prepare students for these tests, especially as they pursue the structural analysis of polysyllabic words.

In the beginning of this book, some suggestions were made about the role of the school and classroom environment to support literacy growth. Let's think briefly again about areas in the school that might be utilized for greater support in vocabulary and word building knowledge.

☑ Cafeteria/Canteen

In some schools, students spend considerable time standing in lines to be served breakfast and lunch. Think about having words and interesting tidbits about words lining the walls where students stand. Just maybe, they'll notice them and make this wasted time more constructive. On a rotating basis, classes might take the assignment of creating the cafeteria display so that no one in particular is burdened with this task.

☑ Hallways

Again, so much time is spent with students walking through the halls to classes before, during, and after school. A thematic Word Wall, important words of the month, or just a few really neat words could catch the attention of students. Every teacher might agree to pick a special word to display on his/her door each week or month. Also, a Literacy Club or Reading Club might take this as a challenge.

☑ Beyond the Language Arts Teachers

For the greatest impact to be made in a school, all teachers must take responsibility for the literacy growth and development of all students. All teachers need to be aware of the approaches for effective word and vocabulary instruction. They need to hold students accountable to standards that have been agreed upon—correct spelling and usage of high-frequency words, for example. They need to have and use books in their classrooms to support their subject areas. When we work together in a school towards the same goals and objectives we have the greatest chance for success.

Reading and literacy development in the upper grades move beyond critical fluency building. The six goals of the Working with Words Block will help students to control language, to communicate clearly, concisely, and effectively, and to learn about the power of words in our lives.

Summary of the Working with Words Block

The purpose of this block:

- To ensure that students will read, spell, and use high-frequency and commonly misspelled words correctly.

- To learn the patterns of words that will enable students to become better spellers and readers.

- To have students apply the strategies they learn about words in the context of real reading and writing.

- To communicate clearly, precisely, and effectively in written and spoken language through students' knowledge of words.

Different from the other blocks, the structure of this block at the upper grades is dictated by the needs of the students as they relate to the six goals for word growth and development:

☑ Learning high-frequency, commonly misspelled words

☑ Learning one- and two-syllable words that follow a pattern, but are used less frequently

☑ Spelling words with two or more possible patterns

☑ Decoding and spelling polysyllabic words

☑ Applying strategies while reading and writing

☑ Analyzing, evaluating, and appreciating words

Segments: Determined by teacher   (Total time: usually 15-30 minutes)

Choose one to three goals daily to emphasize through activities that support these goals.

A Typical Week in an Upper Grades Working with Words Block

Monday (Goals 1 and 2)

The teacher begins this block by presenting two words that will go on the Word Wall this week. These are words that students have been using incorrectly in their writing, and she wants to clarify their confusion about the words. She explains that these words not only are confusing because their spellings are close, but because their meanings are close as well. She has the words *conscious* and *conscience* written on pieces of colored cardstock, one in blue and one in red. She places them in her pocket chart. She pronounces both, carefully enunciating for the class. She writes the word *conscious* on the chalkboard, and uses it in several sentences: "The victim was conscious for a few minutes after the attack, and then lapsed into a coma." "The boy made a conscious decision to improve his grades." "They were conscious of the time as they dashed to catch the plane." Then, the teacher asks a few volunteers to come up to the board. They are instructed to draw sketches around the word or to write a synonym that will help them and others remember the word. The same is done for the word *conscience*. The teacher also notes the spellings of both words, especially that the word *science* is a part of *conscience*. The students are asked to record these words in their portable Word Wall. Then, the students are asked to spell the two words to a partner, twice each, as practice.

The teacher then leads the class in a Making Words activity using the word *telescopes*, as the secret word. This is a word that relates to their science unit on space exploration. They make 14 words leading up to the secret word, giving the teacher the opportunity to stress several spelling patterns (*-ost, -ope, -oss*) and the fact that *lost* and *post* have the same spelling pattern, but not the same rhyme pattern. The class makes words, sorts them, and the teacher prepares four transfer words as well: *except, crept, envelope,* and *ghost.*

Tuesday (Goals 1 and 3)

The teacher works with students to review the two new Word Wall words for the week—*conscious* and *conscience.* She has the students number their papers 1 to 10 and asks them to respond to a number of statements and questions by writing the correct word beside the right number. "*Alert* can be a synonym for this word." "Cartoons often depict this word by having an angel and a devil sitting on opposite shoulders of a person who has a tough decision to make." "*Principles* might be used as a synonym for this word." Ten clues are given before the teacher has them correct their own papers as they run back through the clues.

The teacher then has students take out a sheet of notebook paper and draw a line down the middle. They do the activity called What Looks Right? with the pattern -*ite* and -*ight*. The students are given 10 words to determine what looks right to them and to write in the correct column. Then the students work in pairs to check their guesses in the dictionary. the class then comes back together with each partner group giving the answer to one of the spelling patterns.

Wednesday (Goals 1 and 5)

Today, the class has a quick round of Be a Mind Reader to call attention to all the words that have been placed on the Word Wall to date. The teacher gives them all five clues to which each student must make a guess of a word that fits the clue: a wild guess first, a word that is blue, a word that has eight letters, a word that is an antonym for another word, and a word that has a double consonant. This round goes quickly and leaves time for one additional round of clues for another Word Wall word.

Today, the teacher uses Guess the Covered Word for the greater part of time in this block. She has taken a page from the science chapter that the students have been reading, and has copied it for each student. Strategic words have been blacked out on each copy. She directs the students to work in small groups to make reasonable guesses about the words that are removed, and to jot down their guesses in the margin. She asks them to have one student record for each group. They are reminded to work strategically, recalling the process they've learned in doing this activity many times before. When the students have had enough time to make guesses about the missing words, she gives them a second sheet on which the onset of each word has been revealed (the remainder of the word is still covered). The students are to eliminate the words that don't fit the onset and now have the opportunity to revise their guesses. After sufficient time has lapsed, the teacher works with the whole class. She has a transparency of their text with self-stick notes covering the same words. She calls on each group to supply the word they think fits the hidden text and then reveals the word on her transparency to check their guesses. As they finish the activity, the teacher reminds the class that this activity provides them with the strategies they should use any time they encounter difficult words in text.

Thursday (Goals 4 and 6)

Today, the teacher uses Greek and Latin base words to have the students work in small groups to figure out what the base words are, given four words that share that base word. After the students identify the bases, they will work together to figure out what the words have in common. This will act as a clue to tell them what the base word means. The students work with four sets of these bases and then check their answers in the whole group with the teacher's answers.

The students now have time to continue work on their alphabet book project. This is a project that relates to their history unit on the immigration of people into the United States. Students are working in small cooperative groups to find 26 words that pertain to immigration. They are also responsible for illustrating their books, which will be presented to their classmates. The teacher has constructed a rubric by which the projects will be graded. The rubric includes criteria dealing with originality, relevance, and communication of basic concepts dealing with this topic. The students have approximately 20 minutes to work on this continuing project.

Friday (Goals 1, 2, 3, 4, and 5)

Students have an opportunity to demonstrate their understanding of many of the goals of this block with a simple assessment. The teacher has a sheet on which she has typed a paragraph using old and new Word Wall words, pattern words they've covered, and words with chunks the class has studied. Their task is to correct or edit this draft offered by the teacher—a real-life skill. After time is allowed for this editing, the teacher gives a short paragraph of dictation, again allowing the students the opportunity to pull together what they have learned about words, patterns, and structural analysis of words.

After this assessment, time remains for a round of Wordo, giving the students a chance to review many of the words on the Word Wall.

Chapter 7

Scheduling

In the primary grades, scheduling for implementation of Four-Blocks™ is usually quite simple, especially when classrooms are self-contained. Those teachers have the flexibility to allot time across their whole day to accommodate the blocks. They don't have to worry about finding a solid chunk of two to two and a half hours to instruct the blocks consecutively; however, they try to find creative ways to keep each individual block intact and sometimes to apply the "wiggle room" that they have to the blocks that most need those extra minutes—most likely the Guided Reading Block and the Writing Block.

The upper grades generally provide more of a challenge, and the challenge grows tougher and tougher as the grades rise. It is the uniqueness in schedules—grade-to-grade and school-to-school—that we will explore in this chapter to help teachers deal with various constraints. We will mention that although there are often unavoidable circumstances that prevent schools from utilizing ideal schedules, some of the obstacles are within the control of the school or the classroom. Some schools should be encouraged to "think outside of the box" in being more creative and efficient. The coming and going of buses should not determine the daily schedule that most directly impacts teaching and learning. Such decisions should be based on priorities: How much emphasis should reading receive in our school? How much support does our population of students need? What must we emphasize in our curriculum?

What's Really Needed at the Upper Grades?

The true Four-Blocks™ framework, by its strictest definition, is a balanced approach giving each of the four approaches to reading equal emphasis. The more language and literacy support that students need, the closer to the original model teachers should stick. The following might help differentiate the variations of the basic Four-Blocks™ framework:

Four-Blocks

Four-Blocks is used for populations of students who still need an emphasis on language and literacy development. With Four-Blocks, the schedule and delivery reflect a fairly equal inclusion of the four approaches daily.

> Students who still need an emphasis on literacy, who are still building grade-level fluency, and who need motivation receive a typical Four-Blocks schedule.

Four-Blocks in the Upper Grades

Once most or all students have attained fluency at a third- or fourth-grade reading level, teachers may give more weight to the instruction in the Guided Reading and Writing Blocks. The Self-Selected Reading Block should still be included daily, if students have not established the habit of reading outside of school, and/or if students still lack the motivation to read. The Working with Words Block and Self-Selected Reading Block may be the blocks that offer greater flexibility in the upper grades. They can be rotated or shortened if they aren't still necessary to include as equal components. The needs of the students should drive the time allocation.

Most students exhibit grade-level fluency, are motivated to read and have established reading habits, and core content areas are emphasized.

If all four blocks remain daily and are given a minimum of 30 minutes, even though the Guided Reading and Writing Blocks may be a bit longer, those schedules will be referred to as Four-Blocks. However, when the Working with Words Block and/or the Self-Selected Reading Block are shortened below the 30 minutes, or when the balance of the Four-Blocks is only achieved over the course of the week, those schedules will be called Four Blocks in the Upper Grades.

Chips off the Blocks

Because Four-Blocks offers many opportunities for engaging activities, some teachers choose to borrow some of the good ideas—constructing Word Walls, organizing their writing instruction in a workshop format, offering a Self-Selected Reading time for students, etc.—but have chosen not to implement the model. There's certainly nothing wrong with borrowing good ideas to strengthen existing programs; however, teachers who borrow from Four-Blocks should not say that they're **doing** Four-Blocks.

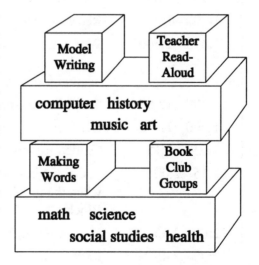

Different Schedules for Different Needs

Let's look below at what schedules have proven successful for Four-Blocks teachers based on different needs:

☑ Intermediate Grades 4-5

Many, if not most, of the intermediate grades may still remain self-contained, which means that teachers meet the instructional needs of the same students for core areas. Students are likely moved for special areas such as physical education, music, and art, if schools are fortunate enough to provide those subjects, even on a rotational basis. Other schools have moved into a departmentalized structure at the intermediate grades where teachers feel that they are more specialized in their content. Whatever the structure might be, there is till an opportunity to include all of the four blocks if teachers determine that their students still need that balance. Below are actual samples from schools around the country that have begun to use Four-Blocks at those grade levels.

☑ Samples Schedules in Intermediate Grades (4-5)

School 1: This school has determined that they need a strong emphasis in language and literacy development because of their high population of English as Second Language Learners. Their typical schedule is:

8:00 - 8:30	All of the beginning of school stuff—attendance, announcements, collecting homework and signing homework logs plus quick math warm-ups and a foreign language lesson.
8:30 - 9:15	Writing Block
9:15 - 10:00	Math lesson
10:00 - 10:15	Recess/Break
10:15 - 11:00	Working with Words Block (These kids need a lot of vocabulary and spelling support since over half are Second Language Learners.)
11:00 - 12:00	Special areas (rotating among: lab, PE)
12:00 - 12:30	Lunch
12:30 - 1:15	Guided Reading Block
1:15 - 2:00	Social studies or science (with hands-on centers when the text has been studied in Guided Reading Block.)
2:00 - 2:35	Self-Selected Reading Block
2:35 - 2:45	Review homework
2:45	Dismissal

School 2: Another school with a high population of at-risk students has made a commitment to increase the time they spend on all of the blocks to build language and literacy skills among their kids. They have also found ample time for special areas, math, social studies, and homeroom activities that include drug prevention, safety exercises, test preparation, among other non-core content subjects.

7:30 - 8:15	Homeroom
8:15 - 9:00	First period: M-music, T-art, W/Th-PE, F-library
9:00 - 9:40	Second period: math
9:40 - 10:25	Third period: science/social studies
10:25 - 11:10	Fourth period: Working with Words Block
11:10 - 11:50	Fifth period: Guided Reading Block
11:50 - 12:15	Sixth period: lunch
12:15 - 12:40	Seventh period: recess
12:40 - 1:30	Eighth period: Writing Block
1:30 - 2:15	Ninth period: Self-Selected Reading Block
2:15 - 2:40	Unit/Theme time
2:40 - 2:50	Homeroom

School 3: This school has a diverse group of students with a fairly equal distribution of low, average, and high achievers. They have generous time for the blocks, especially the Guided Reading Block and the Writing Block.

7:30 - 8:00	Breakfast/preparation/beginning activities
8:00 - 8:50	Guided Reading Block
8:50 - 9:30	Writing Block
9:30 - 10:00	Working with Words Block
10:00 - 10:25	Social studies
10:25 - 11:10	Related arts (M/W-PE, T-library, Th-art, F-music)
11:10 - 12:00	Math
12:00 - 12:25	Lunch
12:25 - 12:40	Recess
12:40 - 1:10	Computer lab
1:10 - 1:45	Self-Selected Reading Block
1:45 - 2:25	Science
2:25 - 2:30	Pack up/dismissal

School 4: These teachers devised a schedule that they felt would allow one segment of time to flow smoothly into the next segment. The Guided Reading Block was placed in the afternoon just prior to the other core content areas so that, quite often, the text for Guided Reading could be the content that students would then explore more fully during the period to follow.

8:00 - 8:15	Morning warm-up
8:15 - 9:30	Math
9:30 - 10:00	Working with Words Block
10:00 - 10:50	Writing Block
10:50 - 11:30	Lunch
11:30 - 12:00	Self-Selected Reading Block
12:00 - 12:45	Guided Reading Block
12:45 - 1:15	Science/social studies/ health
1:15 - 2:05	Special classes (art, computers, music)
2:05 - 2:15	Pack up/Dismissal

School 5: This school has departmentalized at the fifth-grade level. Two teachers share the load of what is to be taught. Each team of teachers teaches their subjects twice. The teachers have time during the week to plan together so that cross-curricular connections can be made. Often the teacher responsible for language arts uses the content material for Guided Reading, uses a content theme for her Making Words lesson, reads aloud something connected to the content theme for the Self-Selected Reading Block read-aloud, and addresses the topics in the model writing lessons, among other connections. Likewise, the content teacher holds the students accountable to the Word Wall words that they bring in on their portable Word Walls, uses some of the vocabulary techniques for content words, and reinforces the skills and strategies students have learned in dealing with text, among other connections. These language arts teachers still want a balanced approach for their students with all four blocks. There is flexibility, though, for time to be borrowed occasionally from blocks to add to other blocks (i.e., most likely borrowing from the Working with Words Block to add to the Guided Reading Block or the Writing Block).

Four-Blocks Language Arts Teachers' Typical Schedule

8:00 - 8:30	Homeroom
8:30 - 10:30	Language Arts Block 1—All four blocks are delivered in fairly equal time segments; however, sometimes these teachers report that they shorten the Working with Words Block to give more time to Guided Reading and/or Writing.
10:30 - 12:00	Planning and lunch (Students have special areas on rotational basis)
12:00 - 2:00	Language Arts Block 2 (all four blocks again to different students)
2:00 - 2:45	Social studies/health and end of the day announcements with homeroom
2:45	Dismissal

Math/Science/Social Studies Teachers' Typical Schedule

8:00 - 8:30	Homeroom
8:30 - 10:30	Math/Science Block 1
10:30 - 12:00	Planning and lunch (Students have Special Areas on rotational basis)
12:00 - 2:00	Math/Science Block 2 (repeated for different group of students)
2:00 - 2:45	Social studies/health and end of the day announcements with homeroom
2:45	Dismissal

School 6: Below are different schedules at one school that teachers have created to accommodate the four blocks.

Teacher 1

8:00 - 8:35	Working with Words Block
8:35 - 9:10	Guided Reading Block
9:10 - 9:45	Writing Block
9:45 - 10:45	Math
10:45 - 11:30	Special area
11:30 - 12:05	Lunch
12:10 - 12:30	Recess
12:30 - 1:20	Self-Selected Reading Block
1:25 - 2:15	Science/social studies
2:15	Dismissal

Teacher 2

8:00 - 8:40	Math
8:40 - 9:30	Special area
9:30 - 10:00	Guided Reading
10:00 - 10:30	Working with Words Block
10:30- 11:15	Writing Block
11:15 - 12:00	Self-Selected Reading Block
12:00 - 1:00	Lunch, recess, water, bathroom
1:00 - 2:15	Science/social studies
2:15	Dismissal

Teacher 3

8:00 - 8:40	Writing Block
8:40 - 9:20	Self-Selected Reading Block
9:20 - 10:00	Guided Reading Block
10:00 - 10:30	Working with Words Block
10:30 - 11:25	Math
11:25 - 12:05	Science
12:05 - 12:50	Lunch, recess
12:50 - 1:15	Social studies
1:15 - 2:00	Special area
2:00 - 2:15	Wrap up, revisit, read aloud chapter book
2:15	Dismissal

Scheduling

School 7: This is a fifth grade that is departmentalized. The language arts teacher also teaches social studies as a part of Guided Reading.

Teacher 1, First Group

8:00 - 8:35	Writing Block
8:35 - 9:25	Special area
9:25 - 10:00	Guided Reading Block/social studies
10:00 - 10:35	Self-Selected Reading Block
10:35 - 11:30	Bathroom break, lunch, recess
11:30 - 11:50	Working with Words Block
12:05	Switch groups

Teacher 1, Second Group

12:10 - 12:40	Writing Block
12:40 - 1:15	Guided Reading Block/social studies
1:15 - 1:50	Self-Selected Reading Block
1:50 - 2:10	Working with Words Block
2:20	Dismissal

And another teacher in this school uses this schedule:

Teacher 2, First Group

8:00 - 8:45	Special area
8:45 - 9:25	Guided Reading Block/social studies
9:25 - 10:05	Writing Block
10:05 - 11:00	Restroom, recess, lunch
11:00 - 11:35	Self-Selected Reading Block
11:35 - 12:00	Working with Words Block

Teacher 2, Second Group

12:00 - 12:40	Guided Reading/social studies
12:40 - 1:15	Writing Block
1:15 - 1:45	Self-Selected Reading Block
1:45 - 2:10	Working with Words Block
2:20	Dismissal

School 8: One school that departmentalizes in grades four and five and that has a high achieving population, offers this schedule for their language arts teachers:

Monday, Wednesday, Friday

8:30 - 10:00	Language Arts Block: Guided Reading Block Writing Block Working with Words Block

(Flexibility in the combination of time devoted to each-sometimes equal time; sometimes longer reading or writing; sometimes an integrated reading and writing time with a 20 minute word exploration.)

Tuesday, Thursday

8:30 - 10:00	Language Arts Block
	Guided Reading Block
	Writing Block
	Self-Selected Reading Block

☑ Middle Grades (6-8):

In some schools, grade six is included in the elementary school, while in others it's included in the middle school. Most schools by the middle grades have departmentalized, as depth of content becomes more of an issue. All schedules below reflect departmentalized schedules. Keep in mind that if a middle school has not departmentalized, the previous intermediate schedules should be helpful.

Here are some samples for teachers in the middle grades (6-8):

School A: This school has made a commitment to literacy development. The population of students has had a history of low performance and is generally difficult to motivate in a low socio-economic region. For the schoolwide schedule to work, they needed shorter blocks of time. Four-Blocks is scheduled at two different time periods. Students may have one or two teachers for these two periods. Grade-level teachers plan together a minimum of once per week to coordinate and integrate the instruction to the extent possible. The Writing Block and the Working with Words Block were grouped together since teachers saw the writing time as application time for what is learned in the Working with Words Block. Also, teachers wanted the Word Wall to be visible during the Writing Block. Each teacher has approximately 60 minutes for the two blocks.

One Teacher's Schedule

7:45 - 8:00	Homeroom
8:05 - 9:00	Guided Reading Block and Self-Selected Reading (Grade 6, Class 1)
9:05 - 10:00	Guided Reading Block and Self-Selected Reading (Grade 6, Class 2)
10:05 - 11:00	Guided Reading Block and Self-Selected Reading (Grade 7)
11:05 - 11:35	Lunch
11:35 - 12:30	Planning
12:35 - 1:30	Writing and Working with Words (Grade 6)
1:35 - 2:30	Writing and Working with Words (Grade 7)
2:35 - 3:05	Career Exploration

School B: This school has divided their day into 90-minute blocks to accommodate the subjects that are defined for them. They feel that students have acquired many of the basics with spelling and decoding and are more focused on Guided Reading and Writing. They want to continue to encourage the development of students' lifelong habits of reading with some regularly scheduled Self-Selected Reading time included in their week. These teachers also require that reading be done outside of school to continue to establish the reading habit.

Scheduling

Monday/Wednesday/Friday

90 minutes:		
	40 minutes	Guided Reading Block
	40 minutes	Writing Block
	10 minutes	Working with Words Block

Tuesday/Thursday

90 minutes:		
	30 minutes	Guided Reading Block
	30 minutes	Writing Block
	30 minutes	Self-Selected Reading Block

School C: In this school, the teams of teachers have agreed on sharing the responsibility for literacy development of their students. They believe that reading and writing are critical skills for the success of their students. Content area teachers have had sufficient training in Four-Blocks to supplement the areas not covered when the language arts teachers rotate between Guided Reading and Writing. The units usually rotate every week and allow the teacher more time for in-depth study of text in Guided Reading, more extensive instruction in focused writing, or more time for in-depth conferencing more with students on their writing.

90 minutes:		
	45 minutes	Guided Reading Block unit
	30 minutes	Self-Selected Reading
	15 minutes	Words Block

90 minutes total language arts time daily, with emphasis on Guided Reading (approximately 1 week)

During the time that these language arts teachers concentrate on a unit of the Guided Reading Block, the science and/or social studies teachers for these students provide writing instruction related to the topics they are covering.

90 minutes:		
	45 minutes	Writing Block unit
	30 minutes	Self-Selected Reading
	15 minutes	Working with Words Block

90 minutes total language arts time daily, with emphasis on Writing Block (approximately 1 week).

School D: This school has made a commitment to teach all four blocks in the upper grades. They serve a high population of disadvantaged children. Teachers are departmentalized and teach three rotations of Four-Blocks or three rotations of science/social studies/math. There is flexibility within the block for Guided Reading and Writing for one to occasionally have longer time and, definitely, for a strong connection between the two when necessary.

This is one language arts teacher's schedule:

7:55 - 8:15	Breakfast and homeroom (roll, paperwork)
8:15 - 8:35	Working with Words Block
8:35 - 9:30	Guided Reading Block/ Writing Block (can be equal time, can go longer in one block, or occasionally eliminate one block to accomplish a task in the other)
9:30 - 10:00	Self-Selected Reading Block
10:00 - 10:45	Planning
10:45 - 11:10	Working with Words Block
11:10 - 11:55	Guided Reading Block/ Writing Block (can be equal time, can go longer in one block, or occasionally eliminate one block to accomplish a task in the other)
11:55 - 12:25	Self-Selected Reading Block
12:25 - 1:10	Lunch and recess
1:10 - 1:30	Working with Words Block
1:30 - 2:15	Guided Reading Block/Writing Block (can be equal time, can go longer in one block, or occasionally eliminate one block to accomplish a task in the other)
2:15 - 2:40	Self-Selected Reading Block
2:40	Dismissal

School E: This is another school, similar to the one above, that rotates between the Guided Reading Block and the Writing Block with content teachers supplementing the reading and writing as they can. Minutes spent on each segment are also shared.

90 Minute Language Arts Block

Working with Words Block	20 minutes Segment 1: 5-10 minutes Segment 2: 10-15 minutes
Self-Selected Reading Block	30 minutes Read-aloud: 10 minutes Students read/conference: 20 minutes Share periodically
*Guided Reading Block	40 minutes Prereading: 10 minutes During reading: 20 minutes Post-reading: 10 minutes
*Writing Block	40 minutes Mini-lesson: 10 minutes Students write/conference: 30 minutes Share once a week
*Alternate Guided Reading Block and Writing Block	

School F: This is another school in the same district that has an additional 10 minutes in their schedule for Four-Blocks in the upper grades.

Monday, Wednesday, Friday

Self-Selected Reading Block	40 minutes
	Teacher read-aloud: 10 minutes
	Independent reading/ conferencing: 30 minutes
Writing Block	40 minutes
	Mini-lesson: 10 minutes
	Independent writing/ conferencing/sharing: 30 minutes
Working with Words Block	20 minutes
	Word Wall segment: 5 minutes
	Word Building segment: 15 minutes

Tuesday, Thursday

Self-Selected Reading Block	30 minutes
	Teacher read aloud: 10 minutes
	Independent reading/ conferencing: 20 minutes
Guided Reading Block	40 minutes
	Prereading: 10 minutes
	During reading: 20 minutes
	Postreading: 10 minutes
Writing Block	30 minutes
	Independent writing/ conferencing: 30 minutes

School G: Teachers in this middle school are experimenting too, with a schedule to rotate between the Guided Reading Block and the Writing Block.

90 Minute Language Arts Block

Working with Words Block	20 minutes
	Segment 1: 5-10 minutes
	Segment 2: 10-15 minutes
Self-Selected Reading Block	30 minutes
	Read-aloud: 10 minutes
	Students read/conference: 20 minutes
	Share periodically
*Guided Reading Block	40 minutes
	Prereading: 10 minutes
	During reading: 20 minutes
	Postreading: 10 minutes

*Writing Block   40 minutes
                                        Mini-lesson: 10 minutes
                                        Students write/conference: 30 minutes
                                        Share once a week (Borrow
                                        5 minutes from modeling
                                        and 10 minutes from writing on this.

*Alternate Guided Reading Block and Writing Block

A Creative Schedule

LaDene Conroy, the principal at Goodwin Elementary School in Charleston, South Carolina, devised a system, along with her faculty, that allows teachers to construct their schedules using a circle graph. This circle graph vividly illustrates how instructional time is being spent in relationship to the whole day. All teachers make two copies of their schedules. One copy is given to the principal, and the other copy is mounted on colored paper outside of their classroom doors. Additionally, they display a large graph of their schedules on poster board in their classrooms. They attach a clothespin to the graph as the day proceeds to show students exactly where they are in the schedule.

Teachers report that this helps them to be more accountable for their instructional time. LaDene said that, "It was surprising to some of the teachers just how they were allocating their time. If we say that literacy is critical to our students, then our schedules should reflect that we value literacy development."

She further reports that the circle graph helps kids to know where they are in the day, especially those special children who have a sense of urgency about when they are to go somewhere—physical education, special areas, or even lunch. The teachers also report fewer interruptions, especially during Four-Blocks, because visitors see the schedule on the door.

Here is a translation of one teacher's schedule from the traditional chart to the pie chart, illustrating its graphical impact:

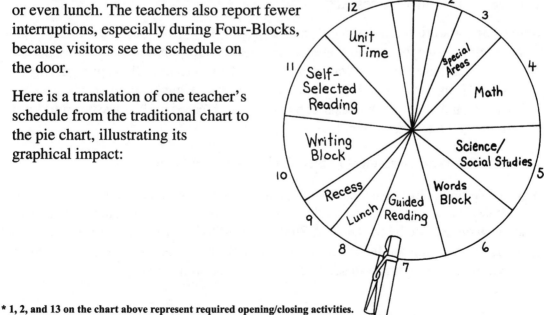

* 1, 2, and 13 on the chart above represent required opening/closing activities.

Chapter 8

Frequently Asked Questions

Some Questions and Answers about Upper Grades

1. Can grades be given with Four-Blocks™ in the upper grades?

Of course! Let's just be sure that the way we give the grades is appropriate for the instruction and philosophy of the framework, and that what we assess is fair to students. Here are some ideas:

Guided Reading Block:

What's being taught during this block?

- ☑ comprehension of printed text at grade level and below grade level
- ☑ specific skills and strategies that are necessary for comprehension
- ☑ vocabulary pertinent to the concepts contained in the text

What is fair to be assessed?

- ☑ the students' ability to apply the skills and strategies that were taught during this lesson
- ☑ the students' understanding of the text
- ☑ the vocabulary that students have learned and applied to the text
- ☑ reasonable guesses of words in a Cloze format dealing with the story (This makes a point of using context clues in reading.)

How can it be formally assessed?

Some fairly traditional assessment measures can be used—multiple-choice, short-answer tests, Cloze format, and/or essay or extended response tests. The teacher can construct a test based on what was actually taught and successfully applied during the days spent on the text. This is far better and fairer than using the publisher's test since neither the publisher nor the basal consultant was present in the classroom to know exactly what the teacher taught that week.

Can a teacher raise assessment in this block to a higher level?

Yes! The ultimate in assessment would be to see if the students could apply the skills and strategies to a piece of text other than the one already read, and in which the students were guided by the teacher. Students need to know that the skills and strategies they're learning are for the purpose of transferring this knowledge to other text they will read at any time—in science, in history, at home, etc.

Self-Selected Reading Block:

Try not to have grades attached to SSR if at all possible. This block is created to instill a desire for reading among our kids. Grades don't usually aid with the intrinsic motivation goal! If a traditional grade must be assigned to "reading comprehension," information gathered during the SSR conference should be considered along with the test described in the Guided Reading section. A rubric can be designed to take into account such things as the student's ability to apply skills and strategies taught during Guided Reading in the context of what is read and discussed during the conference; to self-select appropriate materials; to engage in print; and to make personal connections with the text.

Writing Block:

All of the writing skills, including grammar, mechanics, and usage, as well as the students' growth in writing, can be assessed in the context of their actual writing. Here again, rubrics can be most useful in reflecting students' true growth in written communication. There are numerous publications making good, sound rubrics available to which letter grades can be attached. The best of these also put the conventions—grammar, mechanics, and usage—in proper perspective. They are a part of the whole, where correctness counts but is not the only criterion.

Working with Words Block:

Spelling grades:

Having students memorize long lists of spelling and/or vocabulary words is totally contrary to the philosophy of this block. Memorization is not what will enable students to be good spellers. Learning the patterns of spelling and decoding and about structural analysis of words is what is valuable. If the teacher is spending time daily on new and old Word Wall words, then those words could be a part of the spelling test. Additionally, because transfer and application of the rules and patterns learned is what is really of value, this level of the taxonomy should be included in the test. In the upper grades, something from the additional goals being taught could be included in the assessment. Tests might be designed as follows:

Choose from among:

- Five old and new Word Wall words
- Two to three Nifty Thrifty Fifty words
- Five words written in correct columns as in What Looks Right? activities
- A paragraph for students to edit for Word Wall words, Nifty Thrifty Fifty words, pattern words or words that have been explored in other ways
- Five words written in correct columns as in Brand Name Phonics
- Three to four sentences or a paragraph of dictation incorporating a variety of words (bonus points)

A couple of important issues to be considered related to grading:

- We should perceive grades as an indication of what needs to be done for a student. Too many teachers tend to see grades as a reward or punishment for students—not a gauge for what work lies ahead for the teacher. We must accept the challenge and support each and every individual student. They are in our care.
- We should not sacrifice any more of our valuable teaching and learning time than is necessary to assess students. Far too many teachers have fallen into the practice of testing all day on Fridays. We absolutely cannot afford to give 20% of our instructional time to assessment! There's already not enough time to teach all that must be taught to the depth that it should be delivered. We should rely more on our ability to assess students' progress through our observations of them rather than having as much needless paper and pencil assessment.

2. What is data revealing on the Four-Blocks™ framework in the upper grades?

Schools are currently gathering data, which will be reported soon at *www.teachers.net*. Early reports are as encouraging as in the lower grades. In fact, teachers report that the active engagement of students in the upper grades, alone, has made a tremendous difference.

For the teachers and schools considering the Four-Blocks™ framework in upper grades, there is overwhelmingly convincing research available on the components of the model. The model is comprised totally of what are considered "best practices" in instruction. The framework in the upper grades helps teachers maximize time on task, better organizing the teaching and learning environment. For additional information about the Four-Blocks™ framework in the upper grades, visit the author's column, "Sifting and Sorting through the 4-Blocks," located at *www.teachers.net*.

3. Can a teacher expect to cover all necessary content and implement Four-Blocks in the upper grades?

Yes! Not all content will be covered during the Four-Blocks time; however, the sample schedules in this book should be helpful in showing how many schools and teachers were able to include their other content area subjects with ample time for literacy development. Also, bringing in content text during the Guided Reading Block is an excellent way to teach students how the strategies they're learning during that time can be applied to the texts they read for other subjects. Teachers must be sure that the content of the material is not ignored, though.

As far as covering all necessary language arts content—yes again! There is an appropriate place in Four-Blocks for everything that needs to be taught—grammar is taught in the Writing Block; spelling is taught in the Working with Words Block; vocabulary is taught in the Guided Reading Block when it pertains to the comprehension of the text and in Words Block when the words are being explored or analyzed. There is a place for working with everything related to language arts.

4. Should Four-Blocks in the upper grades be considered for high schools?

Courses are designed differently at the high-school level. Implementing the framework may not serve those students well. "Chips off the Blocks," however, might be the way to go since there are so many good activities, methods, and ideas in Four-Blocks that can be actively engaging for high-school students. We want to be careful not to over-generalize what has worked for grades one to eight.

5. Can we expect that students will perform well on most standardized tests if they've been taught with Four-Blocks?

Yes! If that were not so, then the framework would definitely not be as popular as it is with teachers. Teachers across the country have recognized that Four-Blocks, in many ways, is just a great compilation of good practices put into a structure that makes instruction more manageable for teachers. Most teachers remark that Four-Blocks just makes good sense! If we are teaching students to be better readers and writers, then it's only natural that they'll perform better on tests that require that they read and write.

Even though the organization and activities in Four-Blocks may look simple, realize that Four-Blocks demands **more** of students. Students are active, not passive, participants in the learning process. They are also asked to apply what is learned, not just memorize facts, rules, and words.

The most important issue that teachers and schools must be aware of, in aligning instruction with assessment, however, is that a curriculum must be followed. Four-Blocks will give teachers a more effective way to organize and deliver their instruction—the **how** of teaching. It will not tell teachers **what** to teach. That's up to schools. The **what** and the **how**, though, are both critical components for success.

Chapter 9

Similarities and Differences

For those who wish to compare the upper- and lower-grades models, the simple side-by-side graphics in this chapter may help to clarify the similarities and differences.

Self-Selected Reading Block

Time frames for this block may differ between primary and upper grades.

	PRIMARY MODEL	UPPER GRADES MODEL
Segment 1 **Teacher Read-Aloud**	• All types of texts	• All types of texts, including many chapter books to aid in sustaining interest
Segment 2 **Students Read**	• Free choice of selections • Wide range of materials available in book baskets	• Free choice of selections • Wide range of materials available • Variety in making books available to students • More chapter books available for extended use • Book Clubs as alternative format
	Conferences • Daily; Informal book chat and gather information about fluency, and application of skills and strategies. • Goal of meeting weekly with each student.	**Conferences** • Daily; Discuss books and informally check application of skills and strategies (fluency if necessary) • Goal of meeting every one to two weeks with students so that depth is included where necessary
~~**Segment 3**~~ **Sharing**	• Daily • Variety of formats	• Daily/weekly as time and interest dictate—more time spent reading • Variety of formats

Guided Reading Block

Time frames for this block may differ between primary and upper grades.

	PRIMARY MODEL	UPPER GRADES MODEL
Segment 1 **Pre-Reading**	• Application to text in entirety • All components daily: Prior knowledge/personal connection Vocabulary Mini-lesson Predictions Purpose	• Application to planned sections of text • All components daily: Prior knowledge/personal connection Vocabulary Mini-lesson Predictions Purpose
Segment 2 **During Reading**	• Read, re-read, and re-read again • Three days grade-level and two days below grade-level • Variety of reading formats (partner and playschool frequently) **Conferences** • Fluency, application of strategies, book chat	• Read, re-read (when possible or necessary depending on fluency) • Flexible time at levels according to need • Variety of reading formats (partner and book clubs frequently) • Student Workshop Format as an alternative **Conferences** • Application of strategies • Book chat
Segment 3 **After Reading**	• Alignment with pre-reading elements	• Alignment with pre-reading elements

Writing Block

Time frames for this block may differ between primary and upper grades.

	PRIMARY MODEL	UPPER GRADES MODEL
Segment 1 Teacher Models Writing Daily	• Uses a variety of examples: original works, published authors, students' work (good examples) - mostly own compositions • Some extended multiple day pieces as examples • Editor's checklist used daily • Mini-lesson included	• Variety of examples - more work of others • Many multiple day pieces as examples • Editor's checklist used until no longer needed • Mini-lesson included, more sophisticated
Segment 2 Students Write	• Writers' workshop approach • Free choice of selections with few focused whole-class pieces **Conferences** • Attention to revision and editing • Three to five good pieces to publish one • Some peer conferences	• Writers' workshop approach • Balance free-choice selections with more focused pieces **Conferences** • Status and publishing conferences held; attention to revision and editing • Three to five good pieces to publish one • More peer conferencing • More variety of publishing formats
Segment 3 Sharing	• Daily in a variety of formats	• Daily/weekly as desired in a variety of formats

Working with Words Block

Time frames for this block may differ between primary and upper grades.

	PRIMARY MODEL	UPPER GRADES MODEL
Segment 1	• Work daily with high frequency words on Word Wall	• Six goals to address, reducing number as no longer needed
Segment 2	• Other spelling and decoding activities	• Flexibility in addressing goals and structuring the block

Appendix

Do Not Touch!
Being Read By:

_____

R e s e r v e d

Interesting Words

I wonder... ∘ ∘ ∘

_____

_____

_____

Very Important Points

_____   _____

_____   _____

Book Log

Name:

Date	Title	Pages (From-To)	Genre

Self-Selected Reading Bingo

Science Fiction Title:	Humorous Fiction Title:	Adventure Title:	Nonfiction Title:	Student's Choice Title:
Mystery Title:	Student's Choice Title:	Animal Fiction Title:	Realistic Fiction Title:	Poetry Title:
Student's Choice Title:	Adventure Title:	Historical Fiction Title:	Mystery Title:	Realistic Fiction Title:
Realistic Fiction Title:	Science Nonfiction Title:	Student's Choice Title:	Folk Tale/Fable Title:	Science Fiction Title:
Humorous Fiction Title:	Historical Fiction Title:	Biography Title:	Student's Choice Title:	Mystery Title:

Name _____ Date _____

Teacher's Self-Selected Reading Conference Form

Student _____

Date	Book Title	Level			Connections			Skills and Strategies Demonstrated							
		Easy	Hard	Appropriate	Other Books	Personal Experiences	World Experiences	Decoding Strategies	Literary Elements	Main Idea	Facts/Details	Self-Monitoring	Relationships	Text Structure	Sequence/Plot
Comments:															
Comments:															
Comments:															
Comments:															
Comments:															
Comments:															

Self-Selected Reading Conference Form

Student: _____ Date: _____

Title: _____ Genre: _____

Interest Level:

1   5   10

Passive   Engaged

Comprehension:

1   5   10

Poor   Average   Excellent

Discussion Level:

1   5   10

Literal   Inferential   Analytical

Chosen because: ☐ no reason   ☐ length   ☐ interest

Comments: _____

_____

_____

- -

Self-Selected Reading Conference Form

Student: _____ Date: _____

Title: _____ Genre: _____

Interest Level:

1   5   10

Passive   Engaged

Comprehension:

1   5   10

Poor   Average   Excellent

Discussion Level:

1   5   10

Literal   Inferential   Analytical

Chosen because: ☐ no reason   ☐ length   ☐ interest

Comments: _____

_____

_____

Describe a place that the setting of the book reminds you of.	Describe something you've read that had a setting similar to the setting of this book.
Summarize the main plot of this story. Also, tell about any sub-plots in the story.	Tell about the setting of your book, and read a passage (or passages) that tell something about the setting.
Did the author do a good job in describing the setting so that you can clearly picture it? How? Find passages that defend your choice.	If you were the author, would you have chosen this setting and described it as this author did? If not, what would you have done differently?
Did this plot remind you of anything that you've experienced or that you've heard about? Tell about your experience.	What special techniques did the author use in presenting the plot (flashback, etc.)? Give examples from the text.
Could you successfully predict what was going to happen? If so, how? How did this make it more or less interesting?	Why do you think the author chose this setting? Do you think another setting would have been equally effective? Why or why not?

Tell about something else you've read that reminds you of this selection. Compare the two and explain.

Who was the main character in your story, and how did you make that identification?

How did you learn the most about the main character—through actions, what others said, or what the author/speaker told you directly? Explain.

Read aloud a passage that tells something about your character. Did the author do a good job developing the character? Why or why not?

Tell how the character changed from the beginning of the story to the end.

Tell how another character in your story created some conflict or tension with the main character.

Did the author do a good job of creating and describing secondary characters? Why or why not? Give examples.

Were the characters believeable? Why or why not?

Explain how characters in this book remind you of characters in another book, or how they remind you of people in real life.

What are the characteristics of this book that help you to classify the genre? Be specific.

What similar books on this topic have you read? How do those books compare to this one?

What mood has the author created in this story, and how? What other stories have you read with the same mood?

What message do you think the author is sharing? Can the theme of the selection be transferred into everyday life experiences? How?

What point of view did the author choose for this story? Why do you think the author chose this point of view?

How were you able to tell the point of view? Read aloud from the story as evidence of that point of view.

Did you feel that the point of view for this story was the best choice? What were the advantages and disadvantages?

Do you think the author clearly presented the purpose for writing this selection? Why or why not? Was this the best genre to use to achieve the author's purpose?

What do you think the author's purpose was in writing this selection? Was it to entertain, persuade, inform, etc.?

What is the basic conflict in the story, and what events contribute to it? How does the author build tension in the story? Give examples from the text.

How was the problem solved? Was this a realistic solution? Was the solution one you would have chosen? Why or why not?

Vocabulary Clustering

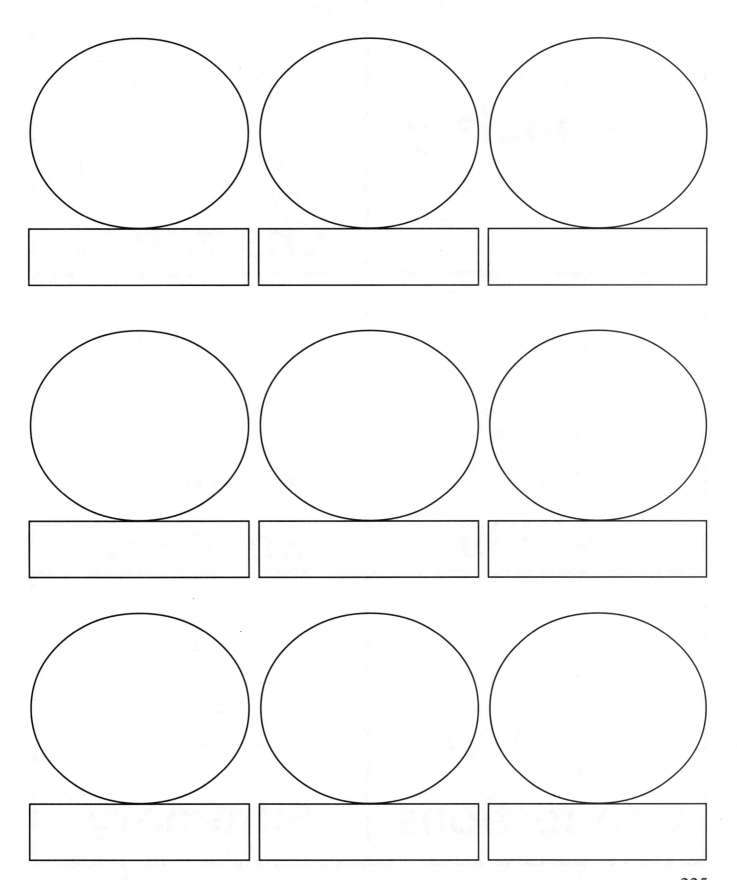

Vocabulary

Characters

Setting

Problem/ Solution

Connections

Summary

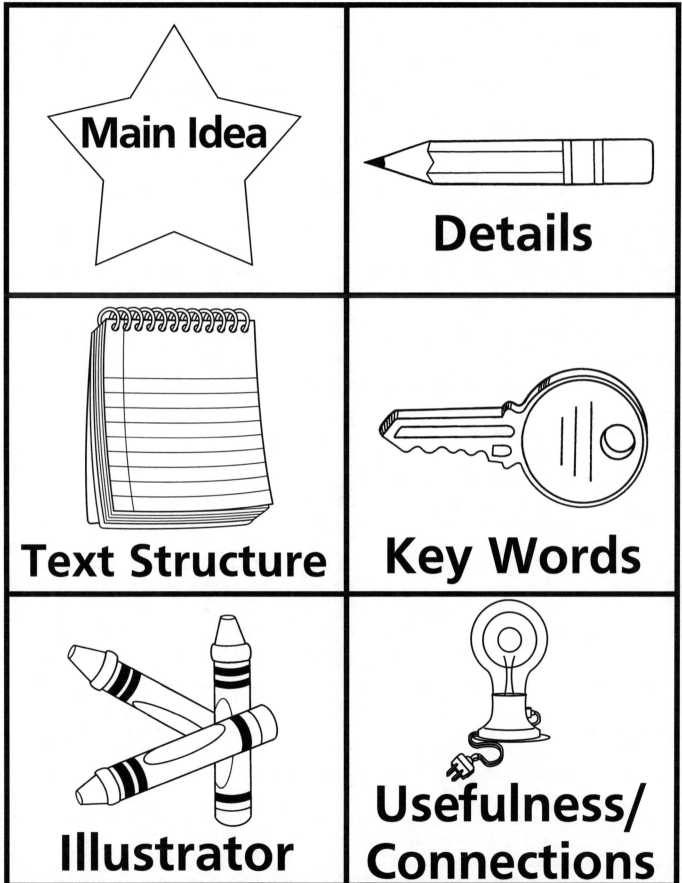

Main Idea

Details

Text Structure

Key Words

Illustrator

**Usefulness/
Connections**

Name	Date

Name	Date

Name	Date

Name	Date

Name	Date

Name	Date

My Record of Writing Lessons

Name: _____

Date	Writing Lesson	How I Apply This in My Writing

My Personal Goals for Writing

Name: _____

Date	Goal	Review Date	Comments/Goals Met?

My Writing Log

Name: _____

Date	Topic	Revising and Editing			Publish Date
		Self	Teacher	Peer	

Teacher's Writing Conference Roster

Student	Status Conference	Publishing Conference

Readers' Response Log

Date I Read It	In response to your writing, I thought...	Reviewer's Name

Aa_____

Bb_____

Cc_____

_____

_____

_____

_____

_____

_____

_____

_____

_____

Gg_____

Hh_____

Ii_____

_____

_____

_____

_____

_____

_____

_____

_____

_____

Mm_____

Nn_____

Oo_____

_____

_____

_____

_____

_____

_____

_____

_____

_____

Ss_____

Tt_____

Uu_____

_____

_____

_____

_____

_____

_____

_____

_____

_____

Dd_____   Ee _____   Ff_____

_____   _____   _____

_____   _____   _____

_____   _____   _____

Jj_____   Kk _____   Ll _____

_____   _____   _____

_____   _____   _____

_____   _____   _____

Pp_____   Qq_____   Rr_____

_____   _____   _____

_____   _____   _____

_____   _____   _____

Vv _____   Ww_____   Xx _____

_____   _____   Yy _____

_____   _____   Zz _____

_____   _____   _____

WORDO

Word Map

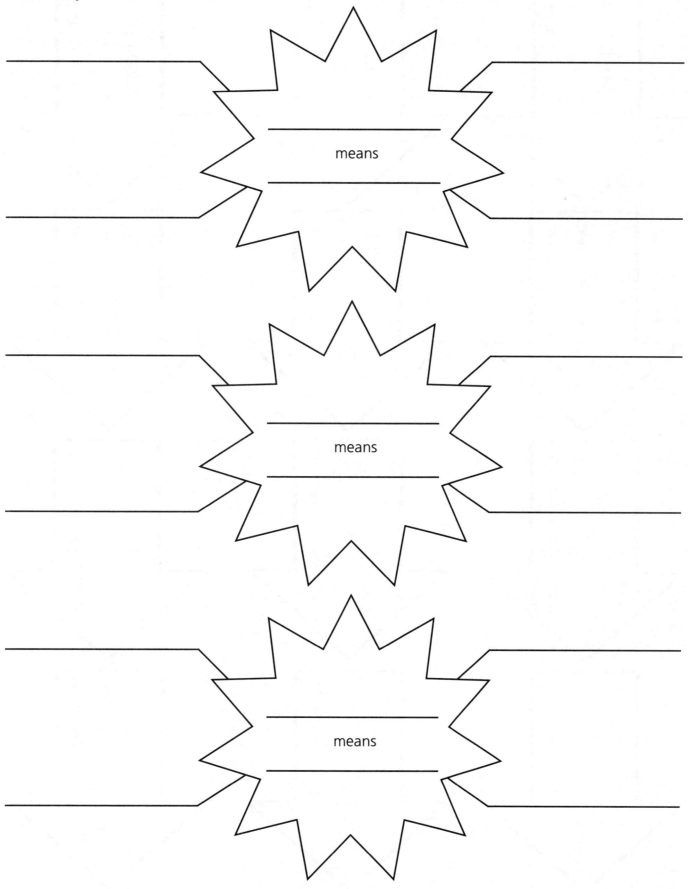

_____ means _____

_____ means _____

_____ means _____

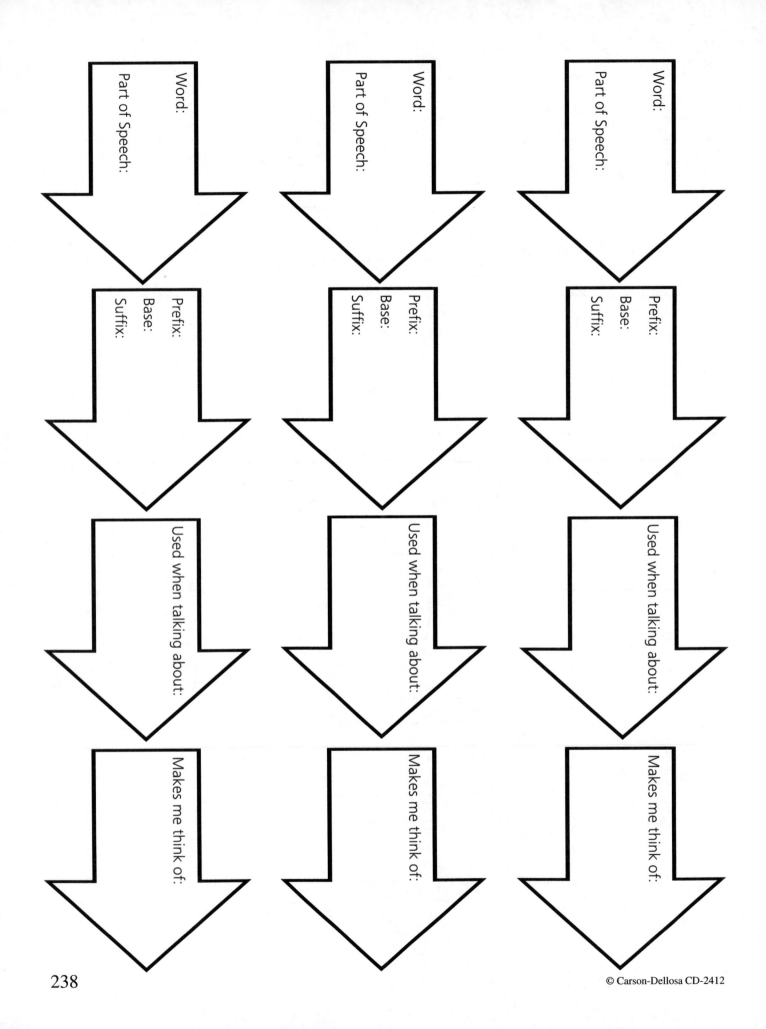

Word:

Part of Speech:

Word:

Part of Speech:

Word:

Part of Speech:

Prefix:
Base:
Suffix:

Prefix:
Base:
Suffix:

Prefix:
Base:
Suffix:

Used when talking about:

Used when talking about:

Used when talking about:

Makes me think of:

Makes me think of:

Makes me think of:

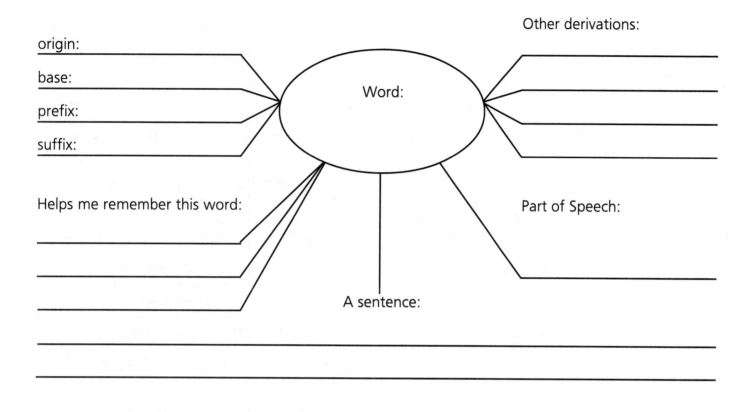

origin:

base:

prefix:

suffix:

Other derivations:

Word:

Helps me remember this word:

Part of Speech:

A sentence:

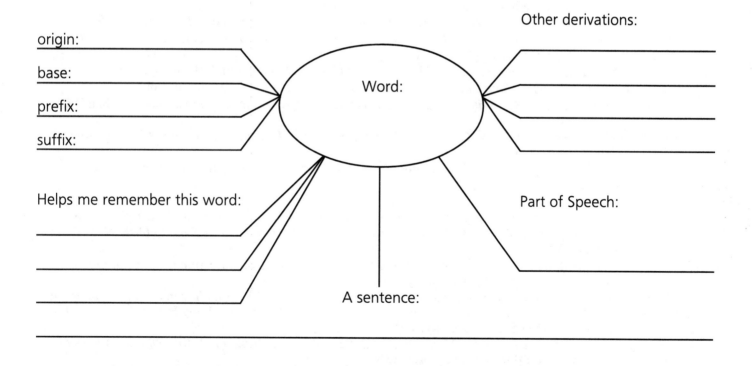

origin:

base:

prefix:

suffix:

Other derivations:

Word:

Helps me remember this word:

Part of Speech:

A sentence:

Professional Works Cited

Allington, Richard L. and Cunningham, Patricia M. (1998) *Classrooms That Work: They Can All Read and Write.* New York: Addison, Wesley Longman.

Anderson, R. C. et al. (1985) *Becoming a Nation of Readers.* Washington, DC: U. S. Department of Education.

Atwell, Nancie. (1998) *In the Middle.* Portsmouth, NH: Boynton/Cook.

Bloom, Benjamin S., et al. (1984) *Taxonomy of Educational Objectives Book 1: Cognitive Domain.* New York: Longman Publishing Group.

Caine, Renate N., and Caine, Geoffrey. (1994) *Making Connections: Teaching and the Human Brain.* New York: Addison, Wesley Longman.

Calkins, Lucy. (1990) *Living Between the Lines.* Portsmouth, NH: Heinemann.

Clay, Marie. (1991) *Becoming Literate: The Construction of Inner Control.* Portsmouth, NH: Heinemann.

Cooper, J. David. (1997) *Literacy: Helping Children Construct Meaning.* Boston: Houghton Mifflin, Co.

Cunningham, Patricia M. (1999) *Phonics They Use.* New York: Addison-Wesley Publishing Co.

Cunningham, Patricia M. and Hall, Dorothy P. (2000) *Guided Reading the Four-Blocks™ Way.* Greensboro, NC: Carson-Dellosa.

Cunningham, Patricia M. and Hall, Dorothy P. (1994) *Making Big Words.* Parsippany, NJ: Good Apple.

Cunningham, Patricia M. and Hall, Dorothy P. (1997) *Making More Big Words.* Parsippany, NJ: Good Apple.

Cunningham, Patricia M. and Hall, Dorothy P. (1998) *Month-by-Month Phonics for Upper Grades.* Greensboro, NC: Carson-Dellosa.

Cunningham, Patricia M., Hall, Dorothy P., and Cunningham, James W. (1999) *The Teacher's Guide to the Four Blocks.* Greensboro, NC: Carson-Dellosa.

Cunningham, Patricia M., Moore, Sharon A., and Cunningham, James W. (1999) *Reading and Writing in Elementary Classrooms: Strategies and Observations.* White Plains, NY: Longman.

Fletcher, Ralph. (1993) *What a Writer Needs.* Portsmouth, NH: Heinemann.

Fletcher, Ralph and Portalupi, Joann. (1998) *Craft Lessons: Teaching Writing K-8.* Portland, ME: Stenhouse.

Forney, Melissa. (1996) *Dynamite Writing Ideas.* Gainesville, FL: Maupin House.

Fry, Edward B., Kress, Jacqueline E., and Fountoukidis, Dona Lee. (1993) *The Reading Teacher's Book of Lists.* Englewood Cliffs, NJ: Prentice Hall.

Gambrell, Linda B. (2000) "Motivation Matters: Fostering Full Access to Literacy." 45th Annual Convention of the International Reading Association, April 30–May 5, Indianapolis, IN.

Gralla, Preston. (1999) *Online Kids: A Young Surfer's Guide to Cyberspace.* New York: John Waley & Sons.

Johns, Jerry and Lenski, Susan Davis. (1997) *Improving Reading: A Handbook of Strategies, Second Edition.* Dubuque, IA: Kendall/Hunt Publishing.

Keene, Ellin Oliver and Zimmerman, Susan. (1997) *Mosaic of Thought.* Portsmouth, NH: Heinemann.

Killgallon, Don. (1997) *Sentence Composing for Middle School.* Portsmouth, NH: Boynton/Cook.

Krull, Kathleen. (1994) *Lives of the Writers: Comedies, Tragedies (and What the Neighbors Thought).* San Diego, CA: Harcourt Brace.

McCarthy, Tara. (1996) *Teaching Genre, Grades 4-8: Explore 9 Types of Literature to Develop Lifelong Readers and Writers.* New York: Scholastic.

Nagy, W. E. and Anderson, R. C. (1984) "How Many Words Are There in Printed School English?" *Reading Research Quarterly.* 19:304-330

Notebook. *Time.* 155: 6: 25.

Routman, Regie. (1995) *Invitations: Changing As Teachers and Learners K-12.* Portsmouth, NH: Heinemann.

Seuling, Barbara. (1997) *To Be a Writer: A Guide for Young People Who Want to Write and Publish.* New York: Twenty-First Century Books.

Tharp, Roland G. and Gillimore, Ronald. (1989) *Rousing Minds to Life: Teaching, Learning, and Schooling in Social Context.* New York: Cambridge University Press.

Well. (1986) "Recent Research Findings Related to the Integrated Teaching of Reading/Language Arts." *Integrated Reading/Language Arts: Implications for Administrators,* by Dr. Mary Ellen Vogt. Long Beach: Department of Teacher Education, California State University, 1990.

Wilson, Elizabeth A. (1995) *Reading at the Middle and High School Levels: Building Active Readers Across the Curriculum.* Arlington, VA: Educational Research Service.

Zemelman, Steven and Daniels, Harvey. (1998) *A Community of Writers: Teaching in the Junior and Senior High School.* Portsmouth, NH: Heinemann.